Family Letters

OF ROBERT
AND ELINOR FROST

Family Letters

OF

ROBERT

AND ELINOR

FROST

EDITED BY ARNOLD GRADE

FOREWORD BY LESLEY FROST

STATE UNIVERSITY OF NEW YORK PRESS

ALBANY, NEW YORK, 1972

Family Letters of Robert and Elinor Frost
First Edition
Published by State University of New York Press,
99 Washington Avenue, Albany, New York 12210
Copyright © 1972 State University of New York

Printed in the United States of America
Designed by P. J. Conkwright

Library of Congress Cataloging in Publication Data

Frost, Robert, 1874-1963
Family letters of Robert and Elinor Frost

Includes bibliographical references
I. Frost, Elinor. II. Grade, Arnold E., ed. III. Title
PS3511.R94Z52 1972   811'.5'2 [B]   71-152518
ISBN 0-87395-087-9
ISBN 0-87395-187-5 (microfiche)

Contents

Illustrations

Following page 168
All photographs are from Frost family sources.

Foreword

THESE letters speak for themselves. As source material, they provide an unusual opportunity to trace the love-coherence of a family, both parental and grand-parental. And it must be remembered that it was a family fraught with and tempered by the powerful complexities of my father's genius. There was the extreme insecurity, emanating from his tragic boyhood, which was to be accentuated by years without recognition, years marked by financial distress. On the New Hampshire farm, there were fears of his own isolation and, correspondingly, an acquaintance with the night. There was an over-burden of death: his father when he was eleven, a first-born child not quite four, a two-day-old daughter — my mother's namesake, a beloved daughter before my mother's death, and later a son by suicide. Nothing without torment.

But, to balance and to restore him continuously, there was a love that by miracle-fortune came his way. There were the boundless moments, a supreme happiness in nature through which the poet discovers that the greatness of love lies not in forward-looking thoughts. There were passionate preferences and laughter, too, always a saving grace. If there is any one sound that returns to me out of my earliest memories it is my mother's rippling laughter at some child's precocity or at my father's turn of a phrase. For instance, it could well have been his remarking, with a smile, "Home is the place where, when you have to go there, they have to take you in." (Yankee accent on the two *haves*!) To which my mother would have answered, with *her* smile, "I should

have called it something somehow you haven't to deserve."[1]
And she was to make her point down the years. With all
their play of mind, they shared a deep innocence, a naivete
common to genius, at once wise and sad, that heartbreaking
insight that recognizes the hairsbreadth between joy into
pain, pain into joy. We find it in all great art, on or off the
canvas or the written page. No tears in the writer, no tears
in the reader.

Even as we children separated into our component
parts—off to school, into marriage, or just up and away—my
mother's letter writing continued to weave the pattern of
home and family. She wrote every absentee child two or
three times a week! After she was gone, the family correspondence was immeasurably reduced and we were to discover that what we had assumed was a patriarchy had
actually been matriarchal. Finally, too soon, came the use
of the telephone, the telephone that has done to good letters
what television has done to good reading.

Although there are many letters missing, it is quite
remarkable that so many remain despite the migrations
and adventures of the descendants. Irma's collection is not
to be found and as many again of those to Carroll and Marjorie must have been lost. As for me, I never saved letters
because my father's name was becoming or had become an
illustrious one. It was, rather, because I had the hoarding
instinct from way back. I just couldn't bear to throw anything away; I truly suffered over the disappearance of
"documentary evidence" of what was going on—personal,
national, or international. Digging down now into seemingly
bottomless trunks and boxes that have survived my numer-
ous cross-country and overseas moves, I find a letter from
a Plymouth, New Hampshire playmate sent me in England

---

[1] Edward Connery Lathem, ed., *The Poetry of Robert Frost* (New York:
Holt, Rinehart and Winston, 1969), p. 38. (*PRF* in later references.)

in 1912; I find the first book I bought on my own, in 1910, in a Manchester, New Hampshire bookshop—the Kate Douglas Wiggin anthology *Golden Numbers*. I find endless lists of groceries with their *prices*, lesson sheets of Latin and French verbs from 1914, theatre stubs and programs from Boston, New York, and London. There are 1908 train schedules for the old Boston and Maine Railroad to the White Mountains, illegible newspaper clippings rusted with age—indeed, an horrendous conglomeration. Oddly enough we never had cameras, so there are few photographs to be treasured, and what there are were taken by others. Instead, we children were encouraged to describe in writing,[2] or to draw or paint, the flowers, birds and scenes we knew at first hand.

With their piercing strokes of sight and insight, the letters are yet another way of seeing a man who was to write, for those who came seeking him out, "They would not find me changed from him they knew—only more sure of all I thought was true"[3] and a woman who bound for him those "silken ties of love and thought."[4] They can be illuminating foot-notes to the poetry itself which says it for both of them and for all time.

LESLEY FROST

[2] See *New Hampshire's Child: The Derry Journals of Lesley Frost* (Albany: State University of New York Press, 1969).

[3] *PRF*, p. 5.

[4] *Ibid*, pp. 331-332.

Editor's Note

Three volumes of Robert Frost's letters have already been published,[1] and additional letters have appeared occasionally in periodical print. *Family Letters*, the first major addition to this literature in eight years, offers 182 previously unpublished letters toward a full and valid assessment of this gifted and protean man. An additional letter—the last one in this book—was included in *Selected Letters of Robert Frost* and is here reprinted with two substantive changes to insure a completeness both chronological and filial. Of the 183 letters all told, 133 were written by Robert Frost (designated as RF), and fifty were written by his wife Elinor (EF). With the exception of considerable time gaps in the early 'twenties and in the latter years of Frost's life, *Family Letters* provides a moving narration of nearly half a century — from 1914 to 1963.

Letter headings have been set within a standard format, although no significant interpolations have been dropped. A bracketed date or point of origin indicates informed speculation. Precise dates within brackets signal the presence of adequate internal evidence or the survival of a postmarked envelope associated with that particular letter. The salutation, body, and closing sentiment of each letter conform carefully to the original. With the exception of infre-

---

[1] Margaret Bartlett Anderson, *Robert Frost and John Bartlett : The Record of a Friendship* (New York: Holt, Rinehart and Winston, 1963); Louis Untermeyer ed., *The Letters of Robert Frost to Louis Untermeyer* (New York: Holt, Rinehart and Winston, 1963); Lawrance Thompson, ed., *Selected Letters of Robert Frost* (New York: Holt, Rinehart and Winston, 1964).

quent bracketed emendations, spelling and punctuation remain untouched. Frost often appended afterthoughts and postscripts in a random, wrap-around fashion. All such marginalia has been placed below the letter proper. Although every effort has been taken to avoid error in transcription and in placement, the editor freely — and with regret — accepts responsibility for any inaccuracies.

The selection of Elinor Frost's letters represents nearly two-thirds of those made available. The decision to exclude some was based on their brevity, lack of pertinence, or duplication of content. Nearly all of Robert Frost's available and as yet unpublished family letters were used; the few not included were at the family's request, and their exclusion serves as a reasonable protection of privacy for people still living. Deletions within letters are rare and clearly indicated.

So as to give full play to the letters, the notes and other editorial apparatus have been kept to a level both moderate in volume and helpful in intent. In these notes, *PRF* refers to placement of a poem within Edward Connery Lathem's *The Poetry of Robert Frost* published in 1969 by Holt, Rinehart and Winston.

Additional assists to the reader include a List of Letters which presents a chronological tabulation of the family correspondence. The Illustrations serve both as a family album and as a means of reproducing selections from the letters. The Frost Family Chronology provides a useful overview; its use may also aid in the placement of a particular letter within a larger and more significant context. The editor's Afterword is both brief and ancillary by design. If it offers a frame of reference or suggests a departure, or if indeed it serves to send the reader back into the letters, then it will have served its purpose. The Index includes a number of sub-headings under "Frost, Robert Lee" following a general pattern established by Lawrance Thompson in his works on Robert Frost. Certain additions to this *schema* are a response to comments by William H. Pritchard.[2]

A word should be said about the editorial stance operative in the preparation of these letters for publication. Although good arguments could be — and were — presented which called for fuller biographical particulars, a decision was made by the editor to minimize material extraneous to the letters themselves. Implementing such a decision is necessarily both a precarious and an arbitrary business. If, contrary to what Lesley Frost has insisted, these letters do *not* speak for themselves, then their publication is hardly justified. It is hoped, therefore, that the reader will accept these letters, together with their apparatus, as working papers toward a fuller appreciation of Robert Frost and his family. The letters *do* speak with a commanding voice; they contain mysteries, insights, apparent contradictions, and the essence of considerable drama. To capture and resolve these are the proper tasks of readers, biographers, and critics. For now and for the future's sake, they are freed to this demanding but exciting task.

[2] William H. Pritchard, "Frost Departmentalized," *The Hudson Review*, vol. 23, no. 4 (Winter 1970-71): 747-753.

Frost Family Chronology

1873	October 25	Elinor Miriam White born in Acton, Massachusetts.
1874	March 26	Robert Lee Frost born in San Francisco.
1876	June 25	Jeanie Florence Frost born in Lawrence, Massachusetts.
1885		RF's father died; mother and two children moved to New England.
1890		RF wrote and published — in the Lawrence (Massachusetts) *High School Bulletin* — his first poem, "La Noche Trieste."
1892	June	RF and Elinor White shared top honors at high school graduation.
	September	Elinor White began studies at St. Lawrence College; RF attended Dartmouth College for three months.
1893		RF began two-and-a-half-year sequence of occasional jobs as teacher, mill worker and newspaperman.
1894		RF had first book of poems privately printed; the only "edition" of *Twilight* consisted of two copies.
1895	December 19	RF and Elinor White were married in Lawrence, Massachusetts.
1896	September 25	Elliott born, first child of RF and EF; died in his fourth year.
1897	September	RF commenced nearly two years of study at Harvard College.
1899	April 28	Lesley born, second child of RF and EF.
1900	October	Family moved to Derry, New Hampshire, where RF farmed and subsequently taught at Pinkerton Academy.

1902	May 27	Son Carol born, third child of RF and EF.
1903	June 27	Irma born, fourth child of RF and EF.
1905	March 29	Marjorie born, fifth child of RF and EF.
1907	June 18	Elinor Bettina born, sixth child of RF and EF; died two days later.
1911	September	Family moved to Plymouth, New Hampshire, where RF taught for one year at the State Normal School.
1912	September	Family sailed for England; first days in London were spent at the Premier Hotel, Russell Square.
1913		RF's first trade book of poetry was published in London by David Nutt — *A Boy's Will.*
1914		RF's *North of Boston* published in London.
1915	February	Family returned to United States accompanied by poet Edward Thomas's son Merfyn. RF purchased farm in Franconia, New Hampshire.
1916		RF's *Mountain Interval* published by Henry Holt.
1917	January	RF commenced teaching relationship with Amherst College which would continue, intermittently, for nearly a half-century.
	September	Lesley attended Wellesley College for one year.
1918	May	RF awarded first of 44 honorary degrees, at Amherst.
	Summer-Fall	Lesley worked at Curtis airplane factory in Marblehead, Massachusetts.
	September	Irma attended Dana Hall School, Wellesley, Massachusetts.
	Winter	Lesley commenced year-and-a-half of studies as Latin major at Barnard College.
1920	Summer	Lesley undertook writing and editorial work in New York.
	Fall	Family made gradual move from Franconia to South Shaftsbury, Vermont.

Irma studied at the Art Students League in New York and made unsuccessful attempts to enter the field of fashion designing. Carol continued his life as poet-farmer.

1921 September   RF began first of three one-year stints in residence at the University of Michigan; severed his relationship early in 1926 to return to Amherst.

1923   RF's *Selected Poems* published.

Carol Frost and Lillian LaBatt married.

RF's *New Hampshire* published; awarded Pulitzer Prize.

1924   Lesley and Marjorie founded The Open Book in Pittsfield, Massachusetts.

William Prescott Frost born, son of Carol and Lillian; RF and EF's first grandchild.

1925 Summer   Lesley inaugurated The Knapsack, a travelling adjunct to the Pittsfield bookstore.

1926   Irma and John Paine Cone married.

1927   John Paine, Jr., born; first child of Irma and John.

1928   Lesley and James Dwight Francis married.

August   RF, EF and Marjorie travelled to England and France.

RF's *West-running Brook* published.

1929   Marjorie entered nurse's training in Baltimore.

Elinor born, first child of Lesley and Dwight.

Jeanie Florence Frost died, RF's sister.

1930   RF's *Collected Poems* published; awarded Pulitzer Prize.

1931   Marjorie entered TB sanitarium in Boulder, Colorado.

Lesley Lee born, second child of Lesley and Dwight.

Carol and his family moved to California.

	September	RF and EF travelled west to Colorado and California.
1932	June	RF and EF made another westward visit.
1933		Marjorie and Willard E. Fraser married.
1934		Marjorie Robin Fraser born, daughter of Marjorie and Willard.
	April	RF and EF rushed to Billings, Montana, because of Marjorie's illness; followed her to the Mayo Clinic in Rochester, Minnesota. Carol and his family returned to Vermont from California.
	May 2	Marjorie died.
	September	Lesley began two-year residence at Rockford (Illinois) College as teacher and director of Maddox House, its cultural center.
	December	RF and EF visited Florida for the first time.
1936		*Franconia*, a book of twenty-six of Marjorie's poems, posthumously printed by Spiral Press.
	Spring	RF gave series of Charles Eliot Norton Lectures at Harvard.
		RF's *A Further Range* published; awarded Pulitzer Prize.
	December	RF and EF began three-month respite in San Antonio, Texas.
1937	September 30	EF underwent cancer surgery in Springfield, Massachusetts; convalesced in Amherst and later in Florida.
1938	March 21	EF died in Gainesville, Florida; memorial service at Amherst one month later.
	September	RF moved to 88 Mt. Vernon Street, Boston. Lesley was teacher and director of Washington's King-Smith Studio School; later established Frost Studio School.
1939		RF's enlarged *Collected Poems* published.
		RF purchased Homer Noble Farm in Ripton, Vermont.

1940		Harold born, second child of Irma and John.
	October 9	Carol committed suicide.
1941	January	RF began construction of "Pencil Pines," his Florida retreat.
	Spring	RF moved from Boston apartment to 35 Brewster Street, Cambridge.
1942	December	William Prescott Frost enlisted in Army; medically discharged the following summer.
		RF's *A Witness Tree* published; awarded Pulitzer Prize.
1943		RF named Ticknor Fellow in the Humanities at Dartmouth College; held post for six years. Lesley commenced four years' service with the Office of War Information and the State Department.
1945		RF's *A Masque of Reason* published.
1947		RF's *Steeple Bush* published.
		RF's *A Masque of Mercy* published.
		Irma and John divorced.
		Irma committed.
1949		RF's *Complete Poems 1949* published.
1952		Lesley and Joseph W. Ballantine married.
1958		RF named to one-year term as Consultant in Poetry, Library of Congress.
1961	January 20	RF took part in inauguration of President John F. Kennedy.
		RF designated "Poet Laureate of Vermont."
1962		RF's *In the Clearing* published.
	August	RF undertook brief trip to Russia as "cultural ambassador."
	December	RF entered Peter Bent Brigham Hospital, Boston for tests and surgery.
1963	January 29	RF died; memorial service at Amherst two weeks later.

Small unresolved discrepancies in dating may be noted in comparing Lawrance Thompson, the Frost family headstone, and John Eldridge Frost's *The Nicholas Frost Family* (Milford, N.H.: The Cabinet Press, 1943), pp. 111-113.

For Once, Then, Something

1914-1928

At the outset of these family letters, Robert Frost was, at forty, a newly discovered poet. After half a lifetime of interrupted college studies, odd jobs, farming, teaching, and the seeking of uneasy clarities, he had sold his first farm and packed his family off to live for a few years in England. Once there, he met and visited with a succession of literary notables. It was in England also that his first two books were published, and he returned to the United States a widely recognized if not established poet. The next thirteen years saw Robert and Elinor's four surviving children growing up. Theirs was a close family life marked by pride and a sense of mutual obligation. Frost commenced the first of a series of college tenures as poet in residence at Amherst and followed this with three one-year terms at the University of Michigan. He was widely sought as poet and performer. When he and Elinor returned to England in 1928 with Marjorie — their only child as yet unmarried or without immediate plans for marriage — it was to be an idyll of their middle years, a warming return to old friends and familiar places. As it developed, the trip was fraught both with nostalgia and a number of anxieties, and they returned to Vermont gladly, just before the publication of Frost's sixth book.

RF to Carol Frost

[Post card]   [West Lothian, Scotland, 1914]

I suppose the Germans would like to do something to this.[1] I have seen a lot of fellows marching about here who will do something to the Germans. [Unsigned]

[1] The face of the card pictures the Forth Bridge, a railway span, as seen from South Queensferry.

RF to Frost Children[1]

DEAR KIDS   [New York, February 1915]

This is where Merfyn[2] suffered imprisonment for five days[3] and got acquainted with the scum of the earth while I got acquainted with a poet who wrote a poem called Scum of the Earth[4]. Poor Merfyn had to be all alone most of the time and he was in the realest danger of being sent straight back in the boat he came by. There was one man down there who shot himself while we were there rather than be sent back. And there were mad people and sad people and bad people in the detention rooms. I don't

[1] Following their English sojourn, RF made arrangements for the family to live, on a paying basis, with the Lynch family in Bethlehem, N. H. He had first made a hay fever retreat there in 1906, and the Frosts had returned a number of times in the intervening years to stay with this charming couple. With his family comfortably settled at the Lynches, RF made a number of side trips — both business and pleasure — before joining them in Bethlehem. They remained there for four months.

[2] Son of the poet Edward Thomas, under the Frosts' care during their return trip from two and a half years in England.

[3] An exaggerated reference to Merfyn's overnight detention on Ellis Island as an unsponsored alien.

[4] Robert Haven Schauffler.

know how I ever got Merfyn out of it. What a liar that American consul in London was to say Merfyn would come in all right. He came in all wrong.   PAPA

RF to Lesley Frost

Franconia, New Hampshire,

DEAR LESLEY: 26 September 1917

You've given us Miss Pendleton[1] and some of the girls (It was terrible about the poor thing with the Hope Chest — terrible that she should have been allowed to make her life out of one expectation. Probably she had been indifferent about her studies and her family had been driven to use every appeal of imagination and sentiment to wake her up.) Next you must give us what seems to be the idea of your course in English. I wonder if your teacher will let you into his mind in the matter or will simply start off with an assignment of work. I began last Thursday with an effort more or less vain I suppose to tell my one class how I wished to be taken. My course is intended for students who like myself write. I shall not judge them by the amount they write during the year but by their one best piece of writing. The theme in which they transcend their ordinary school level — that is for me. But more important than that they achieve anything is that they lead a literary life. The only out and out failure will be failing to convince me that they have failed to lead a literary life. They will naturally ask what they must do to convince me. Why the first thing to do will be to lead the life honestly and not in pretense. I dont see much hope of their convincing me unless they begin by doing that. They may have to talk to me a little so as to show that they have the art of writing at heart and they may have to show me a little of their writing. But a little of both writing and talk will go a long way. I can promise to do them more justice than the world commonly does us if they will do their part and lead the life I ask. And it's for them to find out what I mean by a literary life. One thing I suppose it means is outbursts of writing without self-criticism. You must not always be self-watchful. You must let go. The self-criticism belongs to lulls in inspiration. And it's only when you get far enough away from your work to begin to be critical of it yourself that anyone's else criticism can be tolerable and helpful to you. A teacher's talk is an outrage on fresh work that your mind still glows with. Always be far ahead with your writing. Bring only to class old and cold things that you begin to know what you think of yourself.

This is some of what I said and some of what I shall say tomorrow night when I meet the class again. Writing out this way will make it easier to say it.

Affectionately   ROB

[1] After staying with the John Lynch family in Bethlehem, New Hampshire, the Frosts moved to a farm in Franconia. In January 1917 RF taught his first term at Amherst College, and Lesley graduated from Amherst High School that June. This letter finds Lesley a freshman at Wellesley College. Ellen Fitz Pendleton was Wellesley's president. Although headed "Franconia," the content of the letter suggests that it was written in Amherst where RF was beginning his second term of teaching.

EF to Lesley Frost

MY DARLING LITTLE GIRL:-   [Franconia, fall 1917]

This is at half past nine, Tuesday evening, and I have just finished packing and getting things ready for an early start [to Amherst] tomorrow morning. Papa went yesterday morning and took four trunks with him, and so he will have the house a little bit ready for us when we get there. I am awfully sorry I haven't written much to you lately. It won't happen again, dear, but I have been very, very busy doing a little sewing with the machine while I have it. Marjorie and Irma had to have something to wear. And then there has been packing and getting the house in order to leave.

I feel sorry to go lately because the house seems so cosey and home-like, and I rather dread getting another house in condition to live in. But I rather think the house down there will be nice, too.[1]

Your letter came just before supper, and the children and I have been quite raging about the injustice of the tennis judges.[2] You ought to have heard Irma sputter about it. I have always heard that there was a great deal of injustice in regard to athletic[s] in all colleges and now I can believe it. But don't feel really badly about it, will you? It seems worse, I know, than it would seem if you didn't deserve to get on, but I feel sure that you will have a chance to show what you can do before its all over.

But I can't help shuddering at the thought of your going out to play the second day in spite of the bad cold you had taken the day before. How could you do it? You might easily have taken some serious sickness from it. Remember I care more about your health than about either scholarship or tennis.[3]

I am sending $ 2 in this letter, and I will have papa send you a check at once. I will certainly send you a cake as soon as I get settled down there. I am glad you are eating a heartier breakfast, and you must buy cookies or something to eat between meals when you are so awfully hungry.

Now I must say goodnight, darling, for I must get some sleep tonight. A good hug and lots of kisses from Mama.

[1] EF's references are to the Franconia farm and the Wood house in Pelham, Massachusetts, adjacent to Amherst.

[2] This is the first of many self-explanatory references to Lesley's misadventures as a Wellesley freshman which suggest the depth of RF and EF's involvement in their children's lives.

[3] Illness and the fear of illness are frequent themes in EF's letters. They serve as reminders of her own delicate health, and RF's, and a time of less sophisticated medical knowledge.

RF to Lesley Frost

Pelham Mass [achusetts] but address us at

DEAR LESLEY: Amherst Mass R.F.D. No 2 [Fall 1917]

We don't want to make ourselves obnoxious or even nuisances, but I think we owe it both to ourselves and these girls to find out why you failed to make the team when other girls you defeated have made it and why you were dismissed by that senior from a game you were winning. Either one of three things; you did something you ought not to do or the senior did something she ought not to do or the terms of the contest were not what you thought they were.

It may very well be that the selection wasnt made for skill in tennis but rather for skill in tennis combined with social qualifications we dont know anything about and that that is generally understood in the college. You could ask your sophomore without any show of feeling in a spirit of honest inquiry. Or it may be that the team is made up of as good players as possible who shall be entirely congenial to each other. We really ought to know if you went out under a misapprehension.

Then again in your inexperience you may have overstepped some rule of the game. That hardly seems possible. There must have been some referee to call your attention to any fault you were committing whether accidentally or on purpose. Still I should want to ask.

What I like least is your dismissal from the court in the middle of a game you were winning. How do you know that it doesnt reflect on your honor in some way? The least you could have asked would have been in Cordelias words, "Let me the knowledge of my fault bear with me."[1] Demanding an explanation may get you a chance to give an explanation. There is something to clear up on one side or the other or both sides.

If no one did you an injustice you dont want to do yourself the injustice of looking on yourself as much injured when you are not.

The thing to do is to make a record at once of the names of the girls you beat and the scores you beat them by, and the name of the girl who sent you from the court in the middle of a game you were winning. (Make sure of this girl for my benefit.) Then feel your way toward action. Talk with your sophomore and possibly with the senior at your house. Perhaps one of them will go with you and merely listen while you ask the senior who dismissed you a few plain questions. After that I should carry the matter up to the member of the faculty who has supervision of athletics or to your advisor if you have one.

I shouldn't drag Mr Young[2] into it at all. But I sha'n't refuse to be dragged into it and even to come down to Wellesley unless it is made more intelligible at once. Keep this letter as your warrant to show if there is any question of your judgement in finding out your rights. I may want you to show it to Mr Young before all's said and done.

Very disagreeable — the whole business. My way at your age would have been to shut up in my shell. I was always too inclined to give up wanting anything that was denied me unjustly and take it out in a feeling of injured superiority. I think that was because I took it too seriously. There would be such a thing as not taking it seriously enough to want to understand and be understood. It will be taking it just about right if you follow the course I advise you here. So it seems to me as I write anyway. Say what *you* think. At least you must get me the names and scores I ask for.

Here's ten dollars to use as you think best. I know you wont be ambitious to match pennies with really rich girls. Dont apologise for needing what you need.

Love from us all PAPA

¹ *King Lear.*
² Charles Lowell Young, Professor of English at Wellesley, had kindly assisted Lesley in completing her application for admission there. On a number of occasions thereafter, he became her confidant and advisor in college matters.

RF to Lesley Frost

[Portion of letter missing]   [Amherst, Massachusetts, fall 1917]
... bit. Keep your eye on it and get what you can out of it for the money it costs and try not to let it cost any more than the money. What a show that was at Miss Bates.[1] I should be sorry now if an "opportunity" like that had fooled you. It would be damnable, if it had pleased you. You could have followed me round on my lecturing these last two winters and seen forty such rediculous rites — flatter rapture and all. I doubt if Miss Bates is a very wise person. I doubt if many people we meet are thoroughly sound and wise. We cant afford to be guided by any one but ourselves and thats not because we are perfect but because we are no more imperfect than others and if we are going to be lead by blindness, the blindness may as well be our own. It has the chance of being better suited to our particular cases anyway.

Keep your balance — that's all. Your marks don't matter. I like to have the Latin and French present a good hard resistance. You'll get a lot out of them, marks or no marks. The converting of stories into Latin is just what I should think you would rise to sooner or later. Your memorizing of so much Latin should have stocked your mind with idiom. You'll find it will come out as you work it. Memorize some of the Livy — find time. Read in the grammar a little, I should too, and take special notice of the cases given in illustration. Some of those are worth remembering for their ideas as well as for their interesting forms.

Technical faults! I suppose that would be the reason they would give for putting you off the court. Well what you say sounds sensible. You seem to be taking the right way with such people. We mustn't mind them. Whatever else we do we mustnt be driven into a hole or corner by them. Put not your faith in them but laugh with and at them and beat them at their own game if it's a game you like to play.

We ought not to mind when things don't go too well with you because hard times will tend to throw you back on us.   Affectionately   PAPA

---

1 Katharine Lee Bates, herself a Wellesley graduate, an author best known for "America the Beautiful," and Professor of English at Wellesley.

EF and RF to Lesley Frost

DARLING LESLEY --   [Amherst, fall 1917]

The postman has just left your Sunday letter. I have been waiting to get it before I wrote you. I think your behavior is just fine under it all. *Do not let them make you suffer one bit*, dear. There is evidently a mixture of reasons for what has happened but the chief of them is certainly their commonness and pettiness. It is a pity that your kind of ability and freshness of mind should have to be subjected to their petty judgments. I somehow feel that it might have been better at Smith, but probably not. When you come home Saturday, we will talk over what is best to be done about it. Remember nothing of this sort could make the slightest difference in papa's faith in your ability, or pleasure in it, or mine either. All we care about is the effect it may have on your health and happiness.

I have wanted to make you a cake, dear, but I just haven't been able to do much work since we came down here. [Three sentences deleted.] Now I am feeling a little stronger, and I shall be feeling like myself again in a few weeks.

You must, of course, have more money to buy yourself food. Some fruit and Educator crackers to eat just before going to bed would be good. Now you are coming home Saturday afternoon and stay until Sunday morning. Papa will meet you at Northampton and it will seem *so* good to see you.   With heaps of love   MAMA

Papa went over to Northampton to meet you last night. Your message didn't come until after he had left the house. He was very much disappointed, and wanted to go right on to Wellesley.

Just write the hour when you will leave so [uth] Framingham and I will try to meet you at Springfield

R.[1]

[1] This second postscript is in RF's hand.

EF to Lesley Frost

MY DARLING LESLEY   [Amherst] Friday evening [fall 1917]

I intended to write to you in time for papa to take my letter into the office this evening (he has gone to a fraternity banquet) but I couldn't. However, I think I will write anyway this evening, and the letter will reach you Monday noon, if not tomorrow night. Papa and I were awfully glad to get your letter Wednesday. We were getting worried and on the point of telephoning to you. I am very much afraid, my dear, that you are overworking, and you know I don't want you to do that. It doesn't pay at all in the long run. I will wait as patiently as I can until Thanksgiving and then if I think your health is really suffering (and I can tell as soon as I see you) there will have to be some sort of change.

Don't for a minute worry about what *we* will think of your marks. You know papa is not anxious to have you shine

as a student because he thinks that to shine is more injurious
to one's right development than not to shine. And I think
that marks are a curse, anyway, and not to be worried about.
All I regret is that you have to work in such a rush that you
can't enjoy what you are doing. Perhaps after the Christmas
vacation it will all come easier.

I like this house better and better. I never lived in a
house where the housework seemed so easy. If it wasn't for
the teaching I should have an easy time these days. I think
the children like it, too. Papa is reading "With Fire &
Sword"[1] aloud evenings now, and the children, especially
Carol, are absorbed in it. Somehow, the slaughter in it makes
me feel even worse than it used to, because such things seem
more real and possible to me since this war began. Irma has
begun her knitting for the Red Cross. We went in Wednesday
afternoon and got the yarn for a sweater, and she has got
a lot done on it already. I am going in one afternoon a week
to make dressings. About your going into Boston to do
settlement work — it seems to me that it isn't wise for you
to do it this year. Everyone says that the Freshman year
is made the hardest of all, and so you will probably have
more strength for outside things another year. I would
rather have you rest quietly in your room. However, if you
feel well enough yourself and think it would help to take
your mind off the tyranny of marks, I won't object. I think
perhaps you'd better join the C.A.[2] Of course it isn't
like joining a church.

There was a frightful storm here Wednesday afternoon,
the day Irma and I went into town. We expected to take
the 4.30 car home, but a huge tree blew down across the
track and stopped all traffic on that street. They began to
saw it as soon as the storm lulled a bit, and Irma & I waited
around in the cold and wet for two hours, and as there
seemed no immediate prospect then of their cutting through

it, I hired McGrath, the jitney driver, to bring us home. It cost a dollar, but I felt that I must get home at any cost. I have been awfully tired ever since.

Isn't Mrs. Fobes kind?[3] It won't probably cost $10 to make over the dress she sent, and perhaps you might spend the rest for some evening slippers. Isn't the blue smock just sweet?

I am going to make you a cake, dear, as soon as I have time. We sent the chestnuts but didn't insure them. If they don't come all right, let us know.

I am afraid we left the essay on Mountain climbing up home in one of the pigeon-holes of the desk, but Mr. Glover has the key and we can ask him to go in and send *all* the papers in the pigeon-holes. Irma and I had a vigorous cleaning up and there aren't many papers there and no particularly private ones. I will attend to that tomorrow.

Mrs. Thomas[4] sent a series of drawings that Baba had made for you. I will send them in another envelope, and also the last letter from Mrs. Thomas.

Now, dear little girl, good night with hugs & kisses from

MAMA

[1] The first novel of a trilogy by Henryk Sienkiewicz which RF had originally read in 1894.

[2] The College's Christian Association.

[3] Mrs. J. Warner Fobes, a summer neighbor of the Frosts in Franconia, whose generosity to the family over many years was both considerable and many-sided.

[4] Helen Thomas, widow of the poet Edward Thomas.

EF to Lesley Frost

DEAR LESLEY --

[Amherst] Sunday evening
[11 November 1917]

Company has been here all the afternoon (two college boys and the Johnsons from Hadley) and so I didn't write the long letter to you that I intended to write. I see that

I needn't expect to write to you on Sunday because there is apt to be company all the afternoon, and then in the evening after papa has read aloud until half past eight or nine, I am almost too tired to think of writing.

Do you realize that we didn't get a letter from you all last week? Each day I was terribly disappointed not to get one and had to assure myself vigorously that you were just too busy to write, in order to keep from worrying about you. If you were sick, you wouldn't keep us in ignorance of it, would you? You must promise not to do anything like that.

Last week I was sick in bed all the week and am not the least bit strong yet, but am slowly getting strong again. I was taken sick just as I was planning to go to Springfield to buy some furniture. I went this week Wednesday, however. Papa went with me. I really wasn't strong enough to go but we had all grown so tired of the empty house that I felt I must exert myself and go. We had pretty good luck and bought two good carpets, one exceedingly beautiful table for the sitting room, a luxurious Davenport (a great bargain) and other things besides. So far we have spent $350 for furniture and there is more to buy yet. You will like the house, I know, and will love the woods behind the house. Thanksgiving is 2 weeks from next Thursday. We haven't had a letter from Mrs. Moody[1] since last summer when she sent the invitation and of course something may happen to prevent our going there. In that case you would spend all your time here. Have you taken your "cuts" yet? Couldn't you take some of them the Friday and Saturday after Thanksgiving, so you could stay with us until Sunday. I can scarcely wait until I can see you. My sickness prevented my writing to Mr. Glover to go up to the house and look for the composition you wanted and later papa said he really didn't want Mr. Glover to ransack the desk, but if Miss Drew[2] insisted on having the theme again, he would rather go up and get it himself than have you write another one on the same subject. Tell Miss Drew what he says and perhaps she will relent. I am very glad you are enjoying the English class and glad that you are getting to feel at home in the Latin class. Do you continue to admire the French teacher? What alot there will be to ask you about when you come.

Stark Young[3] hasn't been here yet. I think he will probably wait for an invitation and I think it will be a little while yet before he gets an invitation. He is very pleasant to papa, though, when papa sees him in town, and sends his love to me.

The worst of our life here is that Carol has absolutely no one to play with and as he doesn't care to read or knit or draw as the girls do, he just does nothing a good deal of the time and that drives me almost distracted. I believe that next year, somehow or other, we must send him to a good boys school. I think he is perishing for some pleasant association with boys of his own age. Papa has had him and Irma do quite a lot of writing the last few weeks, and he has written some very good things. He has gone hunting several times in the woods but there seems to be no sight or sound of any game and he has become discouraged and says he won't go any more.

Papa has just agreed to read before the New England Woman's Club in Boston the 11th of April and I am thinking that we'll all go to Boston at that time and take rooms and have a good time all together. You can come in from Wellesley every day and we will go to picture galleries and the theatre.

Well, I must stop for this time.

I do hope nothing has gone wrong with you, darling. I will be restless until I get some word.

Very lovingly   MAMA

[1] Harriet Moody, the enterprising widow of poet-dramatist William Vaughan Moody, maintained a farm near William Cullen Bryant's birthplace in

Cummington, Massachusetts, and a home in Chicago where she entertained Padraic Colum, Carl Sandburg, Rabindranath Tagore, Frost, and other literary notables. She also made a New York City apartment available for the use of friends and writers, and it was here, in early 1919, that RF first met Ridgely Torrence. Her generosity to the Frost family included the gift of a ruby sapphire ring to EF and frequent invitations to visit her.

[2] Helen Drew, Professor of English at Wellesley.

[3] Stark Young, a member of Amherst's English faculty, had hosted RF on his first campus visit in April 1916. Within a matter of months, he travelled to Franconia with an invitation from President Alexander Meiklejohn that RF join the Amherst faculty for a term of teaching. Although both of these occasions had their pleasant side, Frost had reason to take offense at the man's advantage-seeking, and he disagreed with a number of his views.

RF to Lesley Frost

DEAR LESLEY: Amherst, 13 November 1917[1]

If Miss Waite or any other school-fool gives you that chance again by asking what your father will say or said [,] you answer My father knows teachers and my father knows me; and then go on to inform them that your father has delt in marks and dealt with people who delt in marks in every kind of school there is in America.

And you tell the Latin bitch that it is none of her business how you started in Latin: all she has to do is to mark you as low as she can to satisfy her nature. I mean tell her that if she tries anymore of her obiter dicta on you. Or perhaps you might tell her if it was rediculous to start Latin with reading then it was rediculous to teach it the way she teaches it with no sense of literary values.

Dont let them scare you out of what you know must be right. Remember Mr Gardner was on my side and he knew more Latin than all Wellesley put together. Only the other day Prof Litchfield here said he didn't see how any love of Latin was going to be saved or inspired unless by some such way as ours. But it doesnt matter. Your she professor has a right to kill you as an example of what befalls any one who reflects by word or deed on her own little commonness.

The worst is Miss Waites remark that seems to imply belief in the verdict of marks. I was telling Whicher[2] that I supposed we couldnt run a class so as to give all kinds of minds the same chance in it. Every attitude a teacher takes toward a subject is bound to work some injustice and occasionally even great injustice to some pupils. The greatest safeguard then of good teaching is to keep it always before the class that the teachers judgement is ridiculously far from final. I make a business of laughing at my marks all I can. I make light of it all for my own protection and the protection of those who might suffer innocently under me. The understanding is that there is always appeal from my judgement to the judgement of other teachers [,] the judgement of the world (which rather scorns teachers) and the judgement of God. I wish I thought Miss Waite was joking the joke I joke when she said "You have some hope of yourself then?" The chances are that being a woman she wasnt joking.

Now lets look at this as a game to lose a little sleep over but not much sleep. You can win it even with the umpire against you. I mean Latin as one horse teachers would like to make out. But you must just put in a few months now and settle those verbs and declensions and rules.[3] I believe you will have a freer use of them from having come to them the way you have. But you must get them and have the job over with. You must learn the principal parts of every verb in your lesson and you must write out the conjugation from the models in your grammar or beginners book of two a day. Write out the declension of a couple of nouns or adjectives too. Make these extra exercises for yourself. Tend to that list of a hundred rules near the end of the grammar. Keep a little note book of interesting expressions and idioms. Of course measure this to your strength, remembering always that the main thing is the

English and you are free to let everything except that and even including that go to [the] devil when you please.

I was sick all night last night with anger and so was mamma. You ought to have heard what mamma called them all every time she woke up. It's not so much anything as it is our own stupidity in letting such people get one on us. Damn their loathsomeness.

But do it on the highminded. Never be brought to take a low school view of literature, English French Spanish or Latin. English has come up out of that Egypt that Latin is still in within the years since I studied it (a very little) in college. A great many teachers would be ashamed to teach English now as you say Sheffield was mauling that poem. [Sheffield is a clever cut-and-dried mind, but he is a survival. Remember he drove me out of Harvard.][4] English has come to realize that it has a soul to take into consideration. It has in a good many quarters. It can still be pretty awful in the hands of some teachers. And there is this consolation that it is better to have a bad Latin teacher than a bad English teacher. I think I should want to take you away from a bad English teacher whether you wanted to stay in college or not. What you suffer in Latin after all is not right at the center of your being.

Oh and in conclusion be reminded that your safety in a subject you succeed in has to be provided for. You mustn't let praise keep you from stretching away ahead where praise at a given time can't follow you. Good writing is away beyond teachers to do justice to. Write it rich, fill it with everything.

Remember to tell em, if they ask, that I know teachers and I know you.   Affectionately   PAPA

I made it end exactly with the paper!

[1] Although earlier letters from RF and EF commented upon the narrow

and restrictive practices of many teachers, this "position paper" provides a precise and moving exposition of RF's views on the student's freedom to learn.

[2] George F. Whicher, Professor of English at Amherst and a close friend of the Frost family.

[3] See RF to Lesley Frost, 3 December 1917, for portions of their ongoing exchange on the subject of Latin.

[4] Alfred Dwight Sheffield had been a young assistant in English at Harvard during the years 1897-99 when RF was a student there. See RF's first 1934 letter to Lesley Frost Francis for a more charitable reaction to his onetime instructor. The brackets are RF's.

RF to Lesley Frost

DEAR LESLEY: Amherst, 3 December 1917

Be sure to keep a copy of the poem in French. You may be able to use it when you write sometime on A Year in College. And keep everything you do and have done in everything else. You'll live to get some fun out of it yet. I'd like to know if the White chapel Frenchman brought up the subject of your presumption in having attempted a poem in French himself. You could make an audience laugh with the story of that adventure.[1] Prosody (spelled with an o) is the science of versification or meters. It is something most modern poets take pride in professing to know nothing about. There is really very little to it in either English or French anyway. You could learn all that is practicable in it in ten minutes. But the fact is you know it already or your ear knows it and what you would be learning if you turned your attention to it would be merely the technical names for things that are second nature to you. We've talked about it a little already, more as a help to scanning Latin poetry (which we never read without scanning). Hendecasyllables is one of the technical words I mean in prosody. Hexameter is another. But what's the use! You should have heard Wilfrid[2] confessing complete ignorance of the business to the assembled professors of Chicago University last winter. They thought none the less of him but rather the more. Possibly that was because he was an Englishman and a reputation. They might have skun him alive if he had been a mere pupil in their classes. And then again they might not. They were obviously larger men than your White chapel Frenchman.

I wonder if Young[3] got no more satisfaction out of the swab than that. Dont let him make you give two thoughts extra to his course. Tend to the Latin, the algebra, and, then if you have any extra energy left, to the Spanish. And dont let Miss Drew suspect for a moment that you may be neglecting her subject. Enjoy that and give her all the pleasure you can. She at least has something of our view of things and you can be yourself with her. I'm looking forward to the essay on Hiawatha. Remember you are to lay most stress on the source books you go to. Longfellows poem mustn't take too much space in proportions. The reason for that being the nature of the essay called for by the authorities at Wellesley.

I've been looking up aedes. And I find it has that form in the nominative singular (as well as in the plural). It is one of those words with the stem ending i. Most of them have is in the nominative singular but some have es and they dont lengthen in the genitive. Amnis amnis amni amnem etc. They all have ium in the *genitive plural;* whereas the common third declension genitive plural ending is a simple um. (I'd like to bet that once on a time all genitive plurals were orum or arum and they got cramped into um.) See what you can find out in the grammar about these ium genitives. I wish there was some rule about their ablative singular. It isnt always i.

You've got enough material already to write your A Year in College. You dont have to worry.

Rah rah rah for some other college than Wellesley.

PAPA

[1] Lesley's poem — "La Vie et la Mort" — survives. For a Frost poem,

it begins intriguingly "At the edge of the deep woods..." and reflects the influence of symbolist poetry. Along with a full page of conservative corrections, the unnamed teacher has appended a comment — in French — which suggests that the original assignment called for prose: "You obviously have some talent but, for the moment, you should rather concentrate on the very real and very great difficulties of [writing] good prose. It is the best way to acquire the feeling and taste for, and the mastery of, a language; [qualities] without which one cannot write as correctly and elegantly as poetry demands." For Lesley's adventures with another poem, in English, see EF to Lesley Frost, [March 1919] and RF to Lesley Frost, 24 March 1919.

2 Wilfred W. Gibson, Georgian poet and one of RF's good friends in England.

3 See RF to Lesley Frost, [fall 1917], p. 9, n. 2.

RF to Lesley Frost

DEAR LESLEY: Amherst, 9 December 1917

Read Amy's "Men Women and Ghosts"[1] if you can possibly find time right away so that if Amy invites you over to see her you'll be ready for her. You won't perhaps care for the longer poems and of course you won't go far in any poem that doesn't get hold of you. Find something to like though. I know you can. Be fairer to her than some people have been to you. She's not going to examine you and see how well you know and like her. You simply wont want to feel lost in the dark should she happen to illustrate what she means by cadence rythm and such things from her own work. She won't talk about *meter*. She scorns the very word. Prosody, too, she hates the name of. She may try to tell you what determines the ending place of a line in free verse. She'll be interesting. You'll find that there'll be alot in what she says.

But perhaps if she writes to you and invites you just now, you had better say you will feel safer to wait till I can come in and show you the way across the city. Tell her I shall be in town toward the end of the week.

I mean to get to Wellesley on the coming Thursday or Friday.

I don't think you had much of any chance to look at any of my boy's work when you were here. You can let that wait till you are home again. But enclosed is one blessed little poem by someone I never heard of and another of not much worth by Raymond Holden. Keep the good one.[2]

I'm not going to talk Latin every time I write. But I've just been having a good look at conjunctions in coordinate sentences. Coordinates are sentences on equal terms neither one subordinate to the other. Both use the indicative. They are joined together by copulative conjunctions, disjunctive conjunctions and adversative conjunctions. Copulative conjunctives are *et que at que*: they simply hold together the two members — that is to say the two equal sentences. Disjunctive conjunctions sort of put apart at the same time they hold together the two equal sentences. *Aut* and *sed* are examples. Adversative conjunctions connect the sentences but in some way contrast the meaning. They give something of the idea of "on the other hand." I speak of these things mostly to increase your "grammatical vocabulary." We have the same lingo in English, copulative, disjunctive and adversative. They cover the whole subject of coordinate conjunction. Subordinate conjunctions such as *ut* are a little harder because they involve the subjunctive mood and "sequence of tenses". Alii . . . alii . . . and some words used like that amount to adversative conjunction in idea. You translate them some did so and so and others (on the other hand) did something else.

I wrote a rather red letter to Young. But I mean not to keep myself excited any longer. The worst is Miss Fletcher. But the Frenchman annoys me too.

Affectionately   PAPA

[1] Amy Lowell, the eccentric poet-critic, was an admirer of RF's poetry well before they first met in 1915. Her home, Sevenels, was situated in Brookline,

within an hour of Wellesley. *Men, Women and Ghosts* (1916) was Miss Lowell's third book of poetry.

² One clipping is Berenice Van Slyke's "I Stood at Twilight" with RF's marginal comment: "A right sort of subject and just the right handling." Also enclosed is Leslie Nelson Jennings' "Portion" which RF terms "Utter damn fool talk." Part of this page — bearing RF's comments and possibly the Holden poem — has been torn off. Frost and Raymond Holden had first met in 1915 and enjoyed a kinship as poets and academic rebels. Although their friendship was to be sorely tried, each expressed great admiration for the other's poetry over a period of many years.

RF to Lesley Frost

DEAR LESLEY: Amherst, 18 March 1918

We'll all be together again soon telling funny stories.

This is the day in the week when I get a chance to do to others as still others do to you. I wonder if truth were told how many of my underlings suffer from my exactions as you suffer from poor Miss Drew's.

Do you know I half suspect Miss Drew meant to take your sarcasm to herself by her correction of "teacher" to "instructor". It was as much as to say "teacher" is too general. "You aimed at me; so say instructor and be done with it." Were you shooting at her?

First blue bird for us this morning.

Tell us your train of Friday and perhaps we can be at Northampton to meet you.

Affectionately   PAPA

Enclosed is five.

EF to Lesley Frost

DARLING LESLEY,- [Amherst, April 1918]

I certainly felt discouraged when I got your letter telling about your fresh cold. I really don't think, Lesley, that you can do what ordinary girls do, you get sick in various ways so easily. Or else you are thoughtless about yourself. It seems to me that you have been sick nearly all the time this year. I shall be glad when its over. And I am afraid you will have to study pretty hard the rest of the time. They are apt to pile on the work just when the weather gets nice enough to wander about out doors. Well, there are only about six weeks more of class work for you. It's too bad you have that long wait between examinations, but perhaps we can arrange for you to visit friends in Boston then. I know Mrs. Russell[1] would like to have you stay with her two or three days, and I think the Snows would, too, if they knew about it.

Papa starts for the West tomorrow morning. I guess I haven't written to you about Mrs. Moody[2] having arranged readings for him at 3 State Universities out there. Then he will go to Cornell on the way back. If all goes well, he will clear $175 and that will buy a Liberty Bond and settle up our bills here that are getting rather too many for us. It isn't much money for such a lot of hard work but there will probably be some advantage to his reputation in his getting acquainted with certain professors and critics out there. He is going to the Minnesota State Univ. where Joseph Warren Beach teaches and he is going to stay with Joseph Warren.

He will be gone nearly two weeks. I think he intends to write to Miss Cook, of the Dana Hall school, before he goes, to propose reading there the 4th of May.[3] If that arrangement is made, and if he is not too tired to fulfill it when he gets back, we shall all go to Boston the 1st or 2nd day of May and stay there about a week. You could come in and stay with us as much as possible. Carol is much better the last few days. The great question is what we should do with kitty. We have considered many possible plans, but so far we haven't thought of any thing satisfactory.

Papa and I went to the Meiklejohns[4] to supper last night. A Miss Patterson, a teacher in Berkeley College, Cal.

was there, and also Mr. & Mrs. Allis and one or two other people. Mrs. Meiklejohn has on a new evening dress every time I go there.

Have I written to you about the new arrangement for papa's work next year? He is going to get $2500 for about 4 months work, during October, Nov. Dec. & Jan. Then he will have all the rest of the year free for writing. It seems as if something ought to be done in that time.

I must put this letter out before the postman comes. I'll write again in a day or two.

With heaps of love and kisses, darling, from MAMA.

1 Ada Dwyer Russell, a retired actress and companion to Amy Lowell.

2 See EF to Lesley Frost, [11 November 1917], n. 1.

3 This visit undoubtedly offered RF the opportunity to arrange for Irma's admission to the school, in Wellesley, for the following September.

4 Alexander Meiklejohn, president of Amherst College until his resignation in 1923.

RF to Lesley Frost

DEAR LESLEY: Amherst, 13 May 1918

Just as much as this gives room for to tell you a disappointment, namely, that we can't get away before Wednesday and possibly Thursday afternoon on account of ill health in the head of the family who am in bed at this moment with something the doctor doesn't no what to call because he hasn't been called in to look at me. As near as he can make out by telephone it seems to be this here throatal (throtle) epidemic that seems to be epidemic in Amherst. And if that weren't enough there is additional reason in the professional reasoner Ernest Hocking[1] who is to do the Phi Beta Kappa here this week and in whose audience I really ought to show myself. So we may as well say it won't be till Thursday afternoon on the four o'clock from here arriving in Boston at eight in the evening, too late for anything that day. We'll be beginning Boston then

only on Friday and as you will get free the next day you
wont have long to be disturbed by our being so near you
and you unable to see us. Lot of things to tell and listen to,
though except in an academic way I have had an adventureless year. Same with you — adventureless except in an
academic way. But in that way Oh my! I beat you in one
respect. I get an honorary M.A. from Amherst. Then it is
fixed that I am to do 1/3 time for 1/2 pay (that is 1/2 of 5000).
I haven't made myself particularly detested yet — that's
all that means. Give me another year to get into trouble.
I don't suppose I have done anything to distinguish myself
except to do one chapel talk that made talk and got me
chosen to give the talk at what is called Senior Chapel at
the end of the year. Without having distinguished yourself
as a mere student you have apparently made people like
you, or they wouldnt be trying as hard to entangle you in
the next year's courses. After all it's been an exciting and
varigated year for you — really just the kind of experience
mere tuition can't buy. Only fortune can bestow it, and she
cant do it entirely from without: she has to do much of it
from whithin. I don't quite get over my resentment against
some of Wellesley but *nearly* the last vestige goes with the
joke of your agreeing to take Latin Composition with Miss
Fletcher. That puts in on top of it all with a Laugh. *Aint* it
the funny world? Well that is about all I can write in this
position. I can tell you of the ups and downs of my Western
trip later. I personally conducted the elopement of Joseph
Warren Beech that awful sinner with an assistant of his in the
graduate school.[2] I never saw craziness as near the surface
as it is in Beech. He's a darn fool but he makes me laugh
when I'm near him — laugh and cut up. It was cruel of
me to marry him off, but I had to do it. I was cutting up.
It was like some Shakespearean confusion.

Wish we could see you play ball.

Anxious to see the story.

Affectionately PAPA

Boston address by Thursday night 97 Pinkney St.

1 William Ernest Hocking, Harvard philosopher and author of *The Meaning of God in Human Experience* (1912) whom RF had first met following his return from England in 1915.

2 Although here and elsewhere RF frequently exaggerated the circumstances to the point where a written apology was later required, he did urge Beach to press for an immediate marriage, accompanied the couple to Indiana for the ceremony, served as a witness, and feted them with a champagne dinner.

EF and RF to Lesley Frost

DEAR LESLEY,- [Franconia] Sunday evening [June 1918]

I do certainly hope that you won't take another cold just before coming home. And begin your packing Wednesday, so you won't be dreadfully hurried at the last moment. If it looks as if you had too much with you to pack nicely in the trunk, send a good sized bundle by Parcels Post. The express from Boston to Littleton leaves the North Station at nine oclock exactly, so you will have to get an early train from Wellesley into Boston. I think you'd better go to the Wellesley station sometime when you are down town and ask the ticket agent how you are to get your trunk across the city. I have completely forgotten how we did it last fall. Perhaps you can buy your ticket directly from Wellesley to Littleton but I don't think so. I think you go to the Armstrong Express just as soon as you get into the South Station, give them your check and have them check your trunk across the city. Then probably you have to re-check it to Littleton in the North Station. You must find out about it at Wellesley. Cross in the *Elevated* from the South to the North Station. You don't have to go out of the station to get it, you know.

It is Friday you are coming, isn't it? We are so very eager to have you with us. Irma and I have been down to the Red Cross twice. You can go with us when you come. Papa is gaining a little, I think, though he still coughs very badly and sweats so easily that it is almost impossible for him to exercise enough to sleep well without taking more cold.

It seems so strange that you have had roasting weather down there. It has been extremely cool here. People have trembled about a frost the last three nights, but there hasn't been one, fortunately, because there are a lot of potatoes and corn up around here.

Carol has had another accident. Three days ago he was out after pea sticks with his sharp hatchet and cut his leg just over the bone about an inch and a half. The doctor had to put in three stitches. He says it will be all healed in about a week.

Well, dear, I think I must go to bed. I wonder if you are with Mrs. Russell today. I wrote to her if it wasn't *perfectly* convenient for you to come, not to call you up.

Much love & kisses from   MAMA

Ask Mrs. Morse if it would'nt be wiser to send your trunk to the station Thursday night.

If it isnt too much trouble, you might get some needles for the Columbia [phonograph]. I think any of the different kinds are all right, but the last I bought were the Cleopatra, I think. They are $ .10 an envelope. We haven't any way to get them here.

Be sure not to set off on the journey with no money in your pocket for emergencies. You ought to have two or three dollars to spare anyway.   RF

Check for seven enclosed   R.F.

[1] See EF to Lesley Frost, [April 1918], n. 1.

EF to Lesley Frost

[Franconia] Saturday morning
DARLING LESLEY,-   [22 September 1918]

I wrapped up a few things to send you yesterday and took the package down to the office in the afternoon. There was a letter from Irma, giving your address as 25 Front St.[1] So I put that address on the wrapper. I insured the package, and if it doesn't reach you, which I don't suppose it will, you must inquire for it at the post office.

Mr. Parker just came up for the order, and brought your letter. I think that though you may be homesick, there will be interesting things to compensate, but I don't know about Irma. Her letter sounds pretty ominous. She dislikes the girls in her house very much. She wants you to write to her and go to see her as soon as you can. Perhaps you might go on Sunday, a week from tomorrow.[2]

It has rained here incessantly ever since you left, except one day, and it looked as if it might rain any minute that day. Mrs. Johnson had a rather frightful experience that day. A party of three or four people went from Spooner's to climb Kinsman, and when they were about 2/3 of the way up, the man of the party had an attack of acute indigestion. His wife stayed with him, and the other woman hurried back to Spooners, where they telephoned for Mrs. Johnson. She went at once, and climbed the mountain as fast as she could, though she was almost overcome by exhaustion, and found the poor man dead when she got there. She is pretty much worn out, for she has been out night and day ever since the Dr. went away.

Papa and I have been saying that perhaps, if he doesn't have to teach next term, we might get a small furnished house at Marblehead, instead of coming back here.

Well, I'll write again soon,

Lots & lots of love   MAMA

I forgot to tell you that papa & Hendricks[3] came up from Amherst late last night. Papa has hay fever, and Hendricks looks frightfully thin & nervous.

[1] In the last letter, plans were being made for Lesley's end-of-year retreat from Wellesley, to which she did not return. This letter is addressed to her at Marblehead, Massachusetts, where she had begun war work at an airplane factory.

[2] Irma was enrolled at Dana Hall School, in Wellesley.

[3] This is the first of many references to Walter Hendricks who graduated from Amherst in 1917 and was one of RF's admirers. After service in the army air corps, he taught college English and pursued his own poetry. Still later, he founded three Vermont colleges — Marlboro, Windham, and Mark Hopkins — and established himself as a successful publisher. RF to Lesley Frost, 24 October 1918, details a portion of Hendricks's military experience and explains why he looked "frightfully thin & nervous."

EF to Lesley Frost

[Franconia] Wednesday afternoon
DARLING LESLEY:-   [late September 1918]

I am sorry you have been out of money. I'll send $5 in this letter, but you'll have to be careful with it, for we are very short until after the 1st of Oct. and there won't be much to spare then. Its most unfortunate that Mrs. Wanvig[1] should have let you go down without being sure you were wanted, but it can't be helped now. Papa has sent to Rowell[2] for a little money and as soon as it comes I will write to Mrs. Wanvig, enclosing check for your board. Its dreadful that you and Irma both have colds. We haven't any yet, but its a wonder, for it has rained here steadily ever since you went. I hardly think you ought to go to see Irma Sunday. Certainly you mustn't go unless you are absolutely sure that there is no influenza[3] at Dana Hall, and unless you are feeling quite well again yourself. I am sorry about Irma's disagreeable experience, but I don't think it is serious. If she likes Miss Cook, and gets on fairly well in her classes, and especially if she enjoys the drawing and painting with Miss Patterson, I think it will come out all right, because I think the relations with the other girls will settle down into something tolerable after a while.

Hendricks went back to Amherst yesterday morning. He telegraphed for an extension of leave, but had the return telegram sent to Amherst, so he had to go back there. If he gets a longer leave, we shall see him again down there.

There are 72 cases of influenza in Littleton. Mr. Cummings, the lawyer, died of it last Sunday, and his wife is very ill with it. I haven't heard if there are any cases in Amherst or not.

Be as careful of yourself as possible, won't you. The children send much love & will write soon. Heaps of love and a good hug   from   MAMA

Can't you inquire of someone about cheaper board? I'll send your blue dress tomorrow or next day.

---

[1] Mrs. Susan Wanvig, a family friend, had suggested the possibility of Lesley's working in Marblehead and had arranged for rented quarters adjacent to a small restaurant.

[2] Wilbur Rowell was executor of the estate of RF's paternal grandfather.

[3] The worldwide influenza epidemic of 1918-19 claimed 20,000,000 lives, over a half million in the United States alone.

EF to Lesley Frost

My DARLING LESLEY -   Amherst [5 October 1918]

I am wondering a good deal of the time why it is you haven't written. But it may be you have written to Franconia this week. Amherst college changes its mind about as often as I do, apparently. Last Saturday morning Mr. Whicher[1] telephoned that the opening of college had been put off two weeks on account of the influenza. So we settled down comfortably up there, took the trunks back into the bedrooms, bought a cord of wood, Carol got out a hunting license, and we were just getting ready to put in some extra stoves Tuesday, when a telegram came saying that college was to open Thursday of this week. So the trunks were brought out again, and we hustled all day and got ready to come down yesterday. I fully expected a letter from you Tuesday noon and when one didn't come, I was nearly crazy for a while until papa telephoned to Mrs. Wanvig and found out you were all right. My nerves were all on edge and my endurance had about reached the limit, on account of my worry and suspense about Irma. Poor little girl, she has evidently been pretty sick, and it must have been terribly hard for her, all alone among strangers. She has had abscesses in her ears, and I am worried about her hearing. It will be several weeks before she is able to study, I am afraid, and so I almost think it would be better for her to come home. And what about your coming home? I am awfully afraid you'll have it, too, and there is no place for you to be cared for. I don't know how much of it there is in Amherst college. Some say there is none, and some say there are eleven cases today and one of the eleven very seriously ill. The doctors here and the army commandant didn't want college to open but Mr. Micklejohn was determined to have it open.

Guess how we got down here yesterday! Mr. Howes brought us down all the way in his Ford. Papa thought we would run less risk of infection than coming by train, but o, it was a tiresome trip. We were from 9 oclock in the morning until quarter of six in the afternoon, on the way, stopping about half an hour for lunch. It was so bitter cold when we started, and then it rained a cold sleety rain, and I thought we would have to take the train at Woodsville, but it got warmer as we went farther south and finally cleared off.

Miss Marsh's rooms are quite large and pleasant, but I hardly know what we are going to do about meals. They charge so much at the Clover Inn, and there are no conveniences for me to get our meals in [. . .] We haven't decided yet *what* to do.[2]

Have you got heat in your room yet? I think you must be having a hard time, getting up early and working all day, and no comforts. I am waiting with anxiety for your first letter about it. Do you think your position has been sort of created for you by Mrs. Wanvig's friend? If that is so, you hardly ought to stay, for there are many places advertised constantly where you would be really useful.

I think the influenza has got a start in Franconia. Three of the teachers have been sick with what Mrs. Johnson called bronchitis, but the day before we left, one of them, a Miss Folsom was taken to the hospital with bronchial pneumonia, and wasn't expected to live. I imagine it was influenza all the time.

The war news is perfectly splendid, isn't it? Papa & I were walking down after the mail the day Bulgaria unconditionally surrendered, and when we got within hearing distance of the village, we heard a furious ringing of bells. It kept up until we got there and found that Edward Parker and Paul Rich were ringing them because of the good war news. It was quite exciting while papa and I were guessing the reason for it, and quite thrilling when we found it out.

Well, I ought to go to bed because I have been awfully tired all day.

I should have had your every day blue dress all fixed if we hadn't been called down suddenly. I'll try to send it Monday.

You *must* write at least a postal more often, dear. I must know how you are nearly every day just now when everything is as agitating.

With heaps of Love, from   MAMA

1 See RF to Lesley Frost, 13 November 1917, n. 2.

2 Miss Caroline Marsh was a high school Latin teacher who rented rooms to the Frosts in her home at 19 Main Street.

RF to Lesley Frost

Dear Lesley: Amherst, 18 October 1918

Your adventures are partly ours and we enjoy them with you but it seems to us that just your being free from college and exactly where you choose to be in an aeroplane factory ought to be nearly adventure enough for one year for all of us, you and Mamma and Sue[1] and the children, without your casting about for further excitement that we know not of. In other words please try to restrict your adventures to your work, keep them within the walls of the Curtis factory if you care anything for our peace of mind. I liked the propeller episode. But that ought to mark a limit. You surely took risk enough there for all practical purposes. You took a chance and luck smiled broadly on you. That's all clean business and the worst that could have come of it would have made no difference to you or us in the long run. We simply howled with pleasure at the way Mr Lunt came into the story in the nick of time.[2] You were bold and you were rewarded with heaven-sent help. But the yachting with Mr Weeler doesn't yield us the same kind of thrills — if it yields us anything but chills. I wasn't there and don't know all that was in the air, but I doubt very much if Mr Wheeler should have taken you into his boat. In these things there is no sure ground under our feet. We dont want to think too much about them lest we grow too suspicious and even evil-minded, but also we don't want to have too much to do with them. The best way I find is to observe a few simple rules laid down by sensible people for keeping out of danger where men and women meet. Be conventional *pretty* nearly always with men and always with these fellows "old enough to be your father". It's a funny world. You don't want to boast that you have scared as reckless a father as I am into chronic sleeplessness.

College still hangs off. We are grip-bound. The boys march march and that's all.

Amherst gathered on the common yesterday and subscribed its quota of $450000 viva voce. The air was full of money in handfuls and bagfuls. Showers of money all over hats and shoulders like confetti at a wedding. A rivalry got going between the Amherst College army and the M.A.C.[3] army who were drawn up in battle array behind the civilian crowd. I think our boys started it by offering to give a thousand if the Aggies would give a thousand. It looked as if it was going to be rough on someone or someone's fathers before it was over. Probably we could have stood it a good deal better than they could. But someone was sensible to stop it with a joke in time. And anyway just then the hand went to 450,000 on the clock. Money! You'd have thought the town was lousy with it. I went in under the excitement rather too much myself. I dont know what I shall do if there's another loan floated.

There's a good autobiography of Conrad's you ought to read. And I myself like Franklins awfully well. While you're reading either or both of those I'll be thinking up some more. Both James and Howells have written good autobiography. I have forgotten what they call the books. You would probably recognize them somehow by their names.

Remember me cordially to Mrs Wanvig. Tell her I hope your youthful vicissitudes may divert her a little from too much thinking of her part in the war, and so compensate her somewhat for what trouble we have cost her.

Come on with the letters

Affectionately   PAPA

[1] See EF to Lesley Frost, [late September 1918], n. 1.

[2] Under consideration for promotion from factory work to the final shaping of mahogany propellers, Lesley was asked if she had had woodworking experience.

Quickly responding in the affirmative, she then sought assistance in preparing herself for this new position.

³ Massachusetts College of Agriculture, now the University of Massachusetts.

EF to Lesley Frost

DARLING LESLEY,- [Amherst] Monday afternoon [October 1918]

There was no chance to write Sunday letters yesterday, because a poet appeared from New York, and he stayed all night and until the middle of the forenoon today. It was Alfred Kreymborg, the author of that queer poem, beginning, "I have a one room house, You have a two room, three room, four room house." And he is the author of "Mushrooms," the book that Joseph Beach sent papa during the summer. I think you liked it pretty well. He was quite entertaining, and we had a pleasant time last night, and I sat up so late that I am pretty tired today. I have just been writing a long letter to Irma. I have decided to let her stay a little longer. I suppose you saw her yesterday, and I am anxious to know what you thought about her health and sur roundings. Poor child — she has certainly had a painful time.

I am so thankful that you keep well and happy. How splendid it is that you are having a chance to play tennis with good players. You are certainly lucky this year, in having such a nice friend as Mrs. Wanvig, to make things pleasant for you. Be sure, though, that you don't neglect the work any. I rather wish you could have done the propeller work, but of course you know best what the conditions are. Does Mr. Lunt know woodcarving? Probably he knows a good teacher in Boston, if he doesn't do it himself. It would be nice, while work is slack, if you could take a few lessons, to be ready for emergencies. If the war ends pretty soon, what do you suppose will happen to the airplane business? Do you think they might go on with the work in the factory through this year?

Mrs. Wanvig must be wishing the war would end abruptly.

Well, I must take this and Irma's letter to the office. Did you get the outing flannel nightgowns I sent? And the dress?

Lovingly   MAMA

EF to Lesley Frost

[Amherst] Thursday afternoon
DARLING LESLEY:-   [October 1918]

Well, you certainly are living in a whirl of gaiety. It's not much like the picture papa drew of your lonely, unprotected and dangerous existance in a manufacturing town, is it? But now that the celebration is over and the Curtises are gone, probably things will quiet down for the winter. Is Mrs. Wanvig going to stay there this winter? How I wish I could go and see you. But our expenses are so big this fall, with all of us here taking dinners and suppers out, and a pretty continuous outlay for clothes. I don't feel that I ought to spend anything for travelling. Papa took four $100 bonds this time; he paid for one outright, and the other three he is paying for in installments. It is really too much for us to carry, but of course it isn't money spent, only invested. I am sending you $5 for Irma writes you need money to get to Wellesley. Are you all alone now in that teahouse? I am not satisfied with your being there alone, and neither is papa. I have asked you once if you didn't think you could get board near in some family, but you didn't answer. If you could get board for $8 somewhere, you would have something left over for clothes. But I don't know that its possible to find such a place. You ought to get out of the tea house, I think, even if you have to pay as much somewhere else.

If you leave the office, shall you go back into the sewing rooms or try to get the wood carving position. Papa thinks if you *could* get that - if you *could* get that position - it would be more interesting for you, and you would be learning something.

Will they go on making aeroplanes if the war is over?

Mr. Litchfield is in the sitting room and I suppose I ought to go in a little while. I wish I could see you. Try to make Irma take things more easily. She is frightfully nervous.

I'll enclose a letter from Mrs. Haines

[unsigned]

RF to Lesley Frost

DEAR LESLEY: Amherst, 24 October 1918

Didn't we tell you about Hendricks?[1] He had been sick, you know, and I saw at once when he got here, had lost his nerve for flying. He seems to have been a good flyer. He won his commission early and has taught some three hundred men to fly. But the flying field is nearer the front than anything else on this side of the Atlantic. The ships are always getting "cracked up" and hardly a week passes without somebody's getting killed or injured. The service has a reckless fatalistic way of taking itself that would be funny if it wasn't so tragic. It jokes with Death as presiding presence. Two ambulances stand conspicuously waiting for you always on the field. You may fly a month you may fly at best a year. But It will get you soon or late. You will make some day very likely through no fault of your own, what is known as a Mat landing which calls for the *m*otorcycle the *a*mbulance and the *t*ruck. The *a*mbulance or meat wagon is for you personally and maybe for your cadet but not so certainly for him because he rides in the back seat where in the crash he has a good chance, whereas you

are pretty sure to die by "getting the engine in your lap."
It is thrown right back into you, you see when the nose of
the fusilage dives into the ground. The teacher takes the
big risk that the pupil is apt to be the one to incur. Hendricks
had made a number of "forced landings", that is without
power, but had had but one serious smash up. In that he
had made one big hole in the ground, bounced and made
another. The truck took home what was left of the engine
and he walked home on his own legs after having made a
bonfire of the wings and fusilage. But I doubt if it was that
sort of thing that had shaken him or if he ever dreaded a
particular flight. It was just that the shadow of Death over
the whole place had spoiled him for sleep. He got a terrible
shock I suspect from seeing a fellow flyer die in the next
bed to him when he was in hospital. The doctor holding
the poor boys teeth apart to let the blood gush and the last
two or three breaths draw free — that will be a picture
on his mind (and on mine) for life, though in the stamping
of the impression it was no more than a matter of moments.
I wonder if he is going to get back into condition. He can
gamble with the rest of the boys and he can joke and talk the
language of the Morituri, but unless I'm mistaken he's nearly
insane for want of sleep. You'd think the excitement would
bear him up. They all complain that there is no excitement
in flying after you have learned what little there is to it say
half a dozen to a dozen manouvers. You have to learn
straight flying without fussing your controls, you have to learn
to go into a tailspin in order to learn how to come out of one
(because when you stall or go wrong in almost any way you
almost certainly fall into a tail-spin and it's death if you
haven't the art of undoing it) and you have to learn to make
a "three-point landing" that is on your two wheels and skid
simultaneously (because if you bounce ever so little with
the skid you'll tip up on to your crank shaft and spoil a two

hundred dollar propeller. — That's called a "crank-shaft landing") and you have to learn to make a "vertical bank" to turn on and a good loop — this last to go over your pursuer and get behind where you can pursue him. Thats about the extent of it. Theres a "spinning nose-dive" which I believe they don't know how to handle when they get into it. It is death just as the "tail-spin" was for a long time. In the tail spin the whole ship slowly revolves wing over wing and the tail describes great circles. In the "spinning nose-dive" it is the same except that the nose describes great circles. After you get so much learned apparently you perish slowly of the monotony and for want of exercise. The French have a name for the nervous malady flyers suffer from. I didnt get it. But I have been careful with all the technical language I have used and am sure of it all except the "Immel-mann turn" [.] It's Immelmann something, I think "turn". Hendricks has made a reputation for "vertical banks" and landing in small space. He made a forced landing once in a road between two fences facing one of them where there wouldnt have been room to land facing up the road. One pretty thing I forgot to mention: they make a descent with the power off just fluttering the aillerons a little called "falling leaf". But this is so little in the monotony of endless flying. The romance had all gone out of it for him and he doesn't know for sure why. Told about a boy who after his first "solo", flight alone, "tail-spinning" "looping" "banking" and all, got out of his ship swearing and swearing off on that kind of excitement. He never flew again. Hendricks thinks some of the young wives get their husbands out of it and off into other work, lecturing at colleges and such like safe jobs.

Ive told you all this for a glimpse of the unheroic heroic. We are nobody to judge anybody. There are all sorts of ways to go through with danger. We haven't all got to like it, though I have no doubt a great many like it alot. Affectionately PAPA

[1] See EF to Lesley Frost, [22 September 1918], n. 3.

RF to Lesley Frost

DEAR LESLEY: [Amherst, 5 November 1918]

You seem to have more to tell in the way of sheer news than we stay-at-homes or go-from-home-to-homes. My news is nearly all new poems — some of them not so very important and some I hope more so. What do you say to these? The Lynch one [1] is only funny I suppose. You needn't copy them. I seem to arrive at the copying point slowly. You never know what will come to save a poem at the last moment.

I'm supposed to be coming back to N'York on March 15th or so. I may not feel up to it. So if anybody sets up to know more about my affairs than you —

Take care of your feet and your head will take care of itself. Affectionately PAPA.

[1] "The Cow's in the Corn," RF's "sole contribution to Celtic drama," was inspired by conversations with his good friends John and Mary Lynch of Bethlehem, N. H. See RF to Frost children, [February 1915], n. 1. It was first published in *The Dearborn* (Michigan) *Independent* 18 June 1927 and later as a booklet (Gaylordsville, N.Y., 1929) with the addition of a 47-word preface. The text is included in *The Letters of Robert Frost to Louis Untermeyer*, pp. 197-198. Not in *PRF*.

Also enclosed — and reprinted here because of its variant form — was "The Aim Was Song," first published in *The Measure* (March 1921), 22. *PRF*, pp. 223-224.

THE AIM WAS SONG

Before man came to blow it right,
The wind once blew itself around
And did its loudest day and night
To satisfy the need of sound

On every rough place where it caught,
Mast, bridge, roof, steeple, tree, and hill,
Only to wonder what it sought
That left it discontented still.

Man came to tell it what was wrong:
It hadnt found the place to blow:
It blew too much: the aim was song;
And listen — how it ought to go.

He took a little in his mouth
And held it long enough for North
To be converted into South
And then by measure blew it forth.

By measure! It was word and note.
It answered every blowing need.
A little through the lips and throat!
The aim was song, the wind agreed.

                                        R.F.

EF to Lesley Frost

[Amherst] Monday afternoon
                                    [November 1918]

MY PRECIOUS LESLEY,-

Have you been too busy to send the picture? You got
my letter asking for it, didn't you? The other day I bought
two very pretty pieces of "Marblehead Pottery" for the
mantelpiece, over at Miss Cutler's gift shop. She has some
very pretty things over there, and they are not very expensive, either. I think we can choose some Christmas
presents there.

It seems a long time since we had your last letter,
but it isn't a week, of course. I have a letter from Irma
every day, though I have told her not to write if she needs
her strength for other things. But of course it is awfully nice
to hear from her, as long as she seems to like to write. I
write to her every day, also and of course it is something of a
tax, with all the other little things I have to do and think of.
So you won't mind if I don't write to you but once a week,
will you? You are having a better time than she is, and don't
depend on hearing from me in the same way.

Haven't we told you about the Spanish lady who is going to translate "North of Boston." I will send you her letter as soon as papa answers it. She seems very cultured and friendly and would probably be willing to look for a house for us in Madrid, and help us to find the most inexpensive way to live, but papa thinks he would rather not go knowing someone that way, because there would probably get to be social demands just as there are here, and if we go, he wants a whole year to do nothing but write and learn the language.

Papa went to a dinner at Mr. Meicklejohns Friday evening, to meet one of the British Educational Commission. He was a very genial old Welshman, who had been an intimate friend of Prof. Adamson, the father of Sarah and Margot and the rest of them. And he knew A. C. Bradley, and he would probably have known the Gardners, but papa forgot to mention them. Sometimes I want most dreadfully to go back to England.

Carol and Marjorie are studying Latin together. They recite to papa, and I help them learn the lessons. Marjorie takes hold of it very well, and they are going ahead at a good rate. They seem very willing to study this time.

Do you have good meals now? We have very good food indeed, but we have to hurry too much.

Didn't you see that Mr. Wheeler again?

I meant to write a longer letter but I want you to get it tomorrow, so I think I'll send it right over to the office. I'll write again Friday.

Lots of love from us all   MAMA

RF to Lesley Frost

DEAR LESLEY: Ammass [Amherst] 25 January 1919

We've been tempted by various considerations to go away off to Porto Rico and leave you alone to your cheerful

Barnard curriculum.[1] But we probably won't go. It seems too cruel all round. Marg is the most bent on going. I wish the kids *could* do something for excitement. But perhaps they can hold out till next year and we can all get away to Spain together. We've got Baxter[2] enlisted in the Porto Rico scheme. We are committed to it to that extent. He'll probably let us off though if he has to.

You left a fragment of poetry around that you must go on with some day. The one about the cut-over hillside. You were just going to name some of the slain trees when you stopped. It's a good kind of poem.

New York! New York! Not all of it together and all the entertainment of it and the pleasant friends you can have in it are worth one real deed of your own in poetry. It is full of other people's deeds and accomplishments. But those can only give you something and someone to talk about. What we want is to do something for all that silly mob to talk about. Let them talk about the latest. We want to do the latest.

Great — all that about the subterranean rumblings in England. Write more when you have time. And dont fail to write a good off-hand letter to Mrs Whicher saying anything pleasant you can about any of her friends at the college you have met. Or if you prefer tell me about her friends and I will pass the word along. I want to have her feel that you were pleased to have her introduce you down there.

I think it's better for us that Harcourt is staying with the Holts.[3] Where would we be with our books spread over three publishing houses. Of course I'd go out with Harcourt in a minute. And I wouldnt stand too much from Roland[4] if I were in his place.

Carol is taking punching lessons from Tug Kennedy and seems not displeased with himself. He seems to be coming to his assurance. You mustnt mention this in any letter that I'm going to tell you: it might make him too self conscious; but he had a fight on the rink with a college freshman and knocked him down and cut his lip and got altogether the better of him. It was over a hockey stick the fellow had taken from one of the little boys, Carol had asked him several times to give it up and he had said at last "If you don't shut up I'll take yours." Carol said, "I'd like to see you try it." The fellow tried it and got hurt and badly left before all the crowd.

Let's see what else there is for family brag. Miss Bates sent a Madrid paper with the translation of the Hill Wife. She wrote nice things about you. She was one good friend we had there at Wellesley.

We had a talking evening with the Oldses Coteses and Whichers (at the Oldses)[5] the other night and a very pleasant one at the Lancasters to meet the French teacher and his wife from Smith College tonight. The French teacher is a great Emersonian, as am I also. His wife is a Lake Willoughbian as are all of us. She comes from Lyndon. He saw three years service in the French army.[6]

Tell Harcourt about the Madrid paper. I shouldn't mention it to anyone else.

Tell us about the work in the office.

The Chapins are really nice people. I like Chapin.[7] Remember me to him particularly — and to her too of course less particularly.

The one thing I want to ask of you is that you will get your full sleep as a protection against throats. Sure!

There was a nice letter from Nichols but he hasn't blown in yet and Hendricks hasn't.

Carter Goodrich[8] lunched with us and talked politics two or three hours last week. He's bound away. He expects to mix up in English labor politics all next year. He says he has looked and looked, but he sees not one sign of a revolution in America. He hopes for better reward in England.

The Frenchman from Smith College put the way I begin to suspect it will come out. Bolshevism is nothing to speak of in England France and even Germany and will come to nothing. It may serve to take some of the high mightiness out of the too rich and it may *help* in some rather radical changes that are coming. That will be its life. The credit for the changes will go mostly to other political parties who will be too cautious and too interested to forget the rights of property too far. I don't know, but this sounds somewhere near my sense of the situation. Wilson seems to be representative of the sentiment of the world.

Affectionately PAPA.

[1] Lesley had begun midyear studies at Barnard College following her aircraft work in Marblehead.

[2] RF first met Sylvester Baxter, 24 years his senior, in 1915. A Mayflower descendent prominent in Greater Boston's development, Baxter was a poet, editor, and frequent commentator on Pan-American affairs.

[3] Alfred Harcourt, head of Henry Holt's trade book department, had proposed leaving the firm, establishing his own publishing house, and urging a number of Holt authors — Frost included — to join him. As later letters will indicate, Harcourt made his move. RF, however, despite his affection for Harcourt, had good reason to remain with Henry Holt.

[4] Roland Holt, Henry's son and a vice president of the firm.

[5] Amherst faculty friends.

[6] Regis Michaud. RF had visited Lake Willoughby, in northern Vermont, in 1892. Some years later he returned there to camp with his family and botanize a bit.

[7] The artist James Chapin who did portraits of at least four of the Frosts. See Illustrations.

[8] One of RF's favorite students, Goodrich graduated from Amherst in 1918, remained there as a Fellow for four years, and went on to become a prominent economist.

RF to Lesley Frost

DEAR LESLEY: Amherst, 17 February 1919

You can write to them in Franconia and they'll send to me or you can write to me here and I'll send to them — either way or both ways — better both ways.[1]

I shall have to go to the theatre, I also, before it is all over for this year I expect. And the reason is that my play is to be given in Northampton and I suppose it would look funny if I didnt see it. I rather dread the ordeal, though I must say the boys who are to act the two parts do first rate in them.[2] It will be my fault or the audience's if the thing fails. I'm prepared to call it the audience's. I doubt if the play is very bad.

I pity you having to write essays where the imagination has no chance, or next to no chance. Just one word of advice: Try to avoid strain or at any rate the appearance of strain. One way to go to work is to read your author once or twice over having an eye out for anything that occurs to you as you read whether appreciative contradictory corroborative or *parallel* (can't spell). There should be more or less of a jumble in your head or on your note paper after the first time and even after the second. Much that you will think of in connection will come to nothing and be wasted. But some of it ought to go together under one idea. That idea is the thing to write on and write into the title at the head of your paper. As you write you will probably want to turn again to your author for citation and quotation to make the body of your work. One of the boys here had Longfellow to do. He read him till he saw his idea to go by. He expressed that in his title Longfellow and the Middling Virtues. Another thought that the interesting thing that rose naturally in his mind as he read Hawthorne was that some of his mysticism was mechanical for story purposes mere ghost and mystery, but some of it was profoundly religious and real. So he will probably call his paper something like Real and Affected Mysticism of Hawthorne. Then he will go back to the passages in Hawthorne to bear him out in his idea. He wont be very long or at all pretentious if he knows his business. One idea and a few subordinate ideas — its to have those happen to you as you read and catch them — not let them escape you in your direct interest in your author. The sidelong glance is what you depend on. You look at your author but you keep the tail of your eye on what is happening over and above your author in your own mind and nature. I've never written essay, but I have the material often when I read — I'm aware of it making — not in every book by any means but in a few. Nothing happened either corroborative appreciative illustrative or very contradictory when I read Jean's book[3] for instance and that's why I dont write her the little essay she asks for on it. Out of a class of sixty boys only seven have seen what I mean by all this. The rest will put a name at the heads of their papers Hawthorne, Poe, Emerson or Longfellow; and they will simply tell again what these men said and did and wrote. None of their own increment here. Receptivity is all their faculty. They seem incapable of the over-and-above stuff. I think maybe it goes on in their heads as they read but they are incapable of catching it. They are too directly intent on the reading. They cant get started looking two ways at once. I think too they are afraid of the simplicity of many things they think on the side as they read. They wouldnt have the face to connect it in writing with the great author they have been reading. It may be a childhood memory: it may be some homely simile: it may be a line or verse of mother Goose. They want to be big and bookish. But they haven't books enough in their head to match book stuff with book stuff. Of course some of that would be all right. The game is matching your author thought for thought in any of the many possible ways. Reading then becomes converse — give and take. It is only conversation in which the reader takes part addressing himself to anything at all in the author in his subject matter or form. Just as when we talk together! Being careful to hold up our end to do our part agreeably without too much contradiction and mere opinionation. The best thing of all is going each other one better piling up the ideas anecdotes incidents like alternating hands piled upon the knee. Well its out of conversation like this with a book that you find perhaps one idea perhaps yours perhaps the book's that will serve for other lesser ideas to center round. And there's your essay. Be brief at first. You have to be honest. You dont want to make your material seem more than it is. You wont have so much to say at first as you will have later. My defect is in not having learned to hammer my material into one lump. I haven't had experience enough. The details of essay wont come in right for me as they will in narrative. Sometimes I have gotten round the difficulty by some narrative dodge.

Of course this letter is essay. It is material that has come to the surface of my mind in reading just as frost brings stones to the surface of the ground.

I dont know you know whether its worth very much — I mean the essay — when you have it written. I'm rather afraid of it as an enemy to the really creative writing that holds scenes and things in the eye voices in the ear and whole situations as a sort of plexus in the body (I dont know just where). Take it easy with the essay whatever you do. Write it as well as you can if you have to write it. Be as concrete as the law allows in it — concrete and experiential. Don't let it scare you. Dont strain. Remember that any old thing that happens in your head as you read may be the thing you want. If nothing much seems to happen, perhaps another reading will help. Perhaps the book is bad or is not your kind — is nothing to you and can start nothing in your nature one way or another.   Affectionately   Papa

Received cheque. I'm glad you like the Chapins so much.

[1] The family was scattered; RF, recovering from influenza, lingered on in Amherst after the rest of the family had returned to Franconia.

[2] RF's *A Way Out* was to be presented by Amherst students, though not on the campus.

[3] Jean Starr Untermeyer's *Growing Pains* (1918). Her husband Louis, the poet and anthologist, is frequently mentioned in these letters and was one of RF's earliest advocates.

EF to Lesley Frost

[Franconia] Wednesday afternoon
My precious Lesley,-- [24 February 1919]

I am afraid it took my Sunday letter a long time to reach you, because the postman didn't go by on Monday, it being Washington's birthday, and it was so stormy that none of the children went down. The postman took it yesterday morning, but he has such a long trip to make that it wouldn't go over to Littleton until this morning. So of course you haven't got it yet. It seems ages since I put it in the letter box Monday afternoon. The weather is stormy here. Three snowstorms already. But it hasn't been *terribly* cold yet, and I hope it won't be. Papa got up and dressed yesterday, and ate pretty heartily, and had a very restless night. I was afraid he had taken more cold and might be a good deal worse on account of it, but he is resting quietly in bed today and seems much improved.

Carol and Irma have been out doors a good deal, especially Carol, and they are both looking very well. The change of air is doing Irma good.[1] She has fixed up the front bedroom down stairs for her room, and draws in there in peace and security every afternoon. Carol has had a strenuous time getting the snow off the roof. The heat of the furnace melts it, you know, and then it leaks through in various places, so I wanted very much to have it got off if possible. We are in a bad fix for water again. It seems that the ground froze early, and very deep, before the snow came, so our spring has no water in it. We haven't opened up the water system yet, for as there's no water, there isn't much use in doing it. Will Herbert[2] is bringing water again. It's pretty hard not to have the use of the bathroom in winter, and I'm hoping a thaw will come pretty soon.

The house seems awfully cosy and homelike after existance at Caroline Marsh's. The Columbia seems as good as new. The long rest has done it good, I guess.

Marjorie has started school, but I don't know how long she will keep it up. It makes such a long day for her, from 8 oclock until four. I suppose you remember just how it felt. Getting to school has been so easy at Amherst that I am afraid she is a little spoiled for this wild region. She thinks the school seems awfully sleepy and spiritless, too.

Well, enough for today. I must get supper. I'll write again Sunday. I think there will surely be a letter from you tomorrow morning. We have your photograph on top of the desk, and Chapin's picture of you above it.

Lots of love from us all   Mama

[1] Unhappy with life at Dana Hall and ill with influenza, Irma took mid-year leave of the school and returned home.

[2] Willis E. Herbert sold the Frosts their Franconia farm but remained a near neighbor. RF later made humorous reference to the transaction in his poem "New Hampshire." *PRF*, pp. 163-164, ll. 149-158.

RF to Lesley Frost

[Portion of letter missing]   [Amherst, late winter 1919]

[. . .] allowed to try their puzzles on the whole American army. Puzzles is the word — puzzles and traps. American psychology is famed for the trick boxes it has invented to try the intelligence of monkeys guinea pigs and mice. Something is wrong with it all. As the writer of a book I have been reading says probably it is its artificiality. Glazer, one of our best teachers here (that is he is reputed

in his department one of the brilliant men of the country)[1]
passed one of the lab-test-exams recently with the rating
of a child of fourteen years. One of the things he failed in
was imagining the pattern in a square piece of paper when
it should be unfolded after having been folded four times
and cut into in one or two places. He never had seen any
game like that before. I played it when I was young and
so would probably have done better than he with it. His
failure, they told him, proved that he was weak in visual
imagination. He knows himself too well to be decieved
there. Visual imagination happens to be his chief strength
in his particular science. If he were younger and less self
experienced he might be scared by such findings.

But we have to take education as it comes in our day —
awful as it may be. You can always transcend it to a certain
extent even if you get somewhat worse marks for being
independent in your thoughts and actions. To hell with
the marks so long as you know you are better than the best
marks. Think! Have thoughts! Make the most of your
thoughts. That is all that matters. After that you can read
if you have time so long as you make sure to keep on top
of your reading by thinking. Have at least one idea of your
own for every one in the books. Simile analogy example
from life and experience.

The preparation for the examination was good for you
in one way though it didn't help you in the examination
and the examination was probably good for you in another
way though it may not have been the way intended by
your teachers.

Don't mind Knapp and dont mind Boas.[2] Be pleasant
to them but be natural and untruckling. There's no harm
in your asking if the class couldnt translate a little. He may
think the class is too large. All he has to do is say so then.
I can't think he can mean to punish you for so simple a

proposal. The class ought to translate. It is damnable to have to sit in every class and hear nothing but the voice of teachers. At least there's little of that dullness at Amherst.

Prime yourself for old Boas. Go and get some ideas out of Osborn's Men of the Old Stone Age and books mentioned in it. One book will lead to others. You'll only have time to read patches in each of them. You'll stumble on to curious things that may come in handy in class talks. I've just been reading about the most ancient human remains in their order of antiquity. Pethecanthropus Erectus (found in Java) the Piltdown Man the Neanderthal Man and the Cro-Magnon Man ranging from 200,000 to 10,000 years B. C. Good pictures of them in Osborn's book — funny too when you stop to consider what the artist had to go on.

Then one thing more: one of Whichers friends an old pupil of his at Illinois, a sort of poet-reformer-farmer, a really interesting fellow as far as I could see into him has been visiting here and now he writes from Long Island that his sister has met you at Barnard (where she is enrolled too) and wants you to go home with her some time for better acquaintance. The name is Walser. They're English. It would be nice if you happened to like her and thought she wasnt trying to get into poetical society. You wouldn't see Walser, her brother; he's out managing a farm somewhere in the country. The rest of the family may not be as real and out-of-the-usual as he is — or seemed. Gee! Im on my guard against every body.

[Five-line paragraph deleted.]

I'm sorry for Cox.[3] I wish I could do something for him here. But we are full to the back balcony. It looks as if Percy Mackay[4] might teach with us. I like him and I'm glad in a way but it just cuts out William Benet whose name I have been proposing to Mr Meikle.[5] No word of this to Louis[6] or anyone else.

Dont you think it would be nice for Irma to go down to see you for a while. Could she have a room with you or very near you. Poor kid she has had a hard year. Say what you think of this to me, not to them up there. The children may get hold of what you write to Mamma.

Long letter — what?   Affectionately   PAPA.

I wonder if you want any of us down to see the Grecian Games.[7] Let me know soon either way.

[1] Otto Glaser, in his first year as Professor of Biology at Amherst.

[2] Two of Lesley's teachers. Franz Boas was the noted anthropologist who devoted much of his life to a study of North American Indians. RF's subsequent comments reflect his life-long interests in archaeology and anthropology.

[3] Sidney Cox and RF had met in 1911, in Plymouth, N. H., where Cox was a teacher of English in the high school. They kept in touch with each other, both by letter and visit, over many years, with Cox continually chronicling his admiration for the poet and their many discussions on literature and teaching. See his *Robert Frost: Original "Ordinary Man"* (1929) and *A Swinger of Birches* (1957).

[4] Poet-dramatist Percy Mackaye who would later prove instrumental in securing for RF his first appointment at the University of Michigan.

[5] Amherst's President Alexander Meiklejohn.

[6] Untermeyer.

[7] Spring games at Barnard College.

EF to Lesley Frost

DEAR LESLEY-   [Franconia March 1919]

I hope you got papa's check in time to avert starvation, and also that papa's letter to the girls was all right, and was in time to avert the extremity of their wrath. I didn't feel quite sure that you would have wanted him to give as a reason the possibility of your going into the contest, but he had such a gracious and amusing letter written that I didn't say anything.

Papa is afraid the spirit of your poem (bringing in Christianity) might prevent your getting a prize even if you had it in other respects. Have you time to write another? But I shouldn't suppose they would be so narrow. Anyway,

I almost want you to try to publish the one you have written, if it doesn't take the prize.[1]

You must write us all about the Glee Club concert. Didn't you remember that you had promised Hollister to go with him? He had evidently set his heart on it to such an extent that he must have resented your going with somebody else. His letter was very child like and conventional, wasn't it? You would never imagine him a bloody minded Bolshevist. It was very well written, though, I thought.

We have had a long storm, and it hasn't stopped snowing yet. It began with rain for a whole day and night, then it turned to snow, has snowed for two days and nights. The snow is deeper than it has been all winter, I guess, and there is a lot of water in the cellar. Papa is afraid that if the snow melts suddenly, as it is very liable to do, the furnace will be flooded and spoiled. We have never had so much water in the cellar before. The Herberts have made a great quantity of syrup and sugar this year, and they will probably make more after this spell of cold weather and snow. I am going to try to send you some syrup this week.

Papa wants you to spend what money you need to spend in entertaining the other girls. Have you another installment of rent to pay? Tell us what sum you need, more than the $25 he sent.

Take good care of yourself, won't you, dear?

We all send much love, MAMA

1 This is the first of many references to one of Lesley's poems which has survived. As here printed, it reflects revisions suggested by RF in his letter of 24 March 1919.

THE AWAKENING

I heard the morning church-bells ring
Down where the valley dips;
But God was far from people's hearts,
Though he was on their lips.
Out on the hill where dark green brake

And stunted savin grows,
A sudden movement stirred the ferns,
The great god Pan arose.
He left a hard, bare hollow, lined
With dully shining weaves
Of fern and gold-thread roots: a spot
Like that a turned stone leaves.
Dead fern and twigs were in his hair
And in his cloven hoofs.
He rubbed his eyes with wrinkled hands
And looked down on the roofs;
And then he heard the ringing bells,
And laughed because he knew
By something in the sound of them
They were not ringing true.
With bracken stems he cleaned his pipes,
Half choked with earth and moss.
He squinted through them at the sun,
Then passed his lips across.
Perhaps he paused a moment there —
Should he give back to men
A god they had with ease denied?
Should Pan blow pipes again?

But Pan was glad to be awake.
He puffed his wrinkled lips.
They heard his song above the bells
Down where the valley dips.

RF to Lesley Frost

DEAR LESLEY   Franconia, 24 March 1919

The first thing is to ask you to look up Mrs Zorn[1] at the Grenoble Hotel if she hasn't already looked you up. She is there for a week or so with Mrs Stewart. You could locate her by telephone and then take her somewhere for entertainment. Do the honors. Suggest going with her to see Chapin's studio, or to some good play. (How about the French players?) I should have written about this sooner.

The second thing is to ask you what you-all are thinking of to want me to judge in a lyric contest in which you may be entered however unbeknownst to me. Consider the risk of your winning any prize I had the disposal of.

No one would believe I hadnt known what poem was yours. It would never do.

We decided it would never do before Mamma told me you were in fact going in for the lyric prize. Lucky I foresaw the possibility. People would say it takes two Frosts, father and daughter to win one prize — that is if we won it. And we ought to win it on such a good poem as this you have sent home. Gee it is a good one. Prizes are more or less accidents and of course we can't and dont count on them, having more important things to look to beyond them. Just about perfect all down through beginning with the fifth line, I heard the morning church bells ring.[2]

You know how I would be likely to like all that about the dead fern and leaves in his hair and hoofs. It is the kind of poetry I can hardly keep my finger out of. I should like to ask you to get in a stanza saying that where he got up from the ground was a bare spot as where you turn over a field-stone. You see how it excites my imagination. The best place of all perhaps is about the bells not ringing true. That is returning on an old phrase with real effect. I want you to make it the bells outright like this:

because he knew

By something in the sound of them
They were not ringing true.

Everything could stand very well just as it is however for all I see. I see no real defect in the ringing true lines as they stand. But I think you could do something to fill out the meaning of the poem a little by making more of the line "A god they had with ease desired." You could stuff more into that line. The idea is Should he give back to men an older god than the one that had their bells. Why not say just about that? Gee it's a real poem — Pipes against Bells! It doesnt say how he succeeded. He simply saw a chance. But he had great confidence.

Im enclosing part of an examination I gave my boys. The answers are on the back of the sheet.[3] The boys were supposed to have read all the poems in the Oxford Book of Victorian Verse. But they also had the book open before them. They did rather badly. Their answers were strained and far-fetched. They tried too hard to preserve common sense.

I'm glad you did well with James' Varieties.[4]

If you were plumb sick and nauseated in Knapps quiz and the quiz is crucial I should think he might give you another chance. If not I shouldn't mind.

Here's a check for 25 for luck.

Affectionately   PAPA

[1] Mrs. Otto Manthey-Zorn of Amherst.

[2] See EF to Lesley Frost, [March 1919], pp. 55-56, n. 1, for the text of this poem, "The Awakening."

[3] Although misplaced and apparently missing for many years, the examination to which RF alludes was located shortly before this book went to press. Included here is a verbatim transcript with an upside-down answer key — just as RF sent it to his daughter. The spelling is faulty, and a number of titles are incomplete.

FIRST PAPER

On what similarity have the following groups been made?

1

Masefield's Sea Fever   Stevenson's Romance
Carmen's Joys of the Road, Kipling's L Envoi

2

Johnsons Statue of King Charles
Bottomleys To Iron Founders

3

O Shaughnessy's Fountain of Tears
Margaret Woods' The Mariners, Blunt's Desolate City, Swinburne's Hesperia Dobell's Return, Davidson's Runnable Stag, Domett's Christmas.

4

Rossetti's Blessed Damozel   Morris' Sailing of the Sword
Tennyson's Lady of Shalott

5

Ingelows High Tide   Stevensons Christmas at Sea   Davidsons Runnable Stag, Gibson's Flannan Isle.

6

Patmores Ma grea est Veritas   Locky. Lampson's At Her Window,
Christina Rossetti's Italia, Francis Thompson's Daisy, Synge's.
A Question   Flecker's Riouperoux   Davies Leisure   x
Henleys England my England

6. Nothing at all. Just a jumble
5. Narrative
4 Ans Pre-Raphaelite picture-writing.
3 Ans Sonorousness
2. Ans. Spirit of reaction
1. Ans. Wanderlust

4 William James, *The Varieties of Religious Experience* (1902).

EF to Lesley Frost

DARLING LESLEY   [Franconia, March 1919]

Papa & I don't want you to publish the Pan poem
in the college magazine. Please don't do it. The poem is
too good for that. Send me what things you have of your
own that you would wish to put in, and let me choose
something. The Pan poem is much better as you sent it to
me first, without the changes you made at papa's suggestion.
Papa thinks so, too. The line "The God they had with ease
denied" is much better so, than after you changed it. And I
think, also, the poem would be more effective without the
first verse. What do you think? It isn't at all necessary, and
it isn't quite as perfect as the other verses.   MAMA

Will send check in a day or two.

EF to Lesley Frost

DARLING LESLEY - [Franconia] Sunday afternoon [March 1919]

I wish you could be here for a little while and enjoy
this warm house. Its snowing and blowing a gale from the
north east today, and to have this house thoroughly warm
all over in the midst of the white whirling wilderness seems
too wonderful. The furnace works beautifully, and the big
front room upstairs gets the most heat of all, which will

be splendid when papa gets to work up there. Walter [Hendricks] is using it now. He is going to stay with the children while I am away, and he may stay here all through March, until papa comes up for good, but he will probably go up to Bissells when I get home from New York. He is a very nice person to have in the house — so perfectly refined and also quite jolly and witty. He gets along beautifully with the children. Bissell has given him the use of his house through the spring, and after papa comes he won't come down very often, I imagine, because he knows papa wants his time for writing.

You are evidently having a quite lively time, dear. I almost wish you would make it a rule not to go out evenings through the week, because if you do you will be too tired day times for the amount of work you are carrying. Especially until you know what to expect there in the way of marks, I think you ought to be careful. And there wouldn't be any harm in your getting a scholarship, if it didn't mean *too* hard work. But I am glad you are having chances to go out and have a good time.

I hope I shall see you the end of this week. Carol hasn't been patient about staying in the house to get over his cold, and his throat is pretty rough. I don't *think* it will develop a cough, but if it should, I wouldn't want to leave him. It will be fun to have the trip to New York with papa, and to see you. I can *hug* you this time, can't I?

Well, Walter is going down to the office in a minute. Keep well, darling. Lovingly MAMA.

Did you take with you the little chain Stark Young gave us, and the gold heart shaped pin?

RF to Lesley Frost

DEAR LESLEY: Franconia, Mt [.] 3 April 1919

This is returning you the scholarship application blank no longer blank except in the spot which should name what you are asking for. I hadnt the least idea what figure could be put in there. You put in a *reasonable* one. You know better than I do what you can expect.[1]

As to the contest in poetry — tralala! I could have told you — maybe I did tell you — how it would be. You can plunge into a thing of the kind if you like the excitement and the object is to get so you don't care, but you mustn't expect prizes. Probably I would have immunized myself to criticism a little if I had exposed myself earlier to some of that kind of it. One ought to get so he can pursue the evenness of his writing through everything favorable or unfavorable. It may do you good if you can take the smash from those girls for the practice it gives you in not caring as I say. It's not so important what they decide about you. Don't let them see how you feel about it. I wish you hadnt asked them for a look at the successful poems. All is probably quite honest. Only you have to remember that it is not quite impersonal. You labor under the personal disadvantage of being who you are and of not being in any class where writing is done and so not being acquainted with any of the teachers of writing. They probably knew the writing of the two girls who won and had made up their minds that it was likely to be the best before they saw it. And no doubt they liked it better than they did yours. They really may have — we have to remember that even at our maddest. I'd rather you wouldn't say much to Louis about it. To hell with it.

The thing is to write better and better poems. Setting our heart when we're too young on getting our poems appreciated lands us in the politics of poetry which is death. Consider the ways of the members of the poetry societies and be wise. Write write, for this is all there is.

We'll be pleased to see the winning poems, sceptical as we are about their worth.

Lucky I staid out of the jury.

Bully for Miss Drew.

I wish Irma could see the hoop and torch races. We won't send her down before a week from this Saturday. If she gets there on the 12th, does that make it — does she see the games? I wish I could see the games myself. But I feel ill-natured about the poem. So perhaps I had as well not be there.

Ten feet from the plate is like playing up for a bunt.

Hens are laying 10 eggs a day.

Affectionately   RF

Having trouble with New England Poetry Society because I dont accept presidency.

Must send you a poem of mine some day.

Carol has the Blick typewriter all in pieces cleaning it.[2]

Been reading some of Henry James short stories. Simply too good

Deep snow good sleighing very good here.

Grand row about Stark[3] at Amherst.

Did I tell you we had planted twelve apple trees.

Poor Hollister, he should give up red.

Jean [Starr Untermeyer] began a letter to me, Mr Robert Frost.

I dont see much to Walters poetry.

Ask for what money you need. Always.

---

[1] Lesley applied for — and was granted — a scholarship underwritten by the National Association of New England Women.

[2] The Blickensderfer typewriter, one of the earlier "visible writing machines," was purchased by RF around 1900, about the time the family moved to the Derry farm. Although he seldom if ever used the machine himself, his children

found it helpful in learning to read and to write. Lesley used it in England to "publish" *The Bouquet*, an occasional magazine of prose, poetry, and art work, and she typed many of her father's manuscripts upon it.

³ Stark Young.

RF to Lesley Frost

DEAR LESLEY: Franconia, 20 May 1919

You've done enough to satisfy us in having fought your way to first place in your class and second place in your college in tennis. We don't ask you to win the college cup — you've had so little real experience in the game. You've had a good time and you've proved to yourself that you don't need Charles Lowell Youngs help in sports however much you may need it in Latin French and English. What more should you want. It's so much as it is that you will have to be careful not to brag too much when you go visiting at Wellesley.

And while I think of it be sure you tell the same story I do when anyone asks you how you came to elect Miss Fletcher's Latin for sophomore year. Say you elected it to make it absolutely impossible for you to go back to Wellesley. Say you were afraid you might weaken in the summer (melt in the summer heat) and decide to go back if you didnt put an impassable barrier in your way. Say you have a forgiving nature and you were afraid with time you might come to forgive all your other Wellesleyan injuries, but you were sure of yourself on that injury. Sometime I shall tell Miss Bates the so-called psychology of your apparent inconsistancy in electing Miss Fletcher.

I'm glad you liked the Percy MacKay[e]s. It would be fun for you to go West with Arvia¹ if we could spare you and if we could spare the money. I think you'd like Mrs Moody.² Martha Crowfoot³ is what she is. I wonder if she is really as simple silly as she seems. It would be almost an achievement in unsourness to keep so to her age. I wonder if her silliness may not be mechanical and kept up to cover something sour or bitter underneath. I don't believe it is though. She's an unspoiled old sentimentalist.

What do you say to getting in one evening with the Cambridge Brownes — the final e Brownes so to speak?[4] You will be in such a hurry to get home though. Perhaps you had better come right along as soon as you leave Wellesley. Be sure you write at the last moment to let us know definitely when to look for you — on what day and train exactly. Coming up from Boston gets you to Littleton earlier than coming up from New York. I can look up your train from Boston right now. It leaves Boston at nine in the morning and gets you to Littleton at about four in the afternoon.

And be sure you have money enough with you for emergencies.

I have a letter from Harcourt[5] in script to tell me in confidence that he is leaving the Holts to set up for himself. I suppose the script means that not even Miss Eayres is in the secret. He wants to know if we will go with him and I suppose there is only one answer possible after what has passed between us. But by jingo it throws my already confused relations with publishers into still greater confusion. This is a year of unsettlement. I am on the point of making changes here at Franconia too and at Amherst I feel all at sixes and sevens. Out of the general breaking up may come some new beginning that will be exciting and perhaps good and even great for us.

Lets feel darned friendly toward your psychology teacher for liking you to think. People deserve almost more credit for appreciating what we do than we deserve for doing it.

The great things are direct thought and emotion and never to be put off our unforced natural thought and emotion in any circumstances however disturbing — not even in examinations. I never got so I was serenely myself in examination. I have rather to pick and choose my circumstances. The Carter Goodrich[6] kind of boy is the ideal kind of examinee. No Faculty can muddle his faculties.

Powerful flight the CN4 made to the Azores. It makes me feel strong myself. I almost wish Hawker hadn't tried it. It was too wild an adventure. But he was a brave man.[7]

Affectionately   PAPA

Twelve small white chickens hatched yesterday.

[1] The MacKaye's daughter, about Lesley's age.

[2] See EF to Lesley Frost, [11 November 1917], n. 1.

[3] Harriet Moody's companion.

[4] RF first met George Herbert Browne, a co-founder of Cambridge's Browne and Nichols School, in 1915. A figure-skater of some note, Browne later and informally gave a number of skating lessons to Lesley. His Frost material and letters are deposited at Plymouth (N.H.) State College's Lamson Library.

[5] See RF to Lesley Frost, 25 January 1919, n. 3.

[6] See RF to Lesley Frost, 25 January 1919, n. 8.

[7] Attempting a record-breaking transatlantic flight, Harry Hawker made a forced landing in his Sopwith biplane on 20 May and was, for five days, feared dead. The Navy's NC 4 was another contender. Frost's interest in the heroic was a lifelong one. See also RF to Lesley Frost, 24 October 1918.

RF to Lesley Frost

DEAR LESLEY: Franconia, 22 May 1919

You won't be much longer where you have to look for letters from us and some of the time in vain. It's been a vicisitudinous year. This half of it ought not to have seemed long, and it hasn't — and then again it has. It has gone fast and it was only half a year; but it had some of the attributes of a whole year. It has had as much crowded into it for you as most whole years for one attribute. What a lot we owe Mrs. Wanvig for the pretty interval between one college and another. What's the prospect of your seeing her in New York before you start for home.

There must be Hell to pay in the Holts Office. Poor Miss Eayres writes an excited letter. She knows we know and assumes we know more than we do. I take it she doesn't know where she is going next. She's out in the world. Probably in the long run it will be better for her on the Ailleys (sp.) account. Harcourt will set out to be the big publisher. He wont need much office help though for some time I imagine. He'll succeed just the same. Some one will back him where he wants for capital. And I should say he had been the whole literary side of Henry Holt and Co and would take the whole literary side off with him. He's not a person to my taste. But he has something to him. He means to do it on the great. No petty publishing for him. No mere professional standards. National standards! A great publisher with a flock of great authors — all American. Thats his ambition.[1]

Speaking of petty standards, the pettiest and most dangerously so are intramural college standards. I had an adventure with Walter [Hendricks] the other day that I have had many a time with other well educated little college Walters. I had just uttered something of my own that he more than half saw the goodness of but what was his response to it? "Do they say that?" I told him "No, *I* say it but *they* would say it too if I pointed it out to them." They know of nothing not gotten from somebody else. Quotation is the height of scholarship and scores ten. It is best if you have an idea to attribute it to someone else so that they will feel that it has the weight of authority. They are always asking Who is your authority? I suppose their attitude of mind can hardly be helped in college where acquirement is the main object. But it is deadly and deathly. How to escape it! Well anyway we are rid of Walter,[2] and keeping that pretense up for appearance' sake is over. We had to be careful that the neighborhood didnt notice anything.

About now we must be as far along in Spring as you were a month ago. Affectionately PAPA

Ive been trying Hen Dekker syllables but without much luck lately.[3]

[1] See RF to Lesley Frost, 25 January 1919 and 20 May 1919.

[2] See EF to Lesley Frost, 22 September 1918, n. 3 for background information. RF's friendship with Hendricks was dissolved because of a misunderstanding at Franconia involving his care of the children while EF was away for a short trip.

[3] RF's luck apparently improved. On 30 June 1919, he sent Louis Untermeyer a new poem in hendecasyllabics — "Wrong to the Light," later titled "For Once, Then, Something." *PRF*, p. 225.

EF to Lesley Frost

DARLING LESLEY, [Amherst, October 1919]

We were all delighted to hear of your success last Saturday. Do you think you ought to have entered three contests? I can't help thinking of the possible consequences to your health of overdoing. I thought I would let you get through Field Day before I went to see Mrs. Dr. Rockwell. I went this afternoon during her office hours but she was out. I'll try it again tomorrow and let you know what she says. Now I want to discuss finances a little. I don't believe I want you to spend Mrs. Fobes money for ordinary expenses. Your room and board are all paid for this semester, aren't they? And your books all bought. How much do you think you spend a week for odds and ends of things? I think we ought to supply that. And I think you ought to spend some thought on what to go to with Mrs. Fobes money. There ought to be some music, and Irma ought to hear some music, even if she doesn't think she likes it. Find out from Louis or Hollister what there is going on that is worth hearing. The opera will begin by and by, if it hasn't already. You ought to hear some music twice a month and go to two good plays. Its a great thing for you to have this money that you can spend in that way without any hesitation or scruple.

Thursday noon

We had letters from both you & Irma this morning, which was very cheering. Papa says to tell you *not* to go up in an airplane at Coney Island, or at any place when you are off alone this way. Perhaps there will be a flyer around here Christmas vacation. There have been two different ones here in two weeks.

I have one of my dreadful headaches coming on, and probably won't be able to go with papa to Wellesley tomorrow.

I haven't said nearly all I want to say, but think I'll leave the rest for Saturday & Sunday, I am feeling so miserable.   Very, very much love   MAMA

Check for Irma's rent inside.

RF to Lesley Frost

DEAR LESLEY: Amherst, 4 November 1919

Been to Wellesley where I saw Margaret White[1] and to Boston where I saw Amy Lowell and presided over the Poetry Society so it couldnt be said I never do what I dont want to do. Told the assembled girls about my new classroom game "salon" destined to displace the older games of "quiz" "lecture with notes" "lecture without notes" "pupil-teacher," "examination" and "debating society." In "salon" the players come to class determined to show as wise, witty, and well-read (anything else, too, that counts in good company). The scoring, which is my concern, is rather indirect than direct. I incline to give some credit for initial remarks for their face value, but estimate them chiefly by their prevocative and suggestive effect on conversation. Remarks that provoke comment of any kind sympathetic or unsympathetic from four I give A: from three I give B: from two I give C: from one I give D: from none I give E. I told the girls how one of my boys said this would be all right from the point of view of the class but he didnt see where I came in, because the class would simply stand together and see to it that I had to give every one a. It was the greatest surprise to him when I asked what more could I want than to see them help each other get a high mark. Did he suppose any object in teaching would be to make pupils fail? Evidently from the laugh I got out of both boys and girls that was about what he supposed.

I'm speaking for the group of languages (all the languages) here on Friday before the visiting alumni — that is if I'm up and around by that time — I'm in bed now from overexertions in Wellesley and Boston. Shall have to tell them that the mainstays in a language department should always be men who refuse to put a book to any use it wasn't designed for by the author. The best books are to read; the best of the best to read and reread — not to philologize over, not even to study — not to translate any more than need be — the sooner we reach an understanding of them without translation the happier for us and the books. Shall have to tell them a pedagogue is a person who has been willing to do violence to anything in himself or in the great books or even in the student for the sake of making the books pedagogically useful, laborious and disciplinary in class. Shall have to tell them that language courses ought to be most fruitful of all so to call them. They ought to be where most we come into the enjoyment of what we are and of what by pains and more or less ugly effort expended elsewhere we have come to be. In writing and reading we come home with the reminiscent spoils of all our adventure and experience in life and books.

Speaking of books: ask Chapin will you to give you one of the new N.O.B.S with his autograph.[2] Tell him I wont beg a book of Rolan Dolt[3] and I'm damned if I'll buy one. Arent they behaving small?

Ask Miss Eayres where Harcourt is — what address I'm to use in writing him.

I told Young (Chas Lowell) and Margaret White how you covered yourself with blue ribbons. I saw Sheffy[4] and he looked unutterable things about my publicity. Miss Bates was friendly. How she hates Amy [Lowell] the poetic politician.   Affectionately   PAPA

[1] One of Lesley's house mates when she was at Wellesley College.
[2] RF's *North of Boston* was reissued in a special edition of 500 copies in 1919. It was illustrated by James Chapin.
[3] Roland Holt. See RF to Lesley Frost, 25 January 1919.
[4] See RF to Lesley Frost, 13 November 1917, n. 4.

EF to Lesley Frost

DARLING LESLEY,-   [Amherst, November 1919]

I ought to have sent a letter to you Friday or yesterday, but somehow the days pass in a dream like way, and I don't do half what I want to do. I am sorry you have been discouraged lately. Last year you had all the time you wanted to write examinations, didn't you? It was most unreasonable, to expect all those questions to be answered in such a short time. But never mind, dear, perhaps next year's work will be more interesting. You will have all electives next year, won't you? And possibly you will be at Cornell instead of Barnard, though I don't imagine Cornell will be any improvement on Barnard. I hope you have three weeks vacation at Christmas. I haven't invited Margaret White yet. I hardly know what to do. I feel as if we ought to ask her, and yet I am in such a nervous condition with these electric treatments that I don't like to think of the responsibility of entertaining. And it is awkward about the breakfasts. We have to get our breakfasts upstairs in the sitting room. Miss Marsh has some thought of going to Boston to visit her cousin, and if I could be sure of her going, and just when she will go, it would make a lot of difference, for if she goes, we shall have the whole house to ourselves. It is funny that Margaret hasn't written to you. She went up to papa and talked with him a few minutes when papa was at Wellesley. What sort of girl is this Ethel? Wouldn't she be critical of our servant less condition? You know it is a good deal of a burden to get three meals a day for company, and I wanted you to rest and recuperate while you are at home. But if it would really give you pleasure to ask her here for a part of the vacation, I am willing, if you think you are going to be strong enough to get the meals.

The atmosphere here is rather unpleasant. Papa has nothing to do with Mr. Meiklejohn, and I think the end will probably be that Mr. Meiklejohn will make things so disagreeable in return that papa will want to leave. That might not be such a great misfortune, for I feel that he is wasting his life here. The boys are after him nearly every evening, and he is tired all the time. You will probably see him Tuesday.

Monday afternoon

I stopped writing last night because I thought there might be a letter from you or Irma this morning or this noon and I might have more to write about. But nothing has come, and I will get this to the office before the four oclock mail goes out.

Papa isn't starting until tomorrow. He will probably telephone to you tomorrow from somewhere in the evening. I don't know whether he will go to a hotel or to Ridgeley

Torrence's tomorrow night.[1] Wednesday evening he reads in Montclair. Well, dear, no more this time. Keep as well as you can.

Love & hugs from MAMA

[1] See EF to Lesley Frost, [11 November 1917], n. 1.

EF to Lesley Frost

[En route to Amherst] Thursday

DARLING LESLEY-   [December 1919]

I am writing on the train from Arlington home.[1] I found nothing that satisfied me well enough for me to decide on it at once. I walked up to the little house on the hill. Papa had walked to it on the side of the mountain from the Fisher's[2] house, and so couldn't tell much about the distance up from the village road. It is very nearly a mile, and all the way up hill, and a very wind-swept road much of the way, so that farm is quite impossible. When I saw the other farm that was sold, I wasn't a bit sorry we had lost it. The house is quite commonplace looking, & is surrounded by the most ordinary village houses. There are two other possibilities in Arlington, but I am not very enthusiastic about either of them.

The Fishers are both of them *splendid*. It's almost worth while to make the most of some place that isn't exactly what we want, in order to have such real people as neighbors. Their house is tiny, but *so* cosy and home like. I wish I had the faculty of making things seem as cosy as that.

There is a fierce gale and snowstorm today. Mr. Fisher drove me down in the Ford through some fair sized drifts, and over wind swept ice. It was quite exciting. They have used their Ford all winter except about one week.

I wonder how you are feeling. After you went, I felt sorry that I hadn't kept you at home.

Nothing you can get there is worth the risk to your health. If you continue in that tired, dragged state, you must come home, because I *couldn't* stand it to have you break down. It sort of makes me sad to see you so thin, dear, and for my sake I hope you will do the best you can to keep well.

Thursday evening

This is the first time in my life that I have got stranded on a journey, and had to go to a hotel. I am in the Draper, at Northampton. No cars have run between here and Amherst all day. You can imagine how angry and impatient I was when I got here at five oclock and found I couldn't get home. Luckily I had enough money to go to a hotel, and here I am. I only had to pay $1.25 for a comfortable room. I wonder if I shall have any trouble in getting home tomorrow morning.

I think I'll go to bed now and get a long sleep.

Much love, MAMA.

[1] RF and EF had begun their search for another farm, in Vermont.
[2] The author Dorothy Canfield Fisher and her husband Donald.

RF to Lesley Frost

DEAR LESLEY   Amherst, 28 January 1920

You get neglected with things going the way they are. I've been trying to give the boys good measure at the last moment and mama's been taking care of sick children till she's had to give up sick herself. We don't get our minds made up about your going to Paris and if we got them made up in our present state I doubt if we could keep them so. I rather hate to have you go so far off right now. Still I dont want to hang on to you. Can you wait to decide till I am down on the fourteenth of February? Decisions come hard now-a-days. We don't have to decide much on farms, though, because there aren't any. Amherst is as full as the bases in Pussy-wants-a-corner and we are as left out as Pussy. Today we were on the point of telephoning Mr. Glover to make ready the Franconia house to receive us and to the Fishers to ask if they knew of any furnished house in Arlington we could have for the spring. It sounds as undignified as a retreat from Moscow.

And speaking of Moscow, I should think it was about to become one of the great capitals of the world with a government we are going to treat with respect whether we like it or fear it. It only goes to show how easy it is to lie to us till we are thoroughly unprepared for anything that happens.

Marge is being examined here you there. I heard Marge wishing all her history examination would be by maps. She says she can make and fill out all sorts of maps but she can't spell well enough to answer questions in writing. Take it easy and have good luck.

The same notion haunts me that I had last year at this time. If I knew of a furnished flat in New York I should be tempted to try it down there for a month or two. It wouldnt do though. What we need is a home and settled life right off soon. My observations of mama's health convince me of that.

I've been wanting to say the word, Come home for your free week; but I don't know that you wouldn't be better off where you are. You've got an infirmary to go to if you are sick (you neednt think I'm asking you to be sick) and you haven't any responsibility for other sick people. By staying, too, you avoid two train journeys more or less risky the way things are. What do you say?

Joseph Anthony[1] seemed an able-minded boy when I talked with him here. He ought to go a long way.

He said there was no immediate rush for the poems for Harpers. Wells[2] is out of the office for the moment and no one else ought to have the handling of them. I shall send them to you to copy when I have regarded them a little longer. Overhauling them has stopped me writing new ones for the moment. How are the dailies coming — any as good as the rain-wet window?

Here's one Whicher thought too hard. Joseph Anthony got it quickly enough.

PLOWMEN.

I hear men say to plow the snow.
They cannot mean to plant it, though —
Unless, in bitterness, to mock
At having cultivated rock.[3]

R.

I keep trying for the word I want in your line about the withering silver on the back of a looking glass.

Affectionately   PAPA

[1] Joseph Anthony was publicity manager for Harper & Brothers.
[2] Thomas B. Wells, a vice president of Harper & Brothers and editor of *Harper's Magazine.*
[3] This is a variant of the poem as it appears in *PRF*, p. 238. The key change is in the first line which now reads "A plow, they say, to plow the snow."

RF to Lesley Frost

DEAR LESLEY: Franconia, 8 February (circa) [1920]

I write this snowed in by the greatest snow-storm of all time with very little hope of ever mailing it. We are running short of food fuel and water. How long we can last we are not experienced enough in rationing to calculate. (We could last longer of course if Marjorie would eat less.) Rescuing parties have been by with teams of six and eight horses, but these are merely local and neighborly; they are satisfied if they push the snow a little from our doors: they are not intended to establish communication with the outside world. Everybody is frightened but Margerie [and Carol {and Irma (and Mama)}] who doesn't know enough, isn't, I fear, tall enough, to appreciate the seriousness of snow actually half way up our windows. She cooly, nay freezing coldly, calls for paints and brushes and sits down at a window, that has to be shoveled open for her, to do [Mt.] Lafayette in oils. The picture is now declared done and we are justified in saying of it that the only way it betrays the anxiety under which the artist worked is in the coloring of the sky which is very much too dark a blue; and this is partly attributable to the scarcity of white paint in the house owing to our having been robbed during our absence of a whole can of it as well as a Stilson wrench and probably other things we sha'n't miss till we happen to need them as much as Margeries sky does the white paint (I should say so!) In several ways the picture is a success at least as an expression and record of our present plight if not as a lasting work of art that the artist will look with favor on when she knows more. The cloud cap is the more real that you cant be sure it may not be a cap of drifting snow. She had fortunately enough white paint to do this in white rather than blue or yellow. On the whole then it is a meritorious performance that does great credit to our resources when you consider how far we are and how cut off from an artists supply store not to say an ordinary hardware store. You will enjoy looking at it in the heat of the summer if you havent forgotten by then that it was done of and in extreme winter conditions.

Meanwhile (convenient transition word!) I wish you would call up Raymond[1] and tell him from me (what possibly he knows) that there hasnt been a drop of water in his and my water works all winter and, what he probably ought to know, I wouldn't on the present showing go ahead and spend any more money on the water in that place. What's the use of harnessing water that isn't there. Tell him my advice is to stop where he is and wait. He must do as he pleases of course. But tell him I wanted him to have my opinion. Will gathers from the talk he overhears between

Reed and the contractor's boss that Raymond has already
spent more than his estimated $15,000, and the building not
over two thirds done. His road is going to cost him a lot more
before he can enjoy it. He has spent nearly a thousand on
water and nothing so far to show for it. I'd feel sorry for him
if he wasn't in the profession of being sorry for other people.
Don't tell him much. Just say I don't want to see him
venture any more money on that spring that, maybe, isnt
a spring.

I think I told you Louis [Untermeyer] got me to get
Whicher to find Sasoon[2] fifty dollars for appearing before
the class I surrendered to Whicher on leaving. It was all very
personal. Sassoon didn't want much money. What he wanted
was a chance to meet boys and men when his prospects seemed
bad for seeing anything in this country but girls and women's
clubs. Louis was very earnest and personal about it. The
next we knew Whicher was hearing from Pond the agent
instead of Sassoon himself. Not a word from Sassoon to
Whicher who I had told Sassoon would entertain him. And
Pond's tune was this: Fifty would do for talking to the class
but Amherst was a good way off and couldnt Mr. Whicher
make it a hundred and fifty for a class talk and a talk to the
whole college. To hell with such doings. Louis says Whicher
ought not to have minded. Louis means well enough but how
is Sassoon any different in this episode from the other
Englishmen we complain of. [One line deleted.] It's a joke.
I don't suppose Sassoon thought. The English ought to be
taught to be careful over here.

Black's The Great Desire[3] is really a full book. Except
that [it] doesn't go reeling along with emotion it reminds me
of Changing Winds.[4] The method is like that of Changing
Winds. It's a good way to get a lot in. It is charged with the
good American prejudices that will save us if we are saved.
Black has evidently listened to all this foreign talk against

our differences in law and custom from Europe. To be sure we use quarters where England uses shillings; we have a written constitution where they have none; we let our children run around more unattended by nurses; we drink less than they do; and so I might go on. I dont say who the differences are in favor of from God's point of view. From England's I expect them to be in favor of the English. From America's I think I am safe in saying they are in favor of the American. You'll enjoy the wisdom of the book.

I'm sick enough of that wild crowd to settle in Maine rather than in Connecticut.[5] Their hearts may be in the right place and so may some of their other organs but they have no brains.   Affectionately   PAPA.

[1] Raymond Holden, a poet and admirer of Frost's, had purchased the upland half of RF's Franconia farm and commenced building his home there.

[2] The English poet Siegfried Sassoon.

[3] Alexander Black's *The Great Desire* (1919) is a talky, deeply philosophical novel of life in New York as interpreted by a brother and sister caught up in the tensions of World War I. A first-person narrative whose excellent characterization would make it of particular interest to RF, the book argues for man's fundamental goodness. "The great desire" is man's attempt to find God.

[4] A 1917 novel by St. John Greer Ervine.

[5] As part of a slowly unfolding plan to move from Franconia, RF, in addition to his searches around Arlington, Vermont, had looked over property in southern New England. Holden — unaware that Frost was already looking elsewhere — had agreed to purchase the rest of the farm at such time as the family had to move. His promise was soon to be "called in."

EF to Lesley Frost

DARLING LESLEY, [Franconia] Monday morning [February 1920]

We have had the biggest snow storm that either papa or I ever remember seeing. Friday morning it was warmer, with a strong south wind blowing which began to melt the snow very rapidly. Then in the afternoon it rained very hard and by six oclock about a third of the snow was gone and we had hopes of water in the spring before very long but in the night the rain turned to snow, and it snowed hard and drifted all day Saturday and most of Saturday night. Not a soul could get along the roads. Yesterday afternoon a six-horse sled from the village came up past, to make a beginning at breaking out, but the roads are in a frightful state. There is to be no school today, and I doubt if the postman will attempt to get through. It is rather fun to be here for the worst storm in years, but it would be more cheerful if we had coal for the furnace, and plenty of water to use. However, I am not complaining, for we are all well. Papa isn't *quite* as well as he was before his cold, but he is feeling pretty well, and the children are fine. I have never seen Carol look so well, Marjorie is flourishing and Irma is very well for her. I am sleeping splendidly up here, and feeling much less nervous than in Amherst. Of course there isn't much news to tell you about, except the weather. We haven't had a letter from you for a week and a half, but probably there is a letter from you in the post office.

We have plenty to read here these days, for Raymond left a lot of books here, which he bought last summer, a few of last years more important novels, and some other interesting things I have never happened to read.

Well, I'll have Carol put this letter in the box, in case the postman should come along. I will write again in a day or two.   Much love & hugs from   MAMA

I finished the chemise I began last summer, and will send it along together with a white petticoat and some handkerchiefs. You use your handkerchiefs too long, dear. It isn't pleasant to see anyone using a thoroughly dingy handkerchief.

EF to Lesley Frost

DARLING LESLEY-   [Franconia, February 1920]

A lot more weather since I wrote last — a long thaw, so that the meadow was more completely flooded than we have ever seen it — then a heavy rain which turned to snow. It snowed so hard for a while that we supposed it was going to repeat last weeks performance, but it stopped in time, and then turned very cold. Last night was about 20° below again. Well, it can't last much after the last of March, anyway.

I was very sorry to hear about the Latin. How I wish you hadn't taken that course. While I don't care about your getting very high marks, I *don't* want you to fail in any subject, and especially this term, as you have almost decided not to go back next year. You know what people are! Someone would get hold of it and the end of it would be that everyone would believe you left college because you couldn't do the work. It was a little careless of you to leave that day's lesson untranslated, wasn't it ? It wouldn't have taken you more than an hour to do it, probably, and of course you can't take any chances with that sort of a person for a teacher. I don't want you to make yourself sick, studying too hard, but if there is any possibility of making your final mark a C I think you'd better try for it, looking at it in every way. Of course there is something more than pride in my mind, too. Though papa and I haven't much money, still, I think we can manage to give you any chance you want as it is, but if anything should happen to papa, of course I should be left without any provision, and it would be better if one of you children had enough training in some one thing to earn a fairly good living. Even if you don't graduate, three years of college would be something, if your record was a pretty good one. One doesn't think of such a possibility very often, but it would be wrong and foolish never to think of it. I am hoping very much that we can do something with farming, but we know that many fail at farming where one succeeds — and we mustn't count on it to the extent of altogether neglecting other chances of earning a living that we have already won, and you know you have spent some effort on college work, and we have spent some money. But don't let me worry you, dear. Sometimes I feel a little depressed, but not very often. Papa seems happy, and in the mood for writing, and that is very satisfactory.

We are not getting any daily paper now, and so never know if anything important is happening. I don't believe anything important is apt to happen for a while.

Carol is reading aloud evenings out of Shackleton's book about his Antarctic expedition.[1] He reads much better than I thought he could, and is improving all the time.

I must get to work again —

Lovingly,   MAMA.

[1] Sir Ernest Henry Shackleton's two books were *Heart of the Antarctic* (1909) and *South* (1919).

RF to Lesley Frost

DEAR LESLEY: Franconia, 11 March 1920

Two doubts in sending this precious stuff: will it ever reach you? will you have time to do it in type? You dont mention having had a couple of poems from me lately. It makes me afraid that they got lost. We don't seem to know what bundles you speak of sending.

Don't let this MS out of your hands and don't let the typewritten copies go to Harpers till I say the word. I may want to see them.

I'm thinking I ought to get seven or eight hundred dollars for the lot. I shall have settled some things with Wells[1] by the time you are ready with these.

The way to settle these radicals is to confuse them by quoting them to each other — I shouldnt stick at a little misquoting if it was for the purpose of teasing. You should have said to that fool girl "One of my friends who edits the Liberator says —" and then given her any old wild stuff to mix her up. Tell em you are not interested in the things they are going to change. You are willing they should change them. But there must be some things they havent time or inclination to change. You'd like to ask for the humble job of holding on to those while they are changing the others. You could hold some of them in your lap — the lap dogs and the cats for example. I don't suppose there is any scheme on foot to alter the cats and dogs. If your function is simply to hold on to what they don't want to change I dont see how that makes you either a conservative or a radical. To Hell with their inability to think.

Make the poems look as well as possible. Correct my slips in spelling and make none yourself.

Affectionately   PAPA

Check enclosed

Manuscript in big envelope *mailed with this.*

1 See RF to Lesley Frost, 28 January 1920, n. 2.

RF to Lesley Frost

[Portion of letter missing]   [Franconia, March 1920]

[...] I have decided not to go at Wells for the big money but for another kind of thing entirely.[1] I really want him to give me a send off by printing five or six poems in a bunch. They will be as follows and in this order

Fragmentary Blue

Place for a Third

Good-bye and Keep Cold

An Empty Threat

Two Look at Two

For Once Then Something.

So hold these six ready to send in the minute you hear from me.[2]

The sap started yesterday. Some of the buckets are nearly full. Carol and I principally Carol are going to do one mans share of the sugaring this year. You can stock up with sugar and hand the girls cakes of it in place of arguements for or against God, Hoover, Womens Suffrage, Soviets, Sedition Laws, the Treaty Drinkwater or the Pine Tree Blister. "What have you to say to this," you can ask and get them out a cake.

Yes I think Mrs Clark at the Sunwise Turn must have doubted my cold and swollen jaw. She thinks if I'm as cold by nature as they tell about catching cold couldnt make me enough worse so that I'd know the difference. But I was utterly unpresentable. Still I might have tried to set out and got as far as Littleton if Mama hadnt stopped me.[3]

Affectionately   PAPA

[1] See RF to Lesley Frost, 28 January 1920, n. 2.

[2] All but two of the poems — "An Empty Threat" and "Two Look at Two" — were published in Harper's Magazine, July 1920.

[3] RF's reference is apparently to a broken engagement at Madge Jenison's Sunwise Turn Bookshop in New York City. She later authored *Sunwise Turn; A Human Comedy of Bookselling* (1923).

EF to Lesley Frost

DARLING LESLEY - [Franconia] Wednesday noon [March 1920]

Papa says he is going to walk to the village this afternoon, so I think I'll send down a letter to you. Your package of magazines came this morning. Irma is pleased with the International and papa has read Muzzy's article, and says its very good indeed. I will read it this evening. I wonder

how you are getting on with all that typewriting. Carol
is doing some type writing for papa every day now. He does
it quite fast and makes a very clean sheet. I think he'll be
able to do all there is after this.

We are going to subscribe for two or three magazines
and weeklies. Do you think of anything you would specially
like to see through the summer? Do you see the Harper's
sometimes? Are the pictures in it interesting now?

Carol walked up the hill to see Raymond's house for the
first time yesterday and was much pleased with it. He says
it is very pretty in itself, and just suits the spot. I haven't
been up yet. There are three or four men at work on it all
the time now, but Carol says they work so slowly that its hard
to see what they have done from week to week.

There is plenty of water in our spring now, but the pipes
are frozen all the way down. Mr. Wilkins, the contractor,
says that probably the pipes were clogged by sand and
gravel while Raymonds reservoir was being built, and that is
why they froze, so probably we have to thank Raymond for
our being without water all the spring. And if the pipes are
burst, it means a good deal of expense, too.

Have you heard from Mrs. Fobes at all?

It hasn't been very cold here since Sunday. Most of the
snow has gone, but it has gone gradually, and hasn't caused
any damage that we have heard of. I shall be happy to see
the brown fields again, and a few blades of green grass.

Is it very spring like in New York?

Papa is just starting   Lots of love   MAMA

RF to Lesley Frost

DEAR LESLEY: Franconia, 18 March 1920

Do you suppose it would be safe for me not to see the
manuscript again before it goes to Harpers? You're not

afraid you may have misread my handwriting seriously somewhere. If you think I ought to see it why don't hesitate to send it back. Only be very sure to send it in a good envelope and *insure* it for fifty dollars. Things do get lost. We have never seen the drawing paper you sent Irma.

The magazines came all right. Muzzey makes me like him.[1] The trouble with most people we know is, as he says, that they may be very good at catching on to the very latest style in thought but they never even think of such a thing as wanting to set the style themselves as Lenine[2] has set it for so many millions. They have never even tasted the pleasure of starting an idea for themselves however small. They look on ideas as things to take up with and subscribe. They value themselves on the number they have heard of and the radicality of the ones they go partizan for. College is where you are more in the way of *keeping up* on ideas; certain courses in college are where you are more in the way of keeping up. The poor things have been allowed to think that declaring for a more or less new idea is the same as thinking. It would be hard to explain to them what thinking is unless you could catch them sometime in the act of thinking. They must think accidentally sometimes. We all start accidentally and unconsciously We grow in the power to think as we become aware of ourselves, or have ourselves pointed out to ourselves by circumstances and by other people. I suppose it starts too in the realm of plain observation, that is outward observation. From there it goes on to inward observation. There is sight and there is insight. You learn first to know what you see and to put fresh words on it: you learn second to know what you feel and put fresh words on it. That's the whole story. I don't believe there's anything in literature that that doesn't cover.

Would you have time to make a copy of Place for a Third and send it to G.R. Elliott,[3] Founders Hall, Haverford,

Pennsylvania? It would have to reach him there on the 25th, that is not later than the 25th. Just scribble on the bottom of the MS that I asked you to send it.

I haven't heard from Joseph Anthony this week. I wonder if he thinks the track is clear to go ahead.

I am suffering from a loss of interest in revolutions. I'd like to tie together by the tail a couple going in opposite directions and see if it would result in a standstill. Theoretically it ought to. Something up in Germany. We had been watching the stars pretty closely and we hadn't noticed anything out of the usual. Perhaps we should have watched the papers. It just shows how easy it is to look in the wrong place for a thing. Hope nobody escaped unhurt. Up with the Kaiser next I suppose.   Affectionately   Papa

Did I make those lines in An Empty Threat read
No
There's not a soul
For a windbreak
Between me and the North Pole.
Be sure it's that way.

Letter just came from Joseph. Will send letter for Wells by next mail.

[1] The historian David Saville Muzzey's "Chapters in Southern History" appeared in *The Dial* for 12 July 1919.

[2] That is, Nikolai Lenin.

[3] Professor George R. Elliott's "The Neighborliness of Robert Frost" had been published in *The Nation* 6 December 1919, and, as if to prove the truth of the title, the two families kept in close touch over the ensuing years. Elliott was instrumental in RF's return to Amherst in 1926, and he and his wife were among the last recipients, in 1963, of a letter from Frost.

EF to Lesley Frost

Darling Lesley, -   [Franconia, March 1920]
I am writing to you with a pencil generally these days, because I can sit and warm my feet over the register at the

same time if I use a pencil. You see the house wasn't banked up in the fall and the floors are much colder than they were last winter. The deep snow against the house helps some; when that is gone and the breezes blow right through the cellar, I don't know what we shall do.

The weather hasn't been nearly as cold the last three days, and March is wearing on. I guess we shall have some spring weather soon, though papa insists that it will go below zero at least twice more in March. Papa is pessimistic about the weather. He has given up his trip to New York this month. He simply doesn't dare to take that frightful journey again so soon. He has written to Mrs. Mansfield to ask if the engagement can be postponed until April, but I doubt if she can arrange it that way.

No, dear, we are *not* settling down to stay in Franconia all summer. Papa is going down the last week in April to make a determined hunt for a farm in western Connecticutt. Mr. [Warren R.] Brown, in Amherst, the real estate man, you know, is going to drive papa all around in his car. He knows so much about farm land & c. that he will be a great help in making a decision. We hope to decide on something and get settled by the middle of May. In that case, we would have to leave Marjorie alone here for three or four weeks. She has settled down to the Academy ways and seems pretty well contented. The Latin class here is really doing much harder work than her Latin class in Amherst, but the book is more interesting & the teacher pleasanter, and I think she will come out all right. The worst of it is the hard walk home through the snow after the long day.

Your cheerful letter was very welcome. You are having such a lively time, and such a pleasant time in some ways, that I am afraid you will miss it if you stay at home next winter.

I should hardly think your leg was fit for athletics if it creaks all the time, but perhaps you know best.

We all send much love   MAMA.

P.S. We wrote to Mrs. Mansfield that papa was having a bad cold at the *present* time, so if you should happen to see the Sullivan's don't contradict it.

EF to Lesley Frost

[Franconia] Thursday morning

DARLING LESLEY, -   [April 1920]

I am sorry I haven't written for so long. I don't know what is the matter with me. Most of the time I feel as if I *couldn't* write a letter. And its pretty mean of me, too. I know, for you write such splendid long letters home. Papa wrote to you about Jean.[1] Since that happened I haven't been sleeping well. I waken at three or four oclock in the morning & generally don't get to sleep again. How terrible it is going to be if she stays in that condition all the rest of her life, and if she recovers within a year, as the specialist said she very likely would, what are we going to do for her. Even if she recovers her sanity, she will probably never be able to earn her living. I expect it will be our duty to have her with us, for if she starts wandering about the world with Louie again, she will be insane again pretty quickly. For the present, if we could only be sure she was being treated well, it would be something.

We are having the worst weather I ever knew, cold all the time, and alternating between rain & snow. We have hardly seen the sun for three weeks. Yesterday we had a sunny day and began to hope the weather had changed, but it began to rain & blow again in the night, and now the rain has turned to snow. I certainly pity the mail carrier.

Marjorie hasn't been to school yet. After she had the grippe she didn't seem to get at all strong and the very day school began, she woke with a fierce sick headache, and for two days she vomited up all the medicine I gave her, and she couldn't eat a thing for about 4 days. I had to call Dr. Johnson again. She is much better now but has grown rather thin, and is behind in her work. The last two days I have studied with her about 4 hours a day. She will probably begin school again Monday.

Carol reads aloud every evening and seems to enjoy it.

Didn't you get my letter which contained a note from Irma with a request for black water color paint and the purple ribbon Mrs. Fobes gave us once? Do you remember that rather handsome purple & black ribbon. It was in the bureau drawer upstairs last summer, and it is not to be found now. If you carried it off will you please send it back, for Irma wants to make a summer hat of it. And she very much wants a *tube* of *black* water color paint.

The weeks are going pretty fast aren't they, and soon it will be time for you to come home.

Very very much love,   MAMA

¹ RF's only sister Jeanie was arrested in Portland, Maine, for disturbing the peace and was thereafter committed to a mental hospital for the rest of her life.

EF to Lesley Frost

DARLING LESLEY,   [Franconia] Sunday evening [April 1920]

We are not sitting together this evening for Marjorie has a slight cold and is being quarantined in the sitting room. Irma is in her room, papa is upstairs, and Carol and I are in the dining room. It is rather dismal, but it gives me a chance to write to you.

We had quite a hopeful letter from the superintendent of the Augusta hospital, which I will enclose. Either papa or I are going to see Jean the last of this week.

Raymond went down to Boston Friday, but he is coming back tomorrow, and I am very much afraid he will live with us the rest of the week just as he did last week. His effrontery is simply amazing, and I should be too angry for anything if there weren't so much more serious things to worry about. At any rate, papa has sold him the house for $2500,[1] so we are having him around for some purpose. One reason he is coming up so early, and the chief reason, I imagine, is to establish a legal residence here, and so avoid his New York State income tax. The income tax in New York is very high, and would probably be nearly $2000 of his income. There is no income tax in New Hampshire.

Old Mrs. Herbert has been very sick with acute indigestion, but is better now. The old man is very feeble this year. I believe the doctor has said that he may die anytime. He has Brights disease. Will and Joe are both working on Raymonds' road, and getting $4.50 a day for their own work, and Will gets extra for the horses.

Just when do you finish the year at Barnard? Do you think you will have to study very hard for examinations? Marjorie seems to get above 90 in all her history tests, but the Latin remains hard for her. She carries on a vigorous correspondence with about five of the girls in Amherst. I think it takes almost too much of her time, but I suppose it won't last very long.

Your birthday is this week, isn't it? Marjorie has had her 15th birthday, and now you are nearly 21. It seems queer enough to have you all getting so old. I wish we could buy you a really nice watch for a present, but of course it wouldn't be wise to spend money in that way now.

What is Joseph Anthony going to do after he leaves Harper's?

I *must* write to Mrs. Fobes this evening, and I am getting a little sleepy already. I hope you will go on sleeping enough each night. It must be awfully bad for you in the long run to be up late night after night.

Lots of love and a big hug, dear — Goodnight
MAMA.

1 See RF to Lesley Frost, 8 February [1920], nn. 1 and 5.

RF to Lesley Frost

DEAR LESLEY: Franc [onia], 23 April 1920

Raymond buys the rest of the farm for another twenty-five hundred [.] [Substantial portion of paragraph deleted.] So we are out of Franconia before you kids have ever climbed Mt. Washington.

I am almost sorry to be avoiding Raymond's society in this way. He has been good to us in spite of what we say. Carol likes him. They have been shooting woodchucks with the two rifles the last two or three afternoons. But Raymond makes himself almost too much one of the family. He walks in on us when we are eating and is in and out all day. You can imagine the effect on Mama when she is lying around half sick unable to get meals she can invite him to. He cooly waves a box of lunch he has brought down from Pecketts so we wont have to take care of him when I say we can't and propose sending him to Herberts. I tell him all right let him spread his lunch on our table with ours and we will eat together. The darndest mixup! Irma stays in her room while it lasts. Mama swears. She thinks she knows how he regards us that he treats us so informally not to say rudely. I'm only puzzled. I doubt if he means much harm. I think the benefits will about even up if I introduce him to Harcourt. He can't exactly despise us. Still we couldnt live so close to him.

Wells offered me two hundred for the four poems Fragmentary Blue, Place for a Third, Goodby and Keep

Cold, and For Once Then Something. I took it to have a long thing over. It was about a dollar and a half a line which though less than it might have been was more than I have had before I think. I'm sorry Joseph Anthony is leaving me to the other people there. He's sure to be bettering himself though. He is going to take time to write another novel before he hires out again isn't he? Dont have Jean's troubles much on your mind.[1] We will do all we can for her short of darkening our lives with what we are not to blame for. She is where she is for treatment. When she is well enough we will propose putting her on a small place somewhere (not near us) with Louie Merriam;[2] and they can keep hens and bees together. That's when she gets better if she gets better. She has about ten or twelve hundred dollars left which can go toward making her position more respectable in the hospital. We'll keep track of her and see that she's not treated unkindly.

I wish we could have a farm on the edge of a river town where the boats went up and down — down to towered Camelot. I wonder if Wilkinson will be free after May 4 for a ride up Burrough's way. I have put the search for a Connecticut farm in W.R. Brown's hands and shall have to let him go ahead with it. I'll write to Wilkinson that if Brown finds nothing we want I'll take the road with him. I'm afraid I've lost Wilkinson's letter with the address.

Take care of your fingers.

No Hoover this year.

Fishing season seven days off.

Took sugar pails down on Monday.

Be sure to see a ball game or two.

Good luck in tennis.

Louis clamors about Miscellaney.[3]

All his ideas echo Sassoon at present.

Saw some good poetry by a Nora May French.

Overall craze hasn't struck farms yet.

[Thomas B.] Mosher gave me his reproduction of the first edition of Leaves of Grass.

Davy Todd went up to get near view of Mars today.

Raymond's water works cause anxiety.

Spring peepers been going five nights.

Mr. Parker wanted to know if I would take principalship of Dow Academy at a price.[4]

Pretty damned English number of Yale Review.

Louie Merriam writes to say that I now live surrounded by geese.

Sonora would be a sonorous republic.

Who did you address Place for a Third to?

I think I gave you the wrong name.

The Meiklejohns will spend next year in Italy.

Beautiful farms cheap in Maine. Too far off.

Just digging our parsnips and salsify.

Is Chapin happy about the book?

Cant be many weeks before we see you.

Affectionately   PAPA.

[1] See EF to Lesley Frost, [April 1920], p. 89, n. 1.

[2] Jeanie's friend and companion.

[3] Louis Untermeyer edited *A Miscellany of American Poetry 1920* which included selections from their own work made by eleven poets: Conrad Aiken, Robert Frost, John Gould Fletcher, Vachel Lindsay, Amy Lowell, James Oppenheim, Edwin Arlington Robinson, Carl Sandburg, Sara Teasdale, Jean Starr Untermeyer, and Louis Untermeyer.

[4] A school in Franconia, now physically a part of Franconia College.

RF to Lesley Frost

DEAR LESLEY: Franconia, 19 September [1920]

The stone house it is.[1] And Mama has gone along with Margery to the brick house at Arlington to lie in wait for it there. Now if only our things were all packed and on the way. It looks as if I might be settled down to write again by Christmas. But never mind, we've got what we thought we wanted. There's a lot of fun ahead touching it up to our exact ideas. From now on we write ourselves as of South Shaftsbury, Vermont.

Your job sounds funny but not impossible if you can work yourself up to the sort of thing for a short go. Don't take it too seriously or too unseriously. You [could] be worse employed than urging people to buy a book.[2] I spent a good deal of my time as a teacher urging the same thing. I used to say that all our work in literature and composition fails if it doesn't put libraries large or small into homes.

Tell Melcher and Joseph I ran onto the rolling library at Manchester Vt and had a good talk with Miss Frank who seemed to have been getting experience as well as selling books. I was only a little surprised to learn that she had done better in Barre, Vermont, a rabble town, than at Bretton Woods the swell resort. Next time the library should be routed through medium-sized ordinary places when schools are in session. If the right people were interested it could draw up like a lunch cart and do business in front of the schools I should think.

[Paragraph deleted.]

You probably won't have much time to do the article about Gamaliel Bradford's A Prophet of Joy — not if you are going to have to do several articles a week on books in general. Maybe a little later when you are in France.

Hope you have some luck about the flat or apartment for Irma and Mama.

I wonder if some of your business friends wouldn't know how you could buy your French money. I think it possible that you might buy it as we set out to[,] of the American Express. You might ask at some large Express office[.]

Good luck with the propaganding and have a good time with it while it lasts.

Carol and I had a great ride home over the best roads ever. The car pulled like a demon.

Affectionately   PAPA.

¹ Although it would be some time before the family could occupy it, RF had arranged to purchase the Peleg Cole place, a stone cottage in South Shaftsbury, near Bennington, Vermont.

² Lesley had left Barnard and taken a job as writer and publicist for Frederick G. Melcher and the National Association of Book Publishers. Her immediate superior was Joseph Anthony, formerly of Harper & Brothers. An avid reader herself, she enjoyed the work which entailed the preparation of articles on books and the pleasures of reading for publication in various newspapers.

EF to RF¹

[Arlington, Vermont] Monday afternoon
DEAREST ROB, —   [September 1920]

Marjorie has just started for the train to go to school, & I will write you a note before I clean up the rooms. The train service is less favorable than I thought — she has to leave the house at quarter of twelve, and doesn't get home until nearly eight. She didn't want me to go up with her the first day, so I wrote a note to the principal, and one of the girls she has seen a little of was going to introduce her to him.

We had a very pleasant day yesterday. It was a beautifully clear day, and we walked up to the Fishers for lunch. They said they would come for us but I thought we should enjoy the walk — and we did very much. Marjorie thinks it is all fine country around here. She liked Mrs. Fisher & Jimmy but didn't care so much for Mr. Fisher & Sally. About 4 oclock we all went over to the Stone House. Marjorie says she liked it better than she had expected and thinks the surroundings are very attractive. Mr. Beagle was away, but Mrs. Beagle said they had about decided to buy a house in South Shaftsbury. I don't know whether they are going to hurry about getting out or not. I discovered that [...] there is a small bedroom beside the kitchen in the ell, which with the new paper & c. could be made bright and pretty and would be all right for Lesley when she is at home. We also discovered that the lake at North Bennington extends back toward the house so that it cannot be more than half a mile away across lots. It may be rough walking some of the way, but a path could be made. And the apple trees look much younger than I remembered them, so altogether I was pleased.

Mr. Fisher drove home along an older road nearer the upper edge of the valley — a very beautiful road.

I *do* hope you are all getting on well. Carol must n't work too hard. Tomorrow night I shall mail a list of things I don't want forgotten. I wish I could be there this week myself. As soon as you get this I should like Carol to drive up to Fobes' and try to sell the hay to Hodge. I object to leaving that hay for Will Herbert and there might be enough of it to pay the taxes.

If you get a letter from Lesley send it to me at once.

Be careful of yourselves, all of you.

Lots & lots of love   ELINOR

---

[1] This letter from Elinor to RF — one of the few to survive — finds the family scattered again. Lesley was living and working in New York City. EF and Marjorie were in Arlington, awaiting the opportunity to occupy the stone house. RF, Carol, and Irma were in Franconia, attending to the last details of moving. Marjorie's studies required that she take a train to the nearest high school, in North Bennington.

RF to Lesley Frost

DEAR LESLEY: Franconia, 23 September [1920]

The doctor says I am sick with jaundice and not able to be writing and moving. But able or not there are one or two things I must write to you. Raymond [Holden] tells me they have had two letters from you, one to Grace and one to him personally since you went away. This is as many as we have had from your busy self. I can't think you are going on to take your fun out of playing with this sort of fire. I dont think you can be enough aware of yourself. Raymond has given everybody to understand that he is making business in New York an excuse for going down to see you this week. He is taking the Sunday night train down. I simply tell you so that you will have time to decide what to do. My way would be to get rid of him as I got rid of Walter Hendricks, so that not a word was said out about what was the matter.[1] Be away, be otherwise engaged, be anything you please to show your self-possession. He is no sort of person for youthful folly to trifle with. He's been talking all the bold bad stuff of the books he derives his poetry from — talking it right and left. I simply tell you and leave the rest to your common sense.

Look out for Joe [Anthony] too if it is as you seem to suggest in your letter. Damn such people. You say we'll use him and drop him. We'll use him very little longer. You must get away without any ruction. We can't have scenes in our lives. But damn him from now out. I'm all on your side, only be careful, no youthful folly on your part. I'm on Harcourt's side too in the matter of the book, if the thing is as you say.

The five hundred dollars is enclosed in this letter. I dont know about your cashing it and carrying it about in money. I wouldnt dare to carry as much myself and I have safer pockets than you. Best not cash it till on your way to buy the French money. I wonder if after all the American Express money orders would be what you want. Why not ask Melcher to help and advise you, mentioning me to him. I should feel pretty safe in his friendship.

Tell me more about Smythe's proposal. It sounds amusing but not very feasable.

Cheer up about the Stone House. Oh I almost forgot that I have told Mama about the Du Chenes[2] offer of

their apartment for twenty five a month. She may
refuse it.   Affectionately   PAPA

<hr />

[1] See RF to Lesley Frost, 22 May 1919, n. 2. Here, in this letter, as in the
following paragraph, RF reveals his protective concerns for his children.

[2] Aroldo and Eiley du Chêne. A photograph of his bust of RF first
appeared in a 1921 printing of *Mountain Interval*. Housing arrangements were
being made in New York City so that Irma could pursue her studies at the
Art Students League.

EF to Lesley Frost

DARLING LESLEY, -   [Arlington] Thursday afternoon
                                          [September 1920]

Well, we seem to be in trouble of all kinds and descrip-
tions, don't we? Well, never mind. If you could get an earlier
boat without paying too much, it would be better wouldn't
it, both on your account and on Mme Firchbacher's account.[1] I wish we were settled in the Stone House and you
could come right home, until you go.

I will send you a sort of statement that may answer
for a birth certificate, but if it won't, ask someone who is
the proper city official to write to, and what would be the
probable fee, and write yourself. We were living on Summer
St. at the time, but I can't remember the number.[2] Marjorie
went to school again today. Her classes are all mixed up,
and there is altogether too much for her to make up. I may
decide that the best thing to do is to take her out for this
year. It seems to me that we have made mistakes fast and
furiously this last year. I wonder what will be the crowning
blunder. Last night I was awake hours, and it seemed to me
that the only thing to do was for everybody to stay at home
this year and get our bearings again. But of course this
morning that seemed silly. The only thing to do is to struggle
on, and possibly we will come out all right.

Papa writes that the Du Chene's have offered Irma

their flat for six weeks at the rate of $25 a month. Isn't their flat much out of Irma's way? That is too little to pay for it if it is what we want, and it would necessitate either papa or I being with her every bit of the time. I don't know what to do about it. I wish you would call up the Bureau of Girls Boarding Houses at 11 West 37th St. and ask if they have two rooms with a *family* quite near the League. I *wish* she could be near the League.

I must get this out at once.

I washed & ironed your silk dress & linen dress before I came down, and put them in a box for papa to send when he knew your house address. The blue sweater you were knitting I put in, too. If they haven't sent it, give them your house address at once.

With a big hug and lots of love.   MAMA.

[1] The Fischbachers of Sevres — spelled variously in these letters — were friends of Dorothy Canfield Fisher and offered their hospitality to members of the Frost family both in 1920 and in 1928.

[2] At the time Lesley was born, 28 April 1899, the Frosts were living with RF's mother in Lawrence, Massachusetts, where she ran a private school, on Summer Street, one block from the Common.

EF to Lesley Frost

DARLING LESLEY, —
[Arlington] Friday evening
[September 1920]

Your special delivery letter came this noon, and I was amazed and indignant I can tell you. What a way to treat anybody! But it won't do us any good to rail at the McElroys[1] — We have got to consider what can be done. If there is any possible way of your going safely, I want you to go. I would have walked out at once to see Mrs. Fisher but I have been expecting the truck with the furniture all the afternoon. You know papa sent me word that he had engaged a truck to bring down the furniture and sent a check for $100, so I should be ready to pay the driver when he got here. Papa said he was to start yesterday and in that case, he should get here today, but he hasn't come. I will manage to see Mrs. Fisher sometime tomorrow, anyway. What an extraordinary thing to have happen. Was Catherine suitably apologetic?

I am afraid I can't quite make up my mind to have you go back & forth to classes through the Paris streets alone and of course Mme. Firschbacher couldnt be with you a great deal. Would you really enjoy going if you didn't have a companion? Perhaps Mrs. Fisher can suggest something, though I can't imagine what. Of course you couldn't stay in New York if you didn't go[.] I think we shall have to manage your going somehow. Have you heard of anyone going over in the next few weeks, who might look after you?

Marjorie didnt dislike school quite so much today. I think if her stomach can stand the strain of irregular meals until we get settled in South Shaftsbury, perhaps she will work into it. She has lost 7 lbs since last February, and I thought she wasn't very well at that time.

I can't say that I feel *very* much surprised at what you tell about Joe. I really thought it was too much to expect of human nature that he should do all he has done without self interest of some kind. But we had to find out what it was, I suppose [...] I must go to bed.   .

Cheer up, dear. It wouldn't be so *very* bad if you stayed at home this year, would it?

Lots of love,   MAMA

[1] Lesley and her friend Catherine McElroy had planned their European trip together, only to have Catherine's father refuse her permission to go at the last moment.

RF to Lesley Frost

DEAR LESLEY: [Franconia, September 1920]

Damn a father like Catherine's. Not a word to you after letting her work all summer at you to drag you into her scheme.

Don't worry about them though. We'll get you to Paris somehow.

Let me know if you got the 500 dollar check I sent.

We leave here Wednesday or Thursday. Address me at Arlington next.

Mrs Fobes letter is enclosed with her check.

Affectionately   PAPA

EF to Lesley Frost

                              [Arlington] Tuesday afternoon
DARLING LESLEY-   [September 1920]

You seem not to have got the letter I wrote you last Friday. I think you'd better wait until April to go to France and then you can stay with the Firschbacher's all the time, and we can make definite arrangements long beforehand. I find, by thinking of it, that I should feel frightened about you all the time if you were in Paris alone. You can stay all through the spring and summer, and that will be better than being there through the cold winter months when there is not such a shortage of fuel. Papa seems pretty well some of the time, but again a good deal discouraged and I don't believe he realizes how fast the money is going. If he *shouldn't* be able to do any lecturing at all, we would have barely enough to get through the year, after we spend the money for the furnace, and yet he proposes my going to France with you.

Irma is coming down alone on Saturday, and you must not fail to met the same train you went down on, about

half past eight, isn't it? She may not be able to stay, but
I think its best to try it. You must not try to take her out
anywhere in the evening. She will need all her strength for
her work.

Carol hasn't come down yet, and I feel rather forlorn
about his being up there all alone.

Well, there are dishes to wash & the room to clean up.

Am glad you are coming home soon[.]

Lovingly   MAMA

RF to Lesley Frost

DEAR LESLEY   Arlington, Wednesday [September 1920]

Will you find time to go to the [Art Students] League
and make sure that Irma's place is reserved for her in
Bridgemans class. Say she has paid her fee, but has been
delayed in getting to New York by sickness. I assume there
will be no difficulty. You need wire *only if she is refused*
admission to the class.

You should tend to this at once because Irma will
come on the Saturday train (2.54 P.M. standard time —
same one you took) unless warned not to. It looks now as if
neither Mama nor I could get away to go with her. You
will have to meet her at the train and take her to the Du
Chenes house. Why don't you move down there on Saturday
yourself earlier in the day so as to make sure of the key and
admission?

You may have to live with Irma a few days alone
before Mama or I come down. Please take the way with
her that will keep the peace. Remember that her strictness
is part of her nature. Don't try to make her over. Some of
it she will outgrow, but not all of it even by the time she is
eighty. It has its beauty if you know how to look at it.
When you find it a little aggressive, you can disregard it.

This is in great haste to catch the mail.

Good luck with your articles.

Affectionately   PAPA

Keep the five hundred dollar check in a safe place till we decide what to do with it. Also Mrs Fobes' checks.

EF to Irma and Lesley Frost

[Arlington] Sunday evening

DEAR IRMA & LESLEY, — [September 1920]

I hoped for a letter from you last night on the evening mail, but none came. I wish I knew how you both are. Papa and I have been to the Fishers for dinner and to spend the afternoon. We had a fine long walk through the woods. The leaves are just at their prettiest here, a bright yellowish red, much prettier than I expected they would be a week or two ago. A lovely brook runs through the Fishers land at the foot of the hill on the right of the road, and there are beautiful tall pines on both sides of it. It has been such a wonderful day. Tomorrow morning the mason starts to fix the chimney for the furnace at the Stone House. We ought to have the furnace in [the stone house] in about a week and a half, and then we shall go in ourselves as soon as the things come from Amherst. We are so eager to get over there even if things are pretty messy at first. We can't make things look comfortable and pretty until the partition is taken down and the kitchen is plastered & papered. But it is so nice out doors over there that we want to be there.

Carol has picked about 3 barrels of apples and there are four or five more to pick.

Marjorie's cold is pretty bad today. Her head is heavy with phlegm & she is beginning to have a bad cough. I think she won't be able to go to school tomorrow. Papa doesn't seem a bit strong but is more cheerful than he has been all summer. I am a good deal afraid he isn't strong enough to go to Bryn Mawr, but he wants to try it. You will see him about the 30th but please don't tell anyone, Lesley, that he is coming down at that time. He may not feel strong enough to see many people in New York.

I will enclose a check for $25 for Irma, but I'll have it made out to Lesley as it is easier for her to cash a check.

Well, good night, dears. There isn't much to say until I hear from you.   Lovingly   MAMA

RF to Lesley Frost

DEAR LESLEY: Arlington, 14 October 1920

Mama is just home and *she* says *you* say nobody answers your questions; nobody appreciates your long letters: you might as well make them short notes just assuring us you aren't sick. That's a good one. I don't know about the questions but the long letters are in great demand: we want all we can get of them as full of news as they can hold. Mama brought some news with her, as that a menagery had broken loose in the Du Chene's and was running all round over Irma in the dark like bad dreams. But she was painfully short of intelligence on some important heads. She couldn't tell, for instance, what the two articles were about that you were writing for the Sun and Times respectively.

She said you had rounded out your job with the Book Campaign with colors flying.[1] To have staid as long as the business you were in lasted makes an auspicious beginning in life. Now for almost anything else you please, I should think. What a wide free choice you seem to have. I am not the least tempted to plan for you. My satisfaction is all in letting you plan for yourself since you are so able to. Only I could tell you if you asked me what to do with your cooccupants of the Du Chene apartment to set them back temporarily if not to get rid of them entirely. You can get in a kerosene can a gallon of gasolene (price 36 cents) and pour, literally pour, it into every crack and corner of the wood work of the beds or cots and soak the canvass of them all along where it is nailed to the wood. Dont wet the mattresses: they are as uninhabited as the moon. You must do the deed very early in the day when no light or fire is lit in the room or going to be for a good many hours — that is till the gasolene has had time to evaporate and get out the windows. You can leave the windows open for the day. I say this only for your own comfort for the time being, not to save the apartment for Irma. The apartment will have to be given up. It will never do for Irma to go on with it. You may have to buy a cheap kerosene can. It is the best thing to buy the gasolene in and to put the stuff on with. Dont spare it. Make the wood bubble. Go over the beds twice perhaps. Then open the windows and get out.

This is the kind of letter I should hate to mail at the Franconia postoffice for fear Salome would open it for her amusement and keep it as a memorial of our private affairs. Two or more letters that Carol and I sent from there to other members of the family never reached their destination. We are sure of two. I wonder if you got all we wrote to you toward the last of it. I mustnt suspect the Franconia post office too much. I hear that letters are being lost everywhere in transmission.

One of your questions you complain of my not answering was whether I advised your reviewing Louis' Misc. The idea has its attractions especially for the chance it would give you to be funny about your obligations to me that would forbid your dealing with me one way or the other lest you should seem too grateful or not grateful enough. You could go on at a great rate with an ironical sideswipe at people who review their wives and intimate friends. But it would never do. I don't mean that part so much as the rest

of it. You'd be in danger of converting too many friends and
half friends into enemies. It would be going out of the way
to seek trouble. Unless of course you found you had one good
characterizing apiece for everybody in the book that was
neither favorable nor unfavorable and could be delivered
for its intrinsic interest and not seem evasive and non-
committal. That would be a good kind of review: eleven ideas
on art or life suggested by the eleven poets in the book.
You could look the book over and see what it had for you.
Eleven minus me. You could carry on about me, especially
if the review was to be signed.[2]

All this reviewing is by the way for you of course, so you
may as well put stiff while you are at it and find out what
sort of thing it is. Why cant you do some of it from the Stone
House in South Shaftsbury if you come home and dont go to
France? You could run down for fifteen dollars a round
trip once a month or so, making two or three days of it there
if business called for it.

I think I must wish as much as you do you could go to
France. I hate not to have you after all that has been said.
How would it be to go for a shorter time than you intended
— say three months — just to escape the reproach of having
fizzled? You couldnt find someone to go with you? I havent
mentioned it to anyone — I've just thought of it — but
wouldn't it be fine for you to take Margery, for some one
to stick to on the voyage and go round with in Paris. Maybe
this isnt feasable. It might cost too much for the family
purse. I'll see what Mama says. I wish we all could go. I'm
half scared to have you go alone. Mama speaks of the
possibility of typhus over there this winter. And I can tell
from a lot of things the French are out of love with us as are
also all the rest of the world. All the more reason there
should be no League of Nations. Vote for Debs if you want
to, but don't vote for Cox. And by the way how are you

going to vote when you have no residence anywhere unless
it is in Franconia? Or had you been long enough in New
York to establish a residence for registration? I never heard
how long it takes in New York.

Mama amused me with the vagaries of the She-
Untermeyer.[3] Louis socks us to her in the privacy of the
hours when the house is empty of society. She's bent on
punishing someone for my sins of inappreciation. I'm sorry
to have wounded her corpulency, but gee I have to allow
myself the luxury of an occasional critical frankness. If she's
a poet, so's my late uncle. What's the use! She has the merit
of compression. Her poems would pass for tolerable daily
themes in college. The ideas are about as much as you
would expect in such work. The length is suitable. That may
be saying a good deal for her. I can add to it that she's never
nonsensical or strained or overprecious and literary as Carl
Sandburg in most respects greatly her superior, sometimes is.
(Read the dedication of his Smoke and Steel for the kind of
thing: "Listener to new yellow roses." Awful stuff. It
vitiates many a good poem in his book.) And still she
amounts to too little. She hasn't brains enough to think with.
Requiescat ex labore! I was glad Cleveland won (after
seven such well picked games on both sides) and I wasnt
too sorry Lavinski lost, considering the interesting savage
but intelligent man fighting with his tongue out and striking
with the strength of ten because his conscience was so clear
about the war, he lost to. I wish Carpentier were ours so we
could be quite happy in wishing him to lick Dempsey.[4]

I think of another thing you asked about: a book of
Hollister's. It had gone into a box before you spoke. Do you
think he is in a hurry for it? Something about the appreciation of music wasn't it. I'll trust him to appreciate music
a while longer without the help of a book — just as I'll trust
him to go the whole length in music without the help of

Amherst College. I hope he'll take care of his health enough for practical purposes.

Carol lives on his car and its idiosyncracies. He stops and goes as it stops and goes. Last night it came to a standstill in South Shaftsbury just when it was time to come home after having picked apples all day. He cheerfully had it towed to the garage where he put in four or five hours with the garage man over it before they found out that the trouble was with the make and break lever in the magneto. He didnt care [.] He was intending to walk home ten miles after ten oclock at night: but I forebade that by telephone. He likes it as well out of order as in order. He wallows in the dirty oils of it, ruining shirt on shirt.

I'd like a week down there to spend entirely in the Metropolitan Museum where Mama tells me she has been with Irma. I never had enough of such places.

Affectionately   PAPA

[1] See RF to Lesley Frost, 19 September [1920], n. 2.

[2] See RF to Lesley Frost, 23 April 1920, n. 3.

[3] Jean Starr Untermeyer, whom Louis divorced in 1926 and remarried in 1928.

[4] France's Georges Carpentier and "Jack" Dempsey were scheduled for a heavyweight championship bout in early 1921. Dempsey won. Here and elsewhere, RF frequently makes reference to his two favorite sports — boxing and baseball — interests which can be traced to his early years. In 1956, he was commissioned to do an article for *Sports Illustrated*, "Perfect Day — A Day of Prowess." See Hyde Cox and Edward Connery Lathem (eds.), *Selected Prose of Robert Frost* (New York: Holt, Rinehart and Winston, 1966), pp. 87-91.

[*The reader is invited to consult the Frost Family Chronology which provides selected details covering this and other hiatuses in the correspondence.*]

RF to Lesley and Marjorie Frost

DEAR KIDDS: [Amherst, 1924]

Your printed matter received.[1] In reply am giving you a large order for one copy of Canfield's Made to Order Stories which please send promptly as not to a member of your family.

Advise one of your firm keep a scrapbook. Have some letters and stuff to give you good start. Enclosed find couple souvenirs of Harry Kemp author of Tramping on Life. Others to match. Make no mistake: dont neglect important branch of your enterprise.

Yours (off to Chicago to speak a good word for Harriet Monroes[2] poetry) ly

R. F. D. Ph. D.

[1] A brochure announcing the establishment of The Open Book [store], 124 South Street, Pittsfield, Massachusetts, by Lesley and Marjorie Frost and their friend Mary Ellen Hager of Lancaster, Pennsylvania. Actively interested in the project, RF assisted the girls with financial backing, suggestions for advertising in the Berkshire *Eagle* and elsewhere, and other promotional schemes.

[2] Poet and founding editor (1912-1936) of the influential *Poetry : a Magazine of Verse*.

RF to Lesley Frost

DEAR LESLEY: [Ann Arbor, Michigan, late fall 1925]

You needn't be afraid of our failing to appreciate what you have done to Pittsfield. What you have done to Pittsfield you have done also unto us. It makes me feel younger.

But take care of yourself. You'll have to be casting about for more reliable help than your present partners if the business is going further. That's evident. Mary Ellen hasnt the health and Marj of course cant be asked to have the devotion to a thing she isnt really committed to. Shes torn two or three different ways at her age and with her mind. The book store has got to be parttime with her till she sees clearer.

I 've seen a little of them in all three of the bookstores here, Slater's Graham's and Wahrs. Slater seems to be stealing the business from the other two partly by enterprise and partly by book knowledge. He has improved the looks of his store a lot. He gets hold of the professors by giving them all 20% discount. They return the favor by keeping him ahead of their assignments for classes. I like him pretty well. Graham is a gentle charming person who speaks of The Four Horsemen in the same bracket with The Education of Henry Adams as high brow and called someone's protege his protegy (but we all have terrible moments of word blindness like that sometimes). I just met Wahr himself for the first time in his downtown bookstore yesterday. Hes the character. He still supports the Whimsies magazine. Now and then he prints a book. He says he has a whole lot of first editions of poetry in his cellar I might like to see. He bought the lump from an instructor who needed money. I'll tell you if I pick up anything for your shelf of firsts.

I dont believe Vachel[1] wanted to see us much as he wanted an engagement. He didnt come anyway and we dont know where he is. And I cant autograph his books for him. I autographed my own and sent them back.

People often speak of you where I wander. I seldom remember their names. A Miss or Mrs Hinchman talked you and your doings up to us at Grand Rapids. And right here in Ann Arbor who do you suppose called on the telephone for you and Marg but that Canadian Johnson (I think) that worked in the Gen Electric? I didnt ask him to the house. I didnt exactly know how he stood with you folks.

Lawrence Conrad[2] seems the best bet here. Mary Cooley may do something and then again she may turn to active life. She's not madly ambitious in the arts. I shouldn't say there was much stirring. We dont know what to think of the place this time.

Besides the books I have ordered I wish you could get me in a hurry three of [Cornelius] Weygandt's A Century of the English Novel (Century Co) and four of [Hughes] Mearn's Creative Youth (Doubleday?) I want them right off for Christmas presents. Perhaps you could have them sent directly from the publishers to me. The bill could go to you. Or would that mix things up?

Affectionately   PAPA

[1] The poet (Nicholas) Vachel Lindsay was one of many literary figures whom RF sought to speak at Michigan. In this and other ways, he worked with the student editors of *The Whimsies*, an undergraduate literary magazine.

[2] A Michigan student and promising writer who expressed deep appreciation for Frost's work at Ann Arbor. On a number of occasions while there, he assisted by typing RF's manuscripts.

RF to Lesley Frost

DEAR LESLEY: Ann Arbor, 17 April 1926

All over with Michigan but the final disentanglements and reproaches. We are putting off the longest we can our declaration of intention. Effinger knew more than a month ago and Little was supposed to have known. Effinger had promised to tell him. I found yesterday that Effinger hadnt got his courage up. Very embarrassing for me who am already pretty far committed to Oldsie. Like trying to change from one escalator to another going in the opposite direction. May cost me a good hard setdown not to say fall. One thing has led to another till such a point has been reached. Amherst friends merely set out to give me a round of four colleges (Amherst, Wesleyan, Bowdoin and Dartmouth) to earn a living from in eight weeks of the year. In the end Amherst has decided to keep me for Amherst. The thing is practically negotiated. Oldsie will stop over in passing through on Monday and clinch it. But do nothing to spread the news. I wish we might keep out of the papers with it till June.[1]

Right in the middle of everything I get an offer of the Gummere Chair of English at Haverford College. There has been no one found for the place since Gummere died.

It will be a relief to be back in New England and its getting so I cant go without a house and barn of my own a minute longer. It took this bad year to find out what was expected of us here. I wasnt just sure from my memory of talks with Burton how much I was going to be permitted absences.

It has felt to me from hints and attitudes as if we were wanted for constant neighbors and companions. Every time I left town has been noted and remarked on. Mrs Effinger who as yet isnt in on the resignation secret was asking the other day why we didnt summer here. Its a false position. They want us to act as if their charm had prevailed over New Englands. Thats going some and Ive gone as Bert Williams said. Lets not exaggerate anything. We have like[d] a lot of people here and wish they would stay friends (but probably they wont when they find us out[.]) I havent liked the kids as well this time. The young assertiveness prevailing everywhere east and west seems a little more crude and impolite out west. And I find I'm not fond of teaching girls in their new state of mind. They started out escorting me home from night classes and proposing canoe rides and when I blocked that turned on me in some sort of sex resentment and gave me one of the worst classes of wrangle and flat contradictions I ever had. The same critic missies have sat mum at the Whimsies and never helped with an observation or a comparison in the five years I have done my best to entertain them; much less have they ever started any subject of their own. Suddenly out of some sex mischief they break loose and storm me not with subjects, observations and comparisons (such would be welcome) but with contradictions and abuse. I could compose these matters if I cared to. But I seem off such people. I'm willing to grant their equality if thats all they are fighting for. You'll remember that this isnt the first time I ever was off the common people. I'm a great whiffler in my love for the common people. I just naturally seem to shift from some to others and so on to none of them at times.

The new store sounds boss. I wish Marj could have been in on the excitement. She comes on terribly dragging. Mama probably told you the doctor called it a delayed convalescence.[2] Poor comeback I suppose that means as with a person bad at repartee. Miss Murphys exuberance when here yesterday about did for Marj temporarily. Then the Johnson boy held her at the telephone too long. (He spoke from Detroit [.])

Speaking of Pittsfield friends of yours, I saw Gale Sonderguard[3] in Miss Bonstelle's Detroit stock Co do Jessey Lynch Williams Why Not. I talked with her out back about you and Marj and Lulu. I thought she did well though as a whole Williams wasnt very well satisfied with the presentation of his play. Irma and I saw both his plays Why Marry and Why Not.

Marj has been reading Lawrence Conrads novel Figures in the Town — great in part she says preposterous in part. Theres a play here of the Osborn boy's[4] to read: and I must read the poetry (by Negroes) in the Opportunity Prize Contest.

About this passbook and check. Very important to tend to it at once. Deposit the five hundred dollars right off and send the passbook right back to me so I wont be worried about it. Register it carefully. I have reasons for wanting to pull everything out of the Ann Arbor Savings Bank suddenly enough to be noticed by them. Dont let the check lie a minute.

Tell us some more news. Sleep all you can.

Affectionately   [unsigned]

[1] RF was resigning his now-permanent appointment at the University of Michigan to return to Amherst College. Clarence Cook Little was Michigan's President, and George Daniel Olds had assumed the presidency of Amherst in 1923. John R. Effinger was Michigan's Dean.

[2] Marjorie had suffered a series of illnesses and indispositions — including appendicitis and bronchial pneumonia — which required well over a year's convalescence.

3 The actress Gale Sondergaard, active with the Jessie Bonstelle Stock Company between 1925 and 1927.
4 The playwright and film writer, Paul Osborn.

RF to Lesley Frost

DEAR LESLEY: [Ann Arbor, May 1926]

I just want to say in answer to part of your letter to Mama that Dwight[1] has made us all like him. He put the finishing touches on me with the send off he gave Marj when she came away. We can see with our own eyes that he is a gracious and splendid feller. I can see that there are few things that he hasn't a head for. For the rest I am glad to see him as you see him. I take your word for it that he is really good — by which you mean, I suppose, that we could trust him to be good to you.*   Affectionately   R.

*It would have to be very good you understand.

When I get back from Iowa and Illinois I am going to play Seward to your Lincoln and submit serriatim some proposals for the future conduct of your book store administration. Nothing I havent said before orally.

[...] I had the most scratching screeching row of females all over me in my class last night that ever befell me in pedagogy. The little she devils lit into me, as nearly as I could make out, for nothing but to assert their equality to me. Im drawing to the end of such adventures.

1 Lesley's fiancé, James Dwight Francis.

RF to Lesley Frost

South Shaftsbury, Vermont,
DEAR LESLEY: 3 August 1928

A few things in parting:[1] The enclosed check is a present to start the History of Literature bookcase in The Open Book. I had the check through Pierce Cumings for

Atmosphere.[2] I am going to send you home some books for that case from the London bookstands. Tell Canby to make out the check (you keep it.) to you for The Middletown Murder and send the proof to me.[3]

Tell Barbara Young I sent you to make my apologies. Tell her I didnt get her letter till much too late. Marjorie seems so-so and we are off on the Flyer for Queens Hotel Montreal this afternoon (Friday). The Montnairn starts us down stream at three tomorrow. Too bad we werent educated against sea sickness by being lowered suddenly alot when babes in arms.

I had a fine time at the ball game with Dwight. I didnt quite hold my own on the peanuts and hot dogs. Another time I'll go prepared to eat everything. We didnt arrive in time to make my team win the first game. In fact we seemed to throw them into confusion. I supposed we embarrassed them coming in after they had given us up. We made ourselves felt for good in the second game all right. I thought I could make them win if I put my mind on it.

Good bye my dear. We'll write from the boat. Dont let Johnny Farrar[4] trouble you. You trouble him. Such a misleader deserves no consideration [.] I dont forgive him.

The manuscript came all perfected. Be sure to speak to Pat.[5] Tell him he will see me in Dublin.

I'll have to tell you what you can let Davison[6] have. Ask him if he couldnt sell the Middletown Murder to Squier[7] or someone. It doesnt matter except that he seems bent on interceding for me anywhere and everywhere.

Goodbye again. Hold on though. The other enclosed slip is a duplicate list of my wealth in the Bennington First National Bank. Put it in a very safe place. Dont loose it [.]

Affectionately PAPA

---

[1] RF was about to embark with EF and Marjorie on a three-month European trip.

² Otherwise entitled "Inscription for a Garden Wall," this poem was published in the October 1928 *Ladies' Home Journal* and in RF's *West-Running Brook* (1928). *PRF*, p. 246.

³ Henry Seidel Canby was co-founder and chairman of the editorial board of *Saturday Review of Literature* in whose 13 October 1928 issue RF's "The Middletown Murder" appeared. Not in *PRF*.

⁴ RF's dissatisfaction with Farrar was at least twofold; his management of the Bread Loaf Writers' Conference had been questioned, and Lesley was less than happy as his employee. See RF to Lesley Frost, 20 September [1928], n. 4.

⁵ Poet-playwright Padraic Colum.

⁶ Poet and sometime friend of RF's, Edward Davison began a Frost biography but was discouraged from completing it.

⁷ J. C. Squire, poet and editor of *The London Mercury*.

EF to Lesley Frost

[En route to France] Canadian Pacific,
S.S. Montnairn, Friday morning
DARLING LESLEY,-   [August 1928]

Well, the trip hasn't been quite as bad as I expected. The two days on the St. Lawrence were pleasant, and we were not at all seasick. We saw a good sized iceberg, and had a lovely view of Belle Isle going through the strait. But as soon as we were through the strait, trouble commenced, and I have had three horrible days. Today I can take a little interest in things. I have got to get home again, but never again after that will I take an ocean trip as long as I live. Papa & Marjorie had only a touch of seasickness one day. Marjorie has walked a good deal and played shuffleboard some, and has got a grand color — but I think she is growing thinner. She has made acquaintance of a very pleasant Canadian girl about her age. The boat is comfortable, and the sea has been very smooth.

Before the boat started, who should come up to us but "Arty" Cross, of Ann Arbor — history professor, you know, and he has sat at our table and though he tends very much to the anecdotal in conversation, I think on the whole, it has been a gain to have someone we know a little outside the family to talk to.

We land Sunday morning about 7 o clock at Cherbourg, and I will mail this letter at once. Papa gave the letters I wrote on the train between Montreal & Quebec to an official to mail. I hope they got mailed all right. In case my letter to you didn't reach you — I will give our address again. c/o Am. Express. 11 rue Scribe, Paris. I do not believe we shall stay in Europe as long as we planned in the beginning. Unless Marjorie decides to stay over for the year, and I am not really expecting that. I think we shall be satisfied with 2 months over there. I am already homesick.

I will write again as soon as we get settled in Paris. Take care of yourself, won't you?

With lots of love,   MAMA

RF to Lesley Frost

DEAR LESLEY: Paris, 21 August 1928

I don't believe this can last long the way it is going. The French are at their worst, I should imagine, at this time of year with the Americans all over them. We have to try too hard to be fair to them. All we can say is countries never love each other. The detestable thing is the greedy leer and wink everybody has for us and our money. You neednt publish it at home, but what we are most aware of is not the beauty of Paris, but the deceitful hate all round us. Even in Dorothy's friends, the Fishbashers.[1] They are more or less secretly annoyed at our lack of French and I cant blame them for that, as why should we be here incommuniccado? But it goes deeper down still. I suppose it has something to do with the debt — at any rate with our being rich and their being poor, the franc worth four cents that was worth twenty and our dollar as good as it ever was. The question is who is to blame for instituting the comparison. I suppose we are by our presence in their country. The girl usher at the theatre the other night ran off with the stubs of our tickets instead of taking the trouble to hand them to us when we were in our seats and the office sent someone else back to us with them and a demand for more money for the favor — an actual demand before everybody in the audience. I paid. We went to church at the Madeleine on Sunday. The usher there led us to seats and then insolently blocked the entrance with his foot hard down till I had slipped some money into his underhand. Then someone else prowling the congregation with a fist full of paper money, a woman, descended on us and demanded more money. We paid to avoid making a scene when the priests were marching countermarching bobbing and genuflecting up in front. It was loathsome even to me who part with my money too easily. Outside yelling worse then I ever heard them anywhere. The news boys insulted us personally by coming right at us with New York and London papers. "Latest news from Oshkosh and Minnehaha," was their line. As I say our effect on them is bad. We degrade them in some way. I have no doubt among themselves they are like any other nation. Probably their success in the war hurt them somewhat too. The most prominent of the new statuary in the Tuillaries Gardens shows a great falling off in taste and greatness. It is a puffed up, strutting piece of bombast called Victory. I don't believe that as a people they are in a very admirable state. They need to be left to themselves for a while. And I think we will leave them. We'll see how much more themselves the English appear.

I wish you had told us more of the marvelous escape you had in the automobile wreck. There were three cars in the collision, you say, you only speak of two after it. I suppose the third disappeared into thin air — ceased to exist. I think you'll have to do something to break yourself of the habit of being in automobile wrecks. It makes me nervous.

Fine about the store. Isn't Mrs Crane's friendship counting! You got the check I sent to start the new case of old but not necessarily rare books? My heart has always secretly been in the Pittsfield bookstore. I could give it up anytime it seemed really best. But the least turn for the better and it rouses my ambition for it only less than it rouses yours.[2]

Keep us posted.   Affectionately   R.

---

[1] See EF to Lesley Frost, [September 1920], pp. 98-99, n. 1.
[2] See RF to Lesley Frost, [1924], n. 1.

RF to Lesley Frost

DEAR LESLEY: [Paris, 23 August 1928]

Business first. Will you have Ted Davison arange it for me to meet the right person in Longmans for an official talk? I feel as if I wanted to use the opening at this time when I am over here rather to get all my books together than merely to bring out another stray book under a new publisher. Longmans might be willing if Davison put in a word and I had a word too to hold off on me for a year and then do my collected poems simultaneously with Holts in America. That would mean a lot to me and I think it is what Jack Squier has had in mind all along. You might read this much of my letter to Davison over the telephone. Or no you might not because I have called him Davison in it instead of Ted. Just tell him about it in your own words.

Marjorie has been off all afternoon on the Seine and in a gallery looking at Monet's water lillies with Marise Fish-basher and another girl and she reports absolutely on their authority that The French hate us as nationals though they may like us here or there in special cases as individuals. She didnt mention the debt. She blamed our childish behaviour on the boulevards over pleased with ourselves for having reached furthest Paris and making fun of them and their poor depreciated money. She is an educated young lady, you have to remember, of a clever family: yet she is free to maintain that three Americans have been mobbed and killed in Paris for their frank insolence-or insolence with the frank. One man rode all over Paris with his car pasted all over with hundred frank notes. She herself has seen Americans tearing up hundred frank notes (4 dollars) and throwing them into post office waste baskets for show. Let her tell it. At least she thinks she has seen these atrocities. It doesnt matter for the purposes of psychology whether she has or not. I have heard at least two loud Americans making fun of the money. They are too insensitive to know that to the French their money is a sad-a ruin-the poor old inpoverished frank. Marise knew what she was saying. She speaks very good English. So you see what chance we have to be passing friends with the generality. It it werent for the Fishbashers and more especially the Feuellerats[1] and their daughter and son-in-law Mrs and Dr Charles Broquet, not all our philosophy not all our conviction that all nations are alike would have kept us from thinking France was a little worst than America. They have made it up to us for everything. Nevertheless it is a pity we came here at this time of year when the races were both at their terriblest in each others embraces. I saw ten girls come breathless out of one stocking store to consult a moment on the curb before plunging headlong into another. What was their asperation? To be Paris in Ann Arbor, I'll bet. It would be a coincidence if it were Ann Arbor, but I'll bet it. I'll bet they were Alpha Phis. No it is no good to any of us. We were in the wrong boat coming over and we are in the wrong boat still. We throw it off with what health and vitality we have; but it is a mistake from the taxi men to the hags that demand money of you for ushering you into you[r] seat in the opera. The taxi man drives up asking how far are you going? He tells you to walk if he thinks the distance wont pay him. Mama was tired from the Louvre today and I asked four taxi men in vain to take us home. The fifth consented without a murmur. The distance was ten cents. I tipped him fifty and told him why in a mixture of bad English bad French and gestures.

Speaking of the Louvre. That is as redeeming as the Feuillerats of course. We'll remember the good things when we look back. As always. You know how acute our home-sickness always is: and to what mental turns it spurs us. I suppose our realest anguish ensues from our being caught on what looks like touring at all. We ought not to be in France after all we have said from the platform and the throne against tourism literal and metaphorical. By metaphorical I mean in Survey courses in education. We had business in England Ireland. We had a right to go there. We had no business at all here after our plans failed to keep appointments with Babbitt and the others earlier in the year. We have ourselves to blame for weakly having come just because we had got headed and impulsed. Let it amuse you. Have anything you please, preferably some more books for the bookstore, on us.

You dont tell me what Canby says to my vindictive poem.[2] Dont press it on him.

I havent brought myself to see the Untermeyers yet in France Germany or No-mans Land. It wouldnt do to have them here shell-shocking Marj. Pas encore.

Mama is only so so but stoutly denying it. After this folly, rest. I'm all pent up things to do. What the Hell am I so far out of my balliwick for anyway. Elinor needs a place of quiet to rest in and I need one to write in. So whats' this expedition all about? May be Marj. But she doesnt praise it very highly. We could have bought a farm for the price of it. Aint I going strong?

I like your news.

We've had a lot of opera both at the Opera and Opera Comique. There's more good I forgot to mention. We like French bread. The wine doesnt mean much to us. The newspapers such as Le Matin and Le Figaro beat any we ever read for interests of the mind. [...] editorials on ideas are treated as news on the front page.

We shall go along in a few days now — probably on Tuesday or Wednesday [.] Use J.W. Haines house Midhurst Hucclecote Gloucester England as our next address. We dont know just what order we shall follow in visiting places. London may come first.

Think of me sightseeing in spite of all the protective laziness I have developed on principle against it. I deserve to be punished. Upon my soul I never saw anything to match this summer Paris for ugliness not even a White Mountain resort. We're catching it. But never mind. As I say we deserve it. You may say another time we'll know better. Not necessarily. We're not the kind that can be taught. We know instinctively all we are going to know from birth and inexperience.

No mail from any body at home for more than a week.

Marj found a more or less secret building full of eight great pictures of water lillies by Monet who seems to suit her fastidiousness. I think the absence of Americans in the place helped — and tip-exacting Frenchmen.

I've got my writing bag along for fear I shall think of something I want to do. I think of enough, but it is not the right kind. The bag is a reproach.

I picked up one of the biographical figments you say are going out. This one is called La Fayette by Deltiel 1928. You'll see it in translation yet. It begins well by saying La Fayette was only brother to Jean D'Arc and then quoting LaFayette's boast that he conquered the King of England in his might the King of France in his glory and the mob in their fury. It calls him the founder of two republics France and America. So far so fine and Gallic. Thence it goes on to do the regular thing from the laboratories of Vienna by asserting that the Eighteenth century asperation for liberty was sexual. And we are in up to our ankles again head first. No no nothing will do. Mine be a cot beside a rill — or at worst an appartment with no telephone in a back street in N. Y. C. That is contemplatable.

You'll say this is a long letter and more or less unified by mood though it shows joints of being added to from time to time.

Remember me to Dwight. I notice the Giants rose to the surface like a dreg on a bubble got dropped by the bubble when it broke and are now going down to hitch onto another.[3]   Affectionately   R.F.

[1] Professor and Mrs. Albert Feuillerat — of the Sorbonne and Yale — who were, at this point, in Paris. RF had met them in New Haven.

[2] See RF to Lesley Frost, 3 August 1928, n. 3.

[3] See "In a Glass of Cider," *PRF*, p. 468, for RF's later use of this image.

RF to Lesley Frost

Midhurst, Hucclecote, Gloucester
DEAR LESLEY: [11 September 1928]

We dont seem to have had evidence that you have had any letter from us. If the stream keeps on flowing, most of it may sink into the ground and be lost, but some at least must come through sometime to the sea. Be sure to let us know when you are reached.

I've seen a few of the English, J.C. Squier, John Freeman, and the Hainses — not to mention the not least mentionable Badnee or Mrs Hyatt of Ryton Dymmock Gloucestershire. She's all sole alone there now (rent free I suppose by the kindness of the farmer her husband was shepherd for.) The people at the Gallows are at enmity with the neighborhood and drove us off when we tried to look the old place over. Probably they were ashamed of the rundown condition of the property — everything overgrown and the thatch rotted and fallen in. The people at Little Iddens were glad to show us in. That place is better than we left it. The Woods have moved away from the big house.[1]

The Gibsons live at Letchworth where the children can have the advantages of the Quaker schools. Gibson's stock as a poet is quoted very low right now. How he lives is a puzzle to his friends. His third of the income from Rupert Brook's books may still be a big help.

De la Mare[2] is not yet well from an operation that nearly killed him. He is the most prominent one of them all, getting out with both prose and verse to even the unliterary reader. W.H. Davies suffers his worst pangs of jealousy over de la Mare. Davies spends a good deal of his time talking about his own relative deserts. Everybody agrees or concedes that he still writes his best. He has married a very young wild thing of no definable class, but partly gypsy [.]

John Freeman, a well to do head of an insurance firm, has climbed into some poetic prominence. He is so dull that I am tempted again to say my poetry to please me must be sensational. Freeman asked me with too obvious eagerness what I should say Hugh Walpoles article in "Books" on him rating him among the first six was likely to do for him in America. I told him almost anything. Which is no more or less than the truth. He wrote the article about me in The Mercury and I ought to be grateful.[3]

There's nobody new to take our place as the younger poets: or so I heard them lamenting with a false note in the Mercury office. The Sitwells and T.S. Elliott were pointedly left out of count.

Laselles has been too busy and recently too ill to write poetry. Theres a play of his that raised a howl a year or two ago for its immorality. The beginning raised my gorge at its stilted vernacular. I got no further. He has several more children than when we last heard.

Flint[4] is I dont know where. [Harold] Monro has moved his book shop [.] I happened to see on his desk a letter signed by Marion Dodd.[5] He is just getting asked to America by Fekins. About time, he says. He has wondered at not having been asked long since. He treated me very shabily. He always resented my being.

Haines knows and entertains them all now. He may be as much remembered as any. He is full of them all and rich in all their books. He is his whole law firm now and works hard but finds time for correspondence in all directions.

Mrs. Helen Thomas hasnt been heard from yet. She has entirely new friends. She plans more books about Edward. Nobody blames her to[o] hard for that first one [.]

Affectionately   R.F.

[1] Here included are a number of references to the Frosts' various residences in England from 1912 to 1915. The most memorable portion of their stay was their half-year residence at Little Iddens, a timbered country home near the Malvern Hills. The poets Wilfred W. Gibson and Lascelles Abercrombie were near neighbors and frequent companions. Edward Thomas visited nearby in August 1914. After vacating Little Iddens, the family stayed with the Abercrombies at The Gallows until shortly before their return to the U.S.

[2] The poet Walter De la Mare.

[3] "Contemporary American Authors: Robert Frost" in *The London Mercury*, 13 (December 1925), pp. 176-187.

[4] Imagist poet F. S. Flint had introduced RF to Ezra Pound on his first trip to England.

[5] Northampton, Massachusetts, bookstore owner under whom Lesley had apprenticed in 1923.

EF to Lesley Frost

Imperial Hotel, London, Thursday evening,

DEAR LESLEY, — 20 September [1928]

This is gay paper, isn't it,[1] but I don't seem to have

much of any other kind. We came up to London from the Haines' on Monday. Do you remember the Imperial Hotel — next door to the Premier, where we came on arriving in London the other time [in 1912]? This one is very large with many people in it, but we have two quiet rooms on the court. They are small, but very cosy, and a large bathroom opening out of one. For $6.75 per day, breakfast included, I think I can rest here, as well as in the country, and I can see a few people. Tomorrow we are going out to spend the night with the de la Mares, at Taplow, in Bucks. Next week we are going out to Squire's home for the night. Papa has seen two or 3 people whom you wouldn't remember, and met David Garnett[2] at lunch yesterday. We had a pleasant time in Gloucester. Robin is a very nice boy of 15 now. They have a good car and every afternoon we drove three or four hours over the Cotswold hills, and through the villages. All the houses are of grey stone and built in the 14th and 15th centuries, and have hardly been changed since. The houses are positively enchanting.

Marjorie writes [from Sèvres] that she is feeling surprisingly well, but that she has been through the most hellish part of hell, with everybody in the Fischbacher family talking French around her and to her. She feels that she is gaining a little knowledge, I think, and wants to stay until the middle of October, anyway. I shall be, of course, glad to stay until the *end* of October, if she wants me to, but I don't think any longer than that. I am really very homesick. Irma cabled that she expected John in 2 weeks. That would be a week from next Monday. I am so glad of that. I am waiting anxiously to hear from her the details of the Hosmers' getting out.[3]

You must be terribly busy, dear, with so much to do in the office, and so much responsibility of the shop & c.[4] It is lucky you can give up thinking about things, and go right to sleep when you go to bed. I wish I could do that. I am so glad you and Dwight are married. You will feel more pleasantly free, I think. You say you are going on just the same — but are you not going to have an apartment together? I want to give you some money for new furniture & c — but am afraid we cannot spare much until we get home. I can tell better when the bank statement comes. It's lucky I didn't address my letter to Mrs. Francis. I had a sort of instinct you wouldn't wish it for the present.

Papa and I went into the Coliseum for an hour or so one evening to see one of the Russian dances — a fantasy called the Nightingale and the Rose. It was very lovely. We haven't looked up plays yet to find out what are the most interesting things here.

I mustn't tire myself by writing too long a letter. I am not very well, but a little better than I was. Just before we left France I thought I was going to disgrace myself by having to go into a sanatorium. I think we shall probably go back to France, and sail from there.

Well, goodnight, dear, with lots of love from us both.

MAMA

P.S. Squire doesn't seem to advise the new book coming out here — but don't tell Davison that. Papa is going to write to Davison about it today or tomorrow.[5] A little plan has occurred to me, for Carol & Lillian & Prescott having a little fun before winter sets in. They might take the day boat from Albany to N.Y. and stay in your apartment 2 or 3 nights — & go to 2 theatres. Prescott would be enraptured at the trip on the water, and you could take care of him evenings while they are at the theatre. He would also love going to the Zoo. If you approve, and could stay with Lila[6] a couple of nights, you might write to them about it, and I would like to pay expenses for an anniversary present to them and birthday present to

Prescott this year.[7] It really wouldn't cost [a] great deal [.]
You could let me know how much the theatre tickets cost
and I could send them a little check for fare. But if it would
inconvenience you, don't do anything about it.

[1] The heavily scrolled letterhead features shaded lettering and four detailed
views of the hotel's accomodations.

[2] Novelist-bookseller David Garnett was the son of Edward Garnett,
prominent critic and essayist who had been an early and outspoken advocate
of RF's poetry.

[3] Irma married John Paine Cone in 1927, and they moved to Kansas.
Disenchanted with life on a wheat farm, she returned to South Shaftsbury in
the spring of 1928 with a baby son, John, Jr., or "Jacky." Irma's husband was
moving east to attempt a reconciliation.

[4] Lesley was working as an assistant editor, under John Farrar, in the newly
consolidated firm of Doubleday Doran. Although she had moved to New York,
she retained her business interests in the Pittsfield bookstore until 1935.

[5] Gorham Munson's *Robert Frost: A Study in Sensibility and Good Sense* —
for which contracts had been drawn-up by John Farrar — was published in the
U.S. in 1927. Edward Davison had been RF's first choice to write the biography,
but he later had a change of heart while Davison was busily working on his
materials.

[6] Lila Barth, a friend.

[7] Carol Frost and Lilian La Batt had married in 1923; William Prescott,
their only child, and RF and EF's first grandchild, was born a year later.

EF to Lesley Frost

DARLING LESLEY, —

[London] Sunday morning
[September 1928]

We certainly enjoyed your long letter yesterday. It was
simply great, getting it. Your busy life makes us gasp. To
think of your making up that catalogue practically alone.
Where do you get the courage?

I wonder whether you decided on a furnished or
unfurnished flat. I think that a furnished flat would be wiser
for a time. I know by my experience at 10 Dana St.[1] how
difficult and unsatisfactory it is to have to buy furniture all
at once for an unfurnished house. You remember how it was.
It is so much better to buy a piece now and then for a while,
as you see something attractive, or come across a bargain.

As soon as we return, we'll give you $500, so that you can have it ready to buy some things with.

I had a short letter from Irma the same day that yours came. [Irma's husband] John arrived some little time ago, thank goodness. He got a job at once at the Everett Orchards, picking apples, and likes it very much. I am so glad he likes his first job in the East. He is hoping they keep him on through the winter, pruning the trees, and then he can look around in the spring. I think he will eventually want to buy a small farm, which will leave him time in the winter to go on drawing cartoons & c. He has an unusual talent for the drawing of cartoons. His uncle invested $2000, on a 3 yr. mortgage at 7% which has given them $140 a year for clothes & c. The three years are up next fall, I believe, and I hope the money will be forthcoming to invest in something he wants to do in the east. Papa has had a very bad cold since Wednesday. It has interfered very much with our plans. I came down with one Friday. It isn't as bad as Papa's, but on the other hand I haven't as much strength to stand it.

We are going to tea this afternoon at the Mairs. Lucy is the only child at home. I'll tell you about the family in my next letter. We are going to Leeds to spend a day or two with the Abercrombies, and probably on further to Edinburgh to see the Smiths. We haven't communicated with the Gardiners yet, or heard anything about them.

It is almost time for me to change my dress.

Irma says you are going to have a baby. You have always loved children, and will be glad to have one of your own, I am sure, dear. Let me say just a word of caution about not keeping on with your work at Doubleday [Doran] too long. You wouldn't realize, perhaps, how soon you might show your condition, and some men are quick to observe it, and might resent your being there.

If what you surmised about Lillian is true, we shall have more grandchildren very soon. Let us hope there will be at least one girl. Their little clothes are so much more cunning.

We shall probably go over to Paris about the 25th of the month. If you write again, send to Gloucester address, as Haines will always know where we are. I can't tell how long we shall stay in Paris, or whether Marj. will come home with us or not.   Lots of love,   MAMA

The Imperial was a very nice hotel, and it was more lively but here we have large sitting room, with fireplace, and couch and two capacious armchairs and large bedroom & bath. There is no dining room here, but meals are served very nicely in your room if you wish it, more expensively also.

The Imperial forwards mail & cablegrams

As river-boat must now be taken off [,] don't arrange trip for C. & L.[2] this fall [.] The river trip is what I most had in mind.

[1] The Godwin house, the Frost's first residence in Amherst, in 1917.
[2] Carol and Lillian.

EF to Lesley Frost

Georgian House, 10 Bury St. S. W. 1,
DARLING LESLEY, —   London, 1 October [1928]

Papa went to Ireland on Saturday. I don't know just what day he will come back. I am supposed to be resting, but I have been writing letters pretty steadily. I do not, however, make much impression on the number that ought to be written. What a curse is the obligation to write letters! I was not made with the facility about it that some people have, and I often think that trying to write a lot of letters, in addition to my other tasks, is what has brought me down so the last four or five years. When I don't write them they are like a dead weight on my spirits, and that is just a[s] bad as writing them — or almost as bad. We are very comfortable here. The rooms are large, with couch and very comfortable arm chair. The weather is so cold now, we have to keep a coal fire in the grate all day. The smell of coal reminds me so much of the old days at Beaconsfield. It moves me more than the *sight* of the place did, somehow.

We have had pleasant visits at the de la Mares and at the Freemans, and papa has seen [a] number of the literary men at lunch at various times.

Well, this is only a word to say we miss you. A cablegram from Michigan about National English Teacher's Convention at Baltimore came all right yesterday. I dont know if you or Carol gave them the address.

Lots & lots of love   MAMA

I imagine John Farrar is on such bad terms with the Frost family that he will write, or inspire, an unfavorable review of Papa's book,[1] don't you? The thought of reviews close at hand gives me a cold shiver. I believe, really, that what is at the bottom of his unpleasantness to you is the prospect of the book, and then the withdrawal of it.

[1] RF's *West-running Brook* was to be published in November 1928.

EF to Lesley Frost

DARLING LESLEY,— [London] Monday evening [October 1928]

I think it is nearly three weeks since we had that long letter from you, and we are getting eager to hear from you again — just a few words occasionally, perhaps once in two weeks, is all we need, but we *do* want that, for we are sort of homesick for you all. Papa has taken a slight cold and is keeping very quiet for a few days. I hope he will get over it quickly, as there are a few more people we want to see and then we shall plan our departure, which will be around the 1st of Nov. We shall go over to France for a week or two before sailing. Marjorie seems quite contented now, and I think she is learning some French. I feel anxious about Irma. Her last two letters have sounded unhappy, I thought. I am afraid she had a dreadful time with that horrid Mrs. Hosmer. And she has been alone so much.

Papa returned from Ireland last Friday. He had a fine time with Padraic and A.E.[1] He saw a little something of [William Butler] Yeats, and several interesting people. It was too bad he didn't have time to travel inland and see the scenery too.

I hope you will take care not to get colds and grippe as the cold weather comes on.

Lots of love   MAMA

[1] Padraic Colum and the Irish poet-mystic George William Russell.

EF to Lesley Frost Francis

DARLING LESLEY, —   [London, November 1928]

Papa and I were happy to have the news of you and Dwight being married. I think you have so many things you both enjoy, and you know each other so well now, that you have every chance of being happy together.

We are coming home sooner than we expected on account of my not being well enough to see people and go about, and I'll send you our present as soon as we get back. I suppose you'll be furnishing a little flat for the winter. Don't get a too expensive one that will eat up all your income.

Papa and I are going into an inn in one of these Cotswold villages, where I can rest for a week or two until we sail, which will be the last week of the month.

We sent 3 cables today — one to you, one to Mr. Hosmer, and one to Irma, telling her to engage Luella indefinitely, if possible, as I shall want help in the house when we get home.

After this, I shall address you as Mrs. Dwight Francis.

Lots of love   MAMA

EF to Lesley Frost Francis

The Imperial Hotel, Russell Square,
DEAR LESLEY, —   London, 6 November [1928]

Marjorie and I came over to Eng. Saturday. The Channel was glorious — a sky with billowing black clouds, with patches & streaks of light near the horizon, and steely dark water. It wasn't rough, though, and Marjorie and I stood in the bow of the boat the whole hour of crossing without a single qualm of seasickness, and enjoyed it, immensely.

Marjorie and I bought French novels in the station at Paris, and as we traveled 1st class, and had compartments to ourselves, we had quite a nice time. Marjorie has made a big gain in French, but is far from being able to converse easily, of course. She really hasn't any ear for it, and she says it would take her 5 yrs to learn to talk and understand, and by that time she would have lost all her interest to 'go on' with it steadily, without losing any of her English, I think. She can go to the summer school at Middlebury next summer, where they speak nothing but French for six weeks.

If any letter comes to papa in your care, just keep it until we come.

Papa is in bed for two or three days. He did not rest long enough after his cold a month ago, and has been getting too tired. Now he has a bad pain in his temples, either neuralgia or sinus and a peculiar hoarseness. Fortunately he has no temperature. He should have a two weeks complete rest, at least, but we are badly situated for that — with many engagements he has made for this week. He cannot seem to stop and I don't know just what to do. We *may* sail on the Olympic, the 14th. I think I will cable you when we decide, & then will you write a word or two to Carol & Irma, so they will know.

We are back at the Imperial, because they have steam heat here.

I hope you are fine, and that all is going well with you. It will be a rather nervous period for you, I am afraid, with papa's book coming out, being right in the center of things.

Much love —   MAMA.

A Record Stride

1929-1937

For the Frost family, these were mixed years. There were marriages, grandchildren, continued illnesses, the shadow of death, and the first divorce. Robert and Elinor travelled about the country more than they had before, both to seek the sun and to be with their children at times of need. Robert's reputation as poet was established, and he enjoyed his first real financial security. It was a time of good friends and of rivalries real and imagined. He was surer of all he had thought was true, and this assurance met with a mixed reception. He guided and counselled his children, now grown up, without wishing to appear in constant charge of their lives. He husbanded his strength with an eye also to Elinor's always-fragile health. There was a disheartening pendulum-swing to these years; abundant honors alternated with occasions of suffering and loss. Frost's was therefore a double feat — the triumph of his art and the survival of the will.

Frost's 1930 letter to the John Bartletts[1] provides a capsule report on each member of the family at this juncture in the family letters: "[Elinor and I are] not the strength we were, you have to remember, and can't do all sorts of things the way we used to... Marj is in [the] hospital in Baltimore where she lay a hopeless invalid two years ago, now training to be a nurse. Lesley is in New York with her husband and her baby. Carol is farming at the stone house... Irma is going to college at Mass Agricultural College next year with her husband and her baby. Her husband has been farming near us but is turning to landscape architecture so-called. We have three grand children in three different families. One of the grand children starts school this year and so begins again the endless round."

[1] *Robert Frost and John Bartlett : The Record of a Friendship*, pp. 152-153.

RF to William Prescott Frost

[In large block print]

DEAR PRESCOTT   [Amherst, late winter 1931]

You have lots to do this spring, on your fathers farm.[1] But I hope you will find time to take care of my farm too. I dont mean for you to do all the work on both places yourself. Do as much as you can without hurting your appetite and hire a good man like Mr Olin to do the rest. I wish Jack[2] could help you. But I'm afraid he wont get big enough to be any good this year. We'll feed him up and try to bring him along faster. We want him to amount to something. He begins to be quite a talker. But a talker isn't always a worker. Perhaps if he didn't talk so much he would get more done. Some one must put a flea in his ear[.]

I begin to wish I was up there planting pines and clipping birches [.]

I saw a big Newfoundland dog. We must have one to take care of the sheep. Has that last lamb come yet?

Wont it be great when we get the Gully going![3]

Grandma sends a whole train load of love.

Theres a small town near here named Prescott. I want to visit it.   GRANDPA

[1] RF had given Carol and Lillian the deed to the stone house as their wedding gift — with the understanding that they would pay off the mortgage with farm earnings.

[2] Irma's son, 3 1/2. Prescott was 6.

[3] Having endured a series of makeshift arrangements and rentals since deeding the stone house to his son, RF finally purchased a farm about a mile from the stone house which had been protectively built in a gully between two parallel ridges. At this point, he was busily preparing the old house for occupancy.

RF to Carol Frost

DEAR CAROL: Boulder, Colorado, 21 August 1931

Glad you're there[1] all right. Have a look around at the various elevations, and climates. Tell Prescott he'd better be ready to tell me all the differences between New England

and California farming and scenery or I'll — well I'll tell him all the differences, if it takes me an eight hour day.

Affectionately   PAPA

¹ After his wife Lillian contracted tuberculosis, Carol moved his family to Monrovia, California. Marjorie Frost, also pronounced tubercular, entered Mesa Vista Sanitarium in Boulder. RF gave a series of August lectures at the University of Colorado's Writers' Conference which gave him and EF an opportunity to visit with Marjorie and their friends the Bartletts. Then they continued west to visit Carol, Lillian, and Prescott in California.

RF to Carol Frost

DEAR CAROL: [South Shaftsbury] 1 November [1931]

This is an annus mirabilis (wonder year) with us in New England. Here it is November 1st and though it cant be said that we have had no frosts we have had only one or two and those not very severe. We have had no freeze at all. I have had all the grapes I could eat right along since we came home from the West off the Ni[a]gara vine north of the house. Today (November 1st take notice and dont forget) I picked a quart of them for Lesley Mama and myself. They are my witnesses to good grapes on the vine in Vermont so late in the autumn. I may as well call those the last of them, though there are still a few broken bunches for tomorrow and maybe next day. Everything has hung on, the whole month of October has been so quiet. There are still some leaves on the trees.

But it has been rainy enough to make us think how sorry you would have been if you had been here. I havent measured the rainfall or heard the record. It must be bucketsful. Theres a thick mop of very green grass. It probably hasnt grown much but it has some and I never saw it greener at any time of year. Next year's hollihocks have made a rank fall growth. There are still marigolds petunias salvias calendulas and phloxes feebly blooming their last in the piazza garden. I suppose this mild fall is sent to ease us gradually from the heat of your western summer into the rigor of our eastern winter. We deserve some consideration from the elements we are such good parents (we claim, though we cant prove it.)

I can imagine it must be beginning to green up around you if the rains are on. I suppose the water may make some show behind the dam in the canyon (or cañon). What's the coldest you've had it yet? I mean to keep my promise about the weather records: but we havent been rich enough to buy a good thermometer. A lot of expenses have come on us at once this month.

We'll be freer to spend soon.

We are keeping warm on the big ash you felled and cut up and piled for us. I fetch it two pieces at a time one under each arm everytime I come up the hill on foot, though I prefer to do it in the dark so the Hawkinses wont catch me in my unfarmerlike ways and make talk the same as they do about Burdella Buck and the old Lyons man who lives with her. With acres of woods they could burn, they cut nothing except along the walls and drag that in a tree at a time as they absolutely need it to keep from starving and freezing. They say there's tons of manure around the barn and in the barn up there that anyone ought to be able to buy though Burdella might not be willing to sell it cheap. She has taken to drawing and painting lately and sits up till midnight at it — just like me at my books. We ought to have got acquainted with Burdella. Remember how she once wanted Lesley to drive a butchers cart round selling her beef for her?

Before I forget it: a nice thing you could do for the Shaws would be to write them out very carefully and clearly all you know and think they should know about raising cultivating handling and selling sweet peas. I can see they are inclined to go on with your business. Make it simple and easy to follow. Emphasize the important things. Tell them about the rotation you planned and about the brush string and wire supports. I tried to tell them a little but I didnt know enough. Introduce the subject by mentioning me and telling them I told you of their interest.

Mama has probably written you about Dwight and Lesleys new venture with a skiing school at Woodstock Vermont. They are bringing a teacher from Austria. Lesley has moved all her furniture up there and went by here today with her two babies to settle for the winter in a farm house. It sounds exciting and a big change for Dwight from Wall St. to that. May they prosper.

Tell us more about the classes in aeronautics and what all this is about your flying.

We miss your help. I'm having a furnace chimney built from the cellar up on the north side of the big chimney and leading into the big chimney between the first and second floors. If you were within reach I think I would try to save money on the furnace by having you help me put in one from the Montgomery Ward Catalogue. I shall probably fall back on Horton. I got cross with Robinson again on the plastering job in the attic and shall have Bentley on the chimney job. I'll forgive Robinson as I have forgiven him before but it will take time.

You spoke of climbing over into the Sierras. Tell us about that sort of thing.

You are right about Prescotts reading. He must break new ground. But the great thing is not to betray the least impatience with him and get his mind paralyzed with fear or dislike in some part. The way to do is to make the lessons short and lively. Say a few interesting things between his efforts. Let him get *some* satisfaction every lesson, so he will gain or keep confidence.   Affectionately   PAPA

RF to Carol Frost

DEAR CAROL: South Shaftsbury, 19 November 1931

You tell me your feats. I ought to tell you some of mine or my car's. The old thing did the hundred miles from our house in South Shaftsbury to Lesleys in Pomfret (just outside of Woodstock, this state) in less than three hours, and back the hundred miles in two hours and three quarters. We went into second only twice coming and not once going: The average was nearly thirty five miles an hour. I was surprised. I didnt know I was travelling so fast. I must have been creeping up in my speed. I'll have to bring myself down, or first thing I know I'll rival Dwight in his fifty mile average. Dwight had a serious collision with an old man near Manchester on his way up through here. Neither was hurt badly but both cars were pretty completely wrecked. The old man was coming over a rise on the wrong side of the road and I suppose Dwight was speeding. The Manchester police exhonorated Dwight. I'll never forget the speed we got up to in pursuit of the fellow that insulted us that day near Pomona.

The weather is going easy on us because we havent been able to make up our minds what kind of heating plant to put in. We are still depending on the kitchen stove and the big open fireplace. We have had only one killing frost to date (November 19th) though that lasted two days and nights and froze half an inch of ice on the pond. A skunk drowned itself in the pond — I think by running on to the ice when it was thawing too thin to hold it. Very likely Winnie was at its heels.

We changed from Robinson to Bentley for the piece of chimney I told you I was having built from the cellar bottom up to about the second floor against the main chimney and leading into it. Robinson was bad in one way.

There was never finish to anything he did. He was crude. Bentley does neat work but he has his defects. He takes my check in payment for his work and goes down to the dens on Pleasant St in Bennington gets drunk gets knocked on the head and robbed of every cent he has on him including my check for $60. The next day he let me know and I telephoned the bank in Amherst to have them stop payment on it. That saves me any loss. It would be the loss of any bank that was foolish enough to cash it. We have heard that it has been presented at a bank somewhere with a forged endorsement. This is the nearest I ever came to any trouble with a check. Bentley says he was attacked on the street. He may have been. But I think likely he was too drunk to know where he was attacked. The police are trying to make it out it was in a house, a speak-easy. Bentley says he knows or can describe the men — there were two of them — who robbed him. They have one he says was in it. I'd better have stuck to Robinson.

That was a fine letter about the climb into the mountains. I'm reminded of your mountains almost every day by something in the New York Times about the doings in astronomy at Mount Wilson. That is one of the most exciting places in the world just now. Einstein is going back there to work on his theories of the universe. He says gravitation and acceleration (speeding up) are the same thing and gravitation and curvature are the same thing. You can see how gravitation and acceleration may be closely connected by the way you feel heavier when an elevator speeds up with you. I like to think of all this going on over you. I[t] takes the curse off having Hollywood so near.

We are terribly sorry about Lillian's mother being so sick. Elinor saw her and talked with her the day we went to Woodstock. It is the kind of attack that she may slowly recover from. But of course it is serious. She has had a good deal to trouble her I'm afraid.

Did Prescott get my long printed letter?[1] I got a cramp doing all those stiff lines. I'll do it easier next time.

The house looked fine in the picture and almost like home. We lived in it so long ourselves. You got it wreathed just right in the pepper tree and the live oak. We were sure the fresh paint showed. It's a lovely place and a great piece of luck.

We're all glad from here to Colorado that Lillian has decided to go to bed for the cure.

Affectionately   PAPA

We mailed three autographed books from Dorothy to Lillian today.

[1] See RF to William Prescott Frost, [late winter 1931].

RF to Lesley Frost Francis

DEAR LESLEY: [n.p., ca. 1931]

I should be able to say from the sidelines what you ought to do next. I suppose you do and you don't want me to. Your question to decide is whether Dwight's not being right in the mind and his having wronged you come to the same thing for practical purposes.[1] If he has only wronged you because he is not right in the mind it makes it harder to be hard on him. I can see how you must feel. But you must have been all over this ground several times before. And the conclusion you reached was whether he was psychopathic or merely spoiled and misbehaved, you couldnt imagine him becoming possible to live with. I remember the hope there seemed in a country life in Woodstock on some such farm as the next one beyond the one you rented. That was as good a prospect as any you have had. But it dissolved in the complications of daily relations. Only if you can contemplate a life of self-sacrificing and child-sacrificing tragedy could you begin over with him. Some people cant resist tragedy. My mother couldnt. Nothing could have saved her but my father's death. It was wretched, pitiful, wicked, but she was hopelessly committed to it. I from my point of view see you as different and differently situated. You can get out. I should say you were out already. You can tell about that from the inside better than I can from the outside. Without any prejudice either way for or against him you appear to have lost all warmth of feeling for him. But as I say you know that better than anyone else. He's a poor sinner, but theres something disillusioning and chilling in the way he goes on with his talk and his attitudinizing. He leaves your sympathys all used up and turned to resentment.

[Portion of letter missing.]

[1] Lesley and Dwight's marriage was foundering and, somewhat later, they were divorced.

EF to Lesley Frost Francis

[South Shaftsbury] Thursday morning
[Portion of letter missing.]   [January 1932]

[...] I have changed my mind over night[.] Don't write to Carroll[1] until I say the word. It isn't that papa doesn't think there is some good in what Carroll has done. I guess it's more that Carroll isn't willing to be told things, & also that he fears Carroll's ambition will get away with him — precluding patience in collecting enough for a possible book.

The temp. went down to zero last night. We didn't sleep very comfortably. We may order some coal today, and dig in for another week or so. Papa sort of wants to take the car down, and we neither of us want to risk bad roads.

I have been thinking that as we two drive around together, and as there's always a chance something might happen to us, you ought to know about our affairs. Our bank books are in safety deposit box in First National at

Bennington — also deeds to this house and Amherst house. I guess there is now about 13000 in banks. The key to the box is in papa's bill fold which he always keeps in his inside coat pocket. It is in the *long* compartment. The Amherst house ought to sell for $10000 now and there is a mortgage (held by college) of $3000. That would leave $7000 there, and this place ought to sell for $8000 — which would make altogether about $28000 — to be divided between the four of you. Not much, but a little something to turn around on. Don't speak to papa of my telling you about this. It would make him nervous, but I think it's best to be prepared for what *might* happen. Of course if the furniture was sold at auction, and the books at a private sale, there would be more cash to be divided.   Lovingly   MAMA

[1] Carol had come to prefer this spelling of his name, although RF seldom honored the preference. EF refers to Carol's efforts as poet.

RF to Lesley Frost Francis[1]

[n.p., 1932]

Capital in parenthesis.
took up an interest
machinery-worm at its core
to rather relish
birds of a feather-work in the same chanels
Time is one of those things you save
to cruelly pay
mutual agreement 112
Alright Chap 7
147 there was little sign of struggle in parenthesis
118 waste of motives bull by horns? Not sure
122 shudders body — shudders *at* rain?
123 Son on go on

132 Who had killed whom
Who had chased whom

133 the *events* had *synchronized* or the times had coincided.

135 (she had fallen into a restless sleep) parenthesis

138 religious instead of Catholic or else call it strange instead of preposterous.
emerged *in* a new world

147 *sinfully* cruel. I'm surprised shes etc

148 I wondered *when?*

152 flare *in* this business?

171 Doubt if I'd mention that horrid Strange Death of Pres Harding.

174 follow her lead? not leader

18[?] rather to balance

210 recourse

Such grand writing in the three or four kinds needed to build a novel[.] Intensities of imagined scene (you grew up on this)[.] Intensities of imagined dialogue intensities of insight into character and situation. Too good to be a detective story.

[1] Lesley's mystery novel, *Murder at Large*, was prepared for publication by Coward-McCann in 1932. RF agreed to read proof, and these are his notations. The *New York Times* reviewed it as a "... story... recommended to those who like murder in wholesale quantities and who do not mind mingling vicariously with some extremely unpleasant people."

RF to Carol Frost

DEAR CAROL: Amherst, 30 October 1932

One thing in favor of all this travelling back and forth:[1] it has got the country pretty well shrunk, so that we neednt feel very far away from each other. Boston, New York Los Angeles, San Francisco, Omaha, Chicago, Denver, Baltimore and Philadelphia are down to the size of villages in a state of about the size of Vermont. If it werent for the coal dust in trains which catches me colds, I shouldn't mind being on the go between places half the time. I wish the locomotives would use oil or electricity.

In Ann Arbor the foliage was at the height of fall color; here in Amherst it is a little past. The market is flowing with two kinds of sweet cider, one the regular doctored kind that cant ferment and the other the old fashioned natural but, I suppose, illegal kind that can ferment and does almost as soon as you get it home. There was none of the second last year and its appearance shows how we are letting down gradually on enforcing the law.

Kent the Dorset real estate agent is after us for someone in Bennington. He drove clear down here yesterday to see what Elinor and I would say to taking two thousand down and a mortgage for six thousand.[2] The customer who doesn't want his name known till things go further is described as having had the money to pay the whole price last year when Shaw got in ahead of him. He is described as a business man who should be able to raise the mortgage when and if times improve. We didnt seem to think you ought to have so much as six thousand tied up. I told Kent to see if he couldn't get more than two thousand down. I don't suppose anything will come of it. It is nothing to get our hopes up on. It merely gives us something to think over.

As a match for your seeing the theatre once a week I set out in Ann Arbor to see foot ball once a week. The Michigan-Illinois game was my first and it ended satisfactorily enough in a victory for our side 32 to 0. My second was to have been the Aggie-Amherst game yesterday afternoon but my cold and the cold of the weather kept me at home. You'll have noticed the score; Amherst took a bad licking. I dont mind as much as I should if we weren't connected in a way with the [Massachusetts] State College through John and if I werent in a way a farmer myself and always on the side of farmers. The State College has a star half-back, Louis Bush, from Turner's Falls that our boys couldn't lay out or stop. I suppose you are seeing baseball Sundays. Be sure to bring Prescott on in playing and understanding the game all his enjoyment of it permits. I'm glad he liked the play at the theatre. He ought to go whenever there is anything not too much beyond him.

You remember Toggles Thompson the chemistry professor people used to make fun of gently? He's just been in to interrupt me with an interesting story of the depression. He has a Polish tenant of a small place he owns down at Hockanum by the Connecticut River. The man is twenty eight and has a wife and two children. He hasnt had work for more than a year and is more than a year behind on his rent. Something put it into Thompsons head to propose going into the wood business with him. Thompson got him an old truck and bought a wood lot on the side of the Holyoke range — twelve acres. Then Thompson did the soliciting. The pole is not only out of trouble, but making money and so is Toggles Thompson. The idea is to sell good dry wood exactly as ordered in size and kind. The partnership between the retired professor and the down-and-out Pole is being preached about in church. Toggles is a funny sentimental fellow and the whole thing makes him talkatively happy. He came to try to take me over onto the wood lot. It *is* of course a good story. The Pole was desperate and had no good out of this country since he came to it seven or eight years ago. He was unjustly detained in jail a week once on suspicion of having set a fire and when released with apologies found that he had lost his job. Nice to give a hard-luck person something pleasant to think of.

We hear all sorts of amusing things about the new President.[3] He has told the old guard to shut up talking about Meiklejohn as fresh as if the row was still on. He is going to have Meiklejohn here visiting and have his picture hung with the portraits of all the other Presidents of the college. Great stuff!

Keep as active as you can for Lillian and Prescott's sake as well as your own. Go to the theatre and games so you'll have plenty to tell Lillian about.

Affectionately   PAPA.

¹ RF and EF had again travelled across the country to visit Marjorie and the Carol Frosts.

² Carol had decided to sell the stone house.

³ Stanley King, Olds's successor as Amherst's president.

RF to Carol Frost

DEAR CAROL   [Amherst, November 1932]

I forgot almost the chief thing in my last letter. I should hope you would do the Long Trail in prose rather than in verse. It would bring you out right now I think to undertake a considerable thing in prose. It would develope your expression in general and so help you in your verse when you went back to it. You'll find you can load the material more freely into prose. You can say a lot in prose that verse won't let you say, especially rhymed verse. You'll set yourself an example in prose of fullness and straightforwardness that your verse will be the better for having to follow. I haven't published any prose, but I know the prose I have written has made good competition for my verse. You know the weakness of verse: one line of it will be strong and good and the next will be almost anything for the sake of the rhyme. That's why some people cant stand the stuff. The ideal we are always striving for is an even goodness, so that neither line can be suspected of having been deflected twisted or trumpted up to rhyme with the other. That will make the verse as honest as the equivalent in prose. Sometimes I don't think there is any other test of a good poem than to see that not a single rhyme in it has hurt it. Lets see some of the prose when you get it started.

The poem about the tools was one of the richest yet.[1]

Mertins[2] writes that he saw you. Be kind to him for his sake as well as mine. You should see how overcome he was in his letter at a word or two of praise I had given him for some of his poetry. He is a poet who has given up pretty much everything, a considerable position in the pulpit even, to live for poetry.

Where we roasted and passed the summer night without sleep awhile back now all is pleasant furnace warmth and comfort. We got pretty well frozen out up at the farm. It dropped to two below zero the night before we left. Sometimes we wonder seriously if it wouldnt be possible to find farming you would like in a softer climate than this.

I have had not a word out of Kent or Mrs Nevils since I told Kent to advise her to buy the farm outright for the $8000 agreed upon if she wanted to speculate with it: she might get herself into trouble with the law trying to get what amounts to an eleven percent commission on the sale. We hear she rented it to some New Yorkers for the deer hunting season.

Leland Stanford comes out on top on the Coast but I suspect Southern California is the best team in the country. Tell me more about how it goes with the Monrovia baseball team. I had very little satisfaction in thinking of Amherst this year. It lost every important game except the one with Mass State College. The game at Williams was a great disappointment. I'm glad I wasnt there in the cold to watch it. Our team started out with the highest expectations.

Tell Prescott to write me a small letter! Tell him if he'll write a reasonable letter to Santa Claus about what he

wants for Christmas, I'll see that Santa Claus gets it. I'm
so much nearer where he lives in Iceland.

Affectionately   PAPA

[1] In this and succeeding letters, RF offers Carol considerable coaching
in poetry and other modes of fatherly support. The following is a surviving
example of Carol's poetry, complete with Frostian touches:

THE GOPHER, MAN AND MAKER

Yes, this gopher of the west is very apt
To make himself at home without a permit
Being given him to. He's so often rapt
In making them he mustn't be a hermit.
In a lawn I modeled over once he drilled,
Till I had wicked wishes for that gopher.
Just as fast as I could get the holes refilled
He cleaned them out to prove he was no loafer.
Mystified I paused to think if there could be
Some way to please the gopher, man, and Maker,
Till I thought of one that might be well for three
And I not be a ruthless dwelling breaker.
Let him have his home, I said, and I will spread
The dirt the little cuss persists in mounding
Up before his hole, out o'er the ground instead,
Between the blades of grass. The pain of hounding
Him to death was chased before the plan's success;
Replaced by a somewhat more than common pleasure,
With the gopher's, man, and God's content. I guess
He's glad I hit upon a better measure.

[2] Louis Mertins, poet and teacher, had hosted the Frosts at his Redlands,
California home. He and his wife Esther prepared *The Intervals of Robert Frost:
A Critical Bibliography* (1947). His *Robert Frost: Life and Talks-Walking* was
published in 1965.

RF to Carol Frost

DEAR CAROL: [Amherst, December 1932]

I feel more and more the power behind your poems.
It still fails to come through sometimes into ideas altogether
clear to me. "Their Rings Are Cones," for instance, almost
says something I get, but just misses my head at the end.
"Songs" is fine deep and effective. Not a line of that one
eludes me. I should think it was about the best you had done.
The last stanza is really splendid.

The philosophic tone of your letters lately has given us satisfaction. Things cant always move along the single rail serenely balanced for anybody. They get to tipping this way and that very hard for spells, till it looks as if their poise couldnt be recovered and they would have to fall off on to the ground and start over. But some how they stay on and presently are stepping off again even and assured. Your affairs would appear to be walking smooth right now. As you say one of the best prescriptions for mental and bodily health is a regular day of well-arranged variety.

Except for one snap below zero a month ago we've had a gentle winter so far almost a match for Miami El Paso and Los Angeles. The ground has been bare and dry for walking much of the time. Yesterday it snowed and today is sunny and dripping and avalanching off the roof. I tell you this to give you an attack of home-sickness.

Winnie's pup her only child has gone to Michigan University. We never saw it, but it is said to be all black and handsomer than Winnie. Winnie ran wild again for all our efforts to keep her shut in and the Lord knows how many denominations and colors of pup she will have this time. On the whole I liked California its groves its shores its mountains, its Olympics, its Sunday ball games, its tennis and its Pomona Fair. Even Marj's Coloradan talk can't get me down on the other parts of my country. Colorado is a good state. So is Michigan. So is California. And so is Massachusetts. The thing I'm down on right now is the flu. We've had a dose of it. I am prepared to say the worst part of the United States is the part where they have the flu worst. I'd like never to have the damn thing again.

The college wags on under the new President much as ever only somewhat livelier. It cant make much difference to me in my detached position, but still it makes some to have a stirring man over us. I havent been to a class or

Chapel yet and I havent seen a game. A few people drop in, Otto [Manthey Zorn] Roy [Elliott] and George [Whicher] chiefly. I have seen more of this President in three months than I did of the last one his whole administration.

I was sorry you didnt see the Trojans play the Irish. I didnt get the ticket because I was more or less afraid it would involve you with Greever or someone else you didnt want the society of.

Turkey thirteen cents a pound! That alone is enough to make California attractive. It must be the cheapest state in the Union. Speaking of states again I read another British book which took the view that our states were as separate as nations. I guess they'll find out whether we're separate or not. What a complete misunderstanding the war was on our part. We thought the Europeans wanted us to help in it by lending them money keeping them in supplies and finally by sending soldiers. All our mistake. They didnt want us at all. They wanted to win the war by themselves.   Affectionately   PAPA

RF to Carol Frost

DEAR CAROL: Amherst, 11 May 1933

That was another good poem. The difficulties in it dont do it too much harm and even do it some good perhaps in keeping it from flatness and commoness. Your way is certainly your own. And it is not just an artificial originality but comes from the thoughts and ideas you have.

It's getting nearer the time for your journey east.[1] Elinor and I both think the low fare and tourist Pullman rates might make it better for you to come by train. I suppose Prescott would be cheaper than you but I don't know. You realize you can get off the train for stops on any length on the way. You ought to plan to stay a few days somewhere in the west for the cliff dwellings and in Ohio for the mound buildings. Of course Prescott mustn't miss the chance to look at the World's Fair at Chicago. It is to be a sight to judge by the architecture already up when I was there a month ago. He must be made to understand that such architecture is supposed to be what he will see everywhere in the world by the time he grows up. We shall see whether the prophecy come true. Then he must see Niagara Falls.

Theres quite a possibility of our being in California with you late next winter. Perhaps if all goes well and Lillian is fine we can all come east together in May. President [Remsen du Bois] Bird [of Occidental College] said something about my lecturing round among the colleges sometime and he has been following the matter up in letters lately. The only doubt is whether I have the strength for all the sociability it would involve. Its the hospitality that lays me out. The Texas trip has resulted in a week's cold in bed.[2] But I want to see California again. I took a great liking to it for those days at the Olympics and the Sunday ball games. Hamlin Garland[3] tried to talk me out there when I saw him in New York the other day. He asked about you and Lillian with real friendliness and concern.

We dont seem to get to the farm very fast for one reason or another. Wade's[4] still up there keeping dog. I must release him pretty soon or he will come back on me in the summer for not having let him start his spring planting in time. The school year hangs on. I have still a reading or two I ought to do and I have an honorary degree to take at the Dartmouth College I ran away from so impolitely in 1892. At least my manners are better than when I was young and surly.

Have plenty of good maps — you'd better bring your Atlas on the train with you for Prescott.

Affectionately   PAPA

[1] Carol planned to drive to New England, with Prescott, for a summer visit.

[2] RF and EF made a brief trip to Texas in April which included a lecture date practically every day they were there.

[3] Author-interpreter of farm life in the Midwest.

[4] Wade Van Dore, poet acquaintance of RF's since 1922, self-styled hired man, author of *Far Lake* (1930). For a partial account of Van Dore's work at "the gulley" and an insight to RF's character, see his "Native to the Grain" in *Yankee* (August 1970), pp. 172-175.

RF to William Prescott Frost

DEAR PRESCOTT: Amherst, 11 May 1933

You can see from the enclosed material what my travels have been in the last month. When we were in Texas I figure we were more than half way to Monrovia. We were the whole way south and about half way west. April there was exactly like the middle of summer here. The trees were in full leaf and the temperature was 85 night and day.

Grandma has told your father about the round trip tickets that are extra cheap this year on account of the world's fair at Chicago. We think the train is your best way to come. The tickets give you the privilege of stopping off anywhere you please for sight-seeing as many days as you please.

All of us including Winnie will be glad to see you on your native soil again and you will be glad to see all of us including Winnie. Take a good look at the United States of America as you come. There may be some questions I want to ask you about the country. Notice particularly if it looks to you as if it were falling to pieces, opening up cracks between the states.

Too bad Lillian can't come with you. But she wont have long to wait till she can come safely.

Affectionately   GRANDPA

We aren't at the Gully yet.

RF to Marjorie Frost and Willard Fraser[1]

DEAR MARJ AND WILLARD   [Amherst, May 1933]

You children can't be too happy to please us and you
mustn't let your happiness be the least diminished by our
absence from your wedding. We'll come to Montana and
spend some time with you soon. You can make Montanans
of us: we'll stay long enough to give you the chance to
anyway. But you catch us right now, both of us, in no
condition for either travel or festivities. I'm counted out by
the doctor and Elinor is counted out by me. Really she is
worse off than I am. There's no use talking too much about
it and there's no use in your worrying. Plunge ahead into
marriage and progressive politics. We'll be all right with
a little rest. Contemplating you will do us good too. The day
of the wedding we'll do nothing but think of you and read
the grand picture book about Montana. Montana has
always been one of my favorite states and I shall enjoy being
connected with it by marriage. We had a horse in the
mountains once that when we bought it was named Beauty
or Beaute. But I changed its name to Butte Montana. So
you see my inclinations.

Our love to you both

Affectionately   FATHER.

Little check enclosed.

[1] Marjorie and Willard, then a senior at the University of Colorado, were
engaged in March 1932. They planned a June 1933 wedding.

RF to Carol Frost

DEAR CARROLL,   Franconia,[1] 18 September [1933]

Elinor has made a good start which I may as well
finish.[2] The check came from Mrs Nevils today. I enclose
it made over to you. So far so good. I told you in my last

letter she had been talking to Kent as if she were almost ready to buy. Apparently she hasn't found the money yet.

You manage to cross the whole continent without making any mistake. And I cant stay in one place three weeks without making one of the worst mistakes I ever made. I let Winnie out when I shouldnt have in the late evening when the porcupines are all round the house. She went for one and got her face so full of quills there seemed nothing for it but to cloroform her to get them out. She bit so and suffered when we tried it at first without the cloroform. But I overdid the dose and killed her. That spoils this place forever. I shall never come here again. I shall miss her too much at the Gulley to want to linger there very long this fall. Another year I shall have forgotten the bloody and fatal night I had over her. It was a lot my fault. I lost my head seeing her suffer and everybody suffer on her account. We did our best to try to get veterinaries. They wouldnt come in the night — not for people they didnt know. I can see now that I should have roped her whole body to a board and put her through without the cloroform. I wish you had been here to help me judge. It was a bad thing.

We leave Franconia tomorrow. The last few days I have found distraction in exploring some of the roads and side roads in the townships of Stark, Stratford and Columbia above here in Coos county. What took us up there partly was my having noticed on the map a little place up there on the Connecticut River called Cones where I figured Johns ancestors must have come from. We found a brook there and also a district school called Cones. The last of the family had just gone to live in Colebrook after having been ruined in his lumber mill business by his wife's interference. On our way back we turned in for luck at a side road that climbed to a shelf of farm land where once had lived twenty six families filling two district schools with their children, but now live only six families with almost no children. We were a good deal attracted by the place. Potatoes were still green and growing. Untouched by blight (Sept 17) and by the recent frost that swept New England. There were all sorts of brooks and streams running away.[3] It occurred to me we might have a certified seed potato farm up there that would leave you free to go south to camp winters.   Affectionately   PAPA

[1] Although the Frosts had moved from Franconia in 1920, their friend and former summer neighbor Mrs. J. Warner Fobes had regularly offered them the use of a guest house adjacent to her home.

[2] EF had written the salutation when RF took over.

[3] For an interesting parallel, see RF's poem "Directive," first published in 1947. *PRF*, pp. 377-379.

RF to William Prescott Frost

DEAR PRESCOTT: Amherst, 21 December 1933

How you have come on! I guess I don't have to print you any more letters to read if you can write a letter like that. Let's have another when you aren't too busy. Great luck to win prizes at ball games in which your side wins too. I wish we could sit out doors and watch things. We are behind closed windows for good. What we see through the window today is every single branch of every tree with a thread or ridge of snow along it. Snow can only stick and pile up that way when it starts as rain. I always think of you as three thousand miles from snow. You are not really more than ten or fifteen I suppose. Very likely you can see snow on Mt Wilson right now. Heres more stamps.

                    Affectionately   GRANDPA

RF to William Prescott Frost

DEAR PRESCOTT: Amherst, Washington's Birthday 1934

Out in Kansas they have cyclone cellars they go down

into when there is a tornado. (They ought to call them tornado cellars.) I hear you have been going to school in an earthquake cellar in California.[1] I dont see what good a cellar would do in an earthquake. The children are better off who have been going to school in tents, I should say. If I were you I should work hard and get promoted from the cellar. I dont take much stock in an earthquake cellar, to tell the truth.

Tell me when you get so you can read my writing so I wont have to print any more.

Heres a mess of stamps to examine for good ones.

We have snow piled higher than your head all along the pavements where it has been pushed in both directions by the snowplows. You've missed the deepest and coldest winter in forty years. But all you have to do is go up Mt. Wilson to see more snow than we ever thought of seeing.

Affectionately   GRANDPA

[1] The Long Beach, California, earthquake of 10 March 1933 killed 115 and did $ 40,000,000 damage. Schools in Monrovia suffered structural damage, and therefore Prescott's classes were, for many months, transferred to temporary quarters in a church basement.

RF to William Prescott Frost

DEAR PRESCOTT: [Amherst, 23 February 1934]

Just a word to tell you I have been within a third of the way to where you are this last week. Two thousand miles more and I should have been in California where the earth quakes like jelly. I enclose this Pullman ticket for proof. I ought to have started sooner sending you my Pullman tickets for you to make a collection of. My wandering days may be about over and then again they may not be over. You never can tell about a restless fellow like me. Anyway you may as well keep this ticket in a safe box or book a while till we see whether I have any more to add to it. The time may come before you grow up when there will be no more Pullman cars and no more railroads; in which case any mementoes of them will be a curiosity worth showing.

One way or another we are going to see you soon. It is still undecided whether you are coming east[1] in a Ford or we are coming west in a Pullman.

Affectionately   GRANDPA

[1] In a few months, Carol and his family — grateful that the sale of the stone house had never been consumated — were to move back to South Shaftsbury.

RF to Lesley Frost Francis

DEAR LESLEY: [n.p., 1934]

The difficulty of a job like that is to keep it from getting out of your mind for a single instant that you are speaking for Us the Frost Family and not just for yourself.[1] In the last year or two owing to a nasty slap I got from an American follower of Eliots, I confess I have several times forgotten my dignity in speaking in public of Eliot. I mean I have shown a hostility I should like to think in my pride unworthy of my position. I could wish you would do better for us. For the most part describe rather than judge, or seem to judge only in a occasional ironical shading or lightly and unvenomously toward the end. Present them nearly as they would present themselves. Remember you are my daughter you are speaking in Cambridge and Eliots sister Mrs Sheffield the wife of my instructor in English at Harvard[2] may very well be in your audience. Show no animus. Be judicial. Don't take anybody *alive* too seriously.

Let me tell you a few things about the new Movement you may or may not have taken in amid all the talk you have had to listen to.

Ezra Pound was the Prime Mover in the Movement and must always have the credit for whats in it. He was just

branching off from the regular poets when we arrived in
England. His Διόpia (Doria) had won second prize in a
contest where Rupert Brooke's Dust had won first. Διόpia
was a more or less conscious departure. The coming in
second made it very conscious.

One of the first things Pound thought of was that rhyme
and meter made you use too many words and even subsidiary
ideas for the sake of coming out even. He and his friends
Flint H.D. and Aldington[3] used to play a game of rewriting
each others poems to see if they couldnt reduce the number
of words. Pound once wrote to me that John Gould Fletcher
failed as a free verse writer because he failed to understand
the purpose of free verse, which was, namely, to be less free
not more free, with the verbiage.

Pound began to talk very early about rhythm alone
without meter.

I assume you'll find in Reed[4] his latest descendant
a full statement of the doctrine of Inner Form, that is to say
the form the subject itself takes if left to itself without any
considerations of outer form. Everything else is to have
two compulsions, an inner and an outer, a spiritual and a
social, an individual and a racial. I want to be good, but
that is not enough the state says I have got to be good.
Every thing has not only formity but conformity. Everything
but poetry according to the Pound-Eliot-Richards-Reed
school of art. For my part I should be as satisfied to play
tennis with the net down as to write verse with no verse form
set to stay me. I suppose I could display my energy agility
and intense nature as well in either case. That's me. Remember you are speaking for them and do them justice.
But whatever you do, do Pound justice as the great original.

He was the first Imagist too — although I believe our
friend T.E. Hulme coined the name. An Imagist is simply
one who insists on clearer sharper less muddled half realized

images (chiefly eye images) than the common run of small poets. Thats certainly good as far as it goes. Strange with all their modernity and psychology they didnt have more to say about ear images and other images — even kinesthetic.

Pounds tightness naturally tended to stripping poetry of connective tissue. Never mind connections — they'll take care of themselves — if only you make your poetic points. The method gives a very ancient Old-Testament flavor to expression.

The same aspiration toward brevity and undersaying rather than oversaying has led to the poetry of intimation implication insinuation and innuendo as an object in itself. All poetry has always said something and implied the rest. Well then why have it say anything? Why not have it imply everything? Harte Crane has gone to great lengths here. There's some excuse for their extravagances. It is true much poetry is simply flat from being said too fully outright. I suppose Gertrude Stein has come in confluently to encourage the intimators or innuendots. A little of her is fun, but goes a long way. I read that negroes were chosen to sing her opera because they have less need than white men to know what they are talking about. That is a thing that can be reported without malice. "The bailey beareth away the bell" poem is taken by as justification of poetry by elipsis hiatus and hint. It's a fine poem beyond cavil. I wish somebody could write more like it. Gerard Manley Hopkins' obscurities and awkwardnesses are some more of their Bible. Hopkins is well enough. His friend Robert Bridges judged his limitations very fairly. His poem about All Pied Things[5] good as it is disappoints me by not keeping, short as it is, wholly to pied things. I'm sending you this long poem by Perse as a further instance.[6] I read the Proem in Chapel one morning with success. I had to practice up a way to perform it. Most of the boys laughed but some there were who pretended to be subconscious of what it was about. On the same principle a child of two three and four gets legitimate pleasure out of hearing Miltons Paradise Lost read aloud. If the child's legitimate he does. We've got to keep control of our mysteries. Above all things no vindictiveness.

From Pound down to Eliot they have striven for distinction by a show of learning, Pound in old French Eliot in forty languages. They quote and you try to see if you can place the quotation. Pound really has great though inaccurate learning. Eliot has even greater. Maurice Hewlett leaned on Pound for medieval facts. Yates[7] has leaned on him for facts and more than facts. Pound has taught Yates his later style of expression. Not many realize this. There's a significant reference to Pound in the preface to Yeates last book.

Last we come to who means the most, Pound or Eliot. Eliot has written in the throes of getting religion and foreswearing a world gone bad with war. That seems deep. But I dont know. Waste Lands — your great grand mother on the grand mother on your mothers side! I doubt if anything was laid waste by war that was not laid waste by peace before.

Claim everything for America. Pound Eliot and Stein are all American though expatriate.

Affectionately   PAPA

You'll notice Eliot translates this

    This Song is what I read the boys

    Auden is their latest recruit

Notice in Eliots Ash Wednesday how he misquotes Shakespeare's

"Desiring this mans art and that man's scope"[8]

Why does he do it if on purpose? Is he improving on Shakespeare or merely giving him an interesting twist up

to date? Ash Wednesday is supposed to be deeply religious
— last phase before going to Rome.

    Send it back[9]

   [1] At this point, Lesley and her two daughters were "just living" on Brown Street, in Cambridge, Massachusetts. She was invited to give a talk on poetry, and RF went to considerable lengths to prepare her for the occasion. This "essay" on the Imagists is a unique example of RF's prose criticism.

   [2] See RF to Lesley Frost, 4 November 1919, n. 2.

   [3] Richard Aldington, his wife Hilda Doolittle, and F. S. Flint.

   [4] The literary critic Herbert Read, author — among other books — of *Form in Modern Poetry* (1932).

   [5] "Pied Beauty."

   [6] RF undoubtedly refers to St.-John Perse's *Anabase*, translated into English by T. S. Eliot (1930).

   [7] That is, William Butler Yeats.

   [8] RF correctly quotes line 7 of Sonnet 29. In "Ash-Wednesday," I, l. 4, Eliot substitutes *gift* for *art*.

   [9] This 10-line postscript, fragmentary as it now stands and written on a separate sheet, apparently relates to other enclosures not found with the letter.

RF to Carol Frost

DEAR CAROL: Billings, Montana, 18 April 1934

    You realize by this time that Marjorie's sickness is that worst disease of all, child-bed fever, and her chances of recovery are small. Our best hope is her having lasted as long as she has. The doctors and various people tell us that patients who stand the fever a month very often get the better of it. Marjorie has stood it a month and three days now.[1] Several times she has been at the point of death. Nothing has kept her alive so far but blood transfusions. Willard's friends have come forward in a host to give their blood for her. I never imagined anything like it for kindness and friendship. But I try not to give way to either hope or fear. I am simply determined in my soul my bones or somewhere that our side shall win. Reason is no help. She is a terribly sick girl. She has been out of her mind most of the time for a week and never completely in her mind, though she seems to recognize us and says some things more or less intelligible. Yesterday was one of her most desperate days. She sank into a stupor that I could see scared the doctors. Today she has rallied again after another blood-transfusion. All her three doctors are with her several times a day and she has three splendid nurses. It's a fight. She's keeping it up for her part with a noble courage that breaks our hearts. We all admire her. Elinor can hardly bear the sadness of it. There is no way of telling how long it may have to go on. The disease has no term. It has been know[n] to last for three months and yet not kill the victim. That however is unusual.

I tell you all this so you will know what threatens. We have veiled the worst of it from Irma and John. Irma is in no condition to face the terribleness of it.

You are beginning to have spring by now. The frost must let go of the water pipes pretty soon I should think. You say nothing about Prescotts game leg; so we assume he is all right.

What ever the outcome there's no prospect of our being back in New England for some time. The thing to keep saying is the longer Marj holds on the likelier she is to pull through.   Affectionately   PAPA.

Will you tell Anson Hawkins to forward mail not to Amherst any more, but to 244 Burlington Ave Billings Montana till further notice. You had better write this out for him.

R.

[1] Marjorie's daughter Marjorie Robin was born 16 March 1934.

RF to Lesley Frost Francis

DEAR LESLEY: Billings, 20 April 1934
This is Friday April 20. So you are getting no later news than my telegrams or not much later. Marj is having

her ninth blood-transfusion now. The donors have been Willard's friends and students at the Polytechnic School — boys altogether and of around twenty. Boys are preferred to girls. No one is being used who hasnt had scarlet fever, which develops resistance to the same streptococci as occur in child-bed fever. It's a bitter fight. Marj has been delirious for more than a week now but even in her delirium she is the same old Marj in her talk, grim ironical and noble. He[r] courage is the hardest part of it for us to bear. I dont know what will become of Elinor if we lose. Or of Willard — I mustnt forget him poor boy. We don't mean to lose, though the score is against us at this point.

I'm going to send you a few letters for answer for us while our hearts are so out of all affairs. Just tell people where I am or we are and why and how sorry. Make them realize it is no light matter without going into details too painfully. Tell them engagements to read will have to wait a while. If all goes well, we shant want to see anyone but Marj this summer. We'll probably stay out here.

Write us about yourself.

Affectionately   PAPA

EF to Lesley Frost Francis

Hotel Zumbro, Rochester, Minnesota

Darling Lesley,   27 April 1934

I should have written to you before this, but my body trembles and my mind is clouded by all this suffering. I wired you that Marjorie came by airplane to the Mayos — The doctors here are working for her in every possible way, but they give us very little hope. They say she is showing the most marvelous resistance, but she got a terrific infection — several kinds of the streptococci germs that cause child-bed fever. The bacteriologist here has succeeded in isolating them, which they were not able to do in Billings. She is being given a new kind of serum. She has been delirious for about three weeks, and while she says heart breaking things, never once has she said anything that revealed other than a pure and steadfast soul. Papa says her courage and nobility will make death seem simpler and easier when it comes to him.

But we are not giving her up. Of course some of the things they do to her to try to save her life *do* augment her distress of body and mind, but we cannot stop trying while there is a ray of hope, can we? And as one of the doctors said miracles do sometimes happen. There are some words of encouragement, and we snatch at every one. Everyone is kind here, just as in Billings. Just think! As many as a hundred boys and girls offered their blood in Billings. They wouldn't have taken money for anything. Only a few could be used, as they had to have had scarlet fever, and the blood had to match Marjories.

Well, this may go on some time longer.[1] You may write us at this hotel. We may change to a small apartment, but can get our mail here.

Tomorrow is your birthday, isn't it, dear? Last year at this time I was just starting for Texas. I seem shut out of the world, without knowledge of the passage of time.

Why don't you and the children go up to the farm? I don't believe Dwight would bother you there, with Carroll around. And you could think of what to do. If Marjorie gets well, you could come up here.

I will send you a $50 check before long, as I imagine you need a little extra at this time.

Papa and I send much love to you and the children.

MAMA

[1] Marjorie died at the Mayo Clinic 2 May.

EF to Lesley Frost Francis

[Amherst] Monday morning

DEAR LESLEY, —   [13 November 1934]

Your letter was very welcome. We are *so* glad to know that things are going smoothly. Very likely Miss Drew and Miss Potts are really feeling more friendly. If they are not, they probably realize that they wouldn't gain anything in the long run by being hostile.

All the things you are doing for Maddox House are very interesting and exciting, and if only you could get more sleep and rest, everything would seem more satisfactory than one could have hoped for. Now that things are so well started I hope you will just make an extra effort.[1]

No, I didn't bring away a black silk slip. I had a black cotton slip with me, which I wear with my black afternoon dress. I didn't notice any black silk slip, either in the closet or bureau drawers. Do you suppose you could have left it in Cambridge?

Papa is going to Exeter [N.H.] next Saturday to be gone two or three days, and I am going down to stay with Irma.

It looks now as if papa really intends going south. I have expected he would back out. We shall probably close this house on the 27th and go to Albany, where he has an engagement that night. He has another in Washington on Dec. 1st to a big English teachers' convention. Then, he has two others at schools near Washington directly after that, and then we shall strike for Florida. We shall probably go somewhere near Miami. I have no spirit for it at all, but it will be fine if papa can escape the grippe.

I will send 2 pairs bloomers for each child tomorrow. I was afraid the green ones for Elinor would be too large. Take a tuck in each seam at front & back, just below the

Frost, Lesley, Marjorie, and Carol with two friends (white shirt and light tunic) on Mt. Lafayette, c. 1916

Lesley at Barnard College, 1919

Irma Frost, c. 1926

Marjorie Frost, c. 1923

Carol Frost at Gainesville, 1938

Franconia Farm House

The Stone House in South Shaftsbury, Vermont

Robert and Elinor in 1928 passport photo

Frost's [February 1915] note to the "Kids"

Dear Kids

This is where Merfyn suffered imprisonment for five days and got acquainted with the scum of the earth while I got acquainted with a poet who wrote a poem called Scum of the Earth. Poor Merfyn had to be all alone most of the time and he was in the realest danger of being sent straight back

The first part of Elinor's [September 1920] letter to Robert

Monday afternoon

Dearest Rob, —

Marjorie has just started for the train to go to school, & I will write you a note before I clean up the rooms. The train service is less favorable than I thought — she has to

James Chapin's drawing of Lesley Lee
Francis, c. 1945

William Prescott Frost, 1943

Willard Fraser and daughter
Marjorie Robin, 1942

Lillian LaBatt Frost
with young friend, c. 1925

Four generations of Frosts: Robert, daughter Lesley, granddaughter Elinor, great-grandchildren (l. to r.) Douglas, Marcia, and Katherine Wilber, c. 1956

Frost tries the heft of a Spanish rake, c. 1961

bands. Then she will grow to them before they are worn out. I have made the fronts a little bit shorter than backs in these, and will mark the fronts at centre band. Then I will get some strong white material and make another pair for each before we leave. Lots of love, MAMA

<hr/>

[1] Lesley had begun teaching at Rockford College, in Illinois. She also directed activities at Maddox House, the school's cultural center.

EF to Lesley Frost Francis

The Webster [Hotel], New York City

DARLING LESLEY, — [November 1934]

It *is* a long time since I wrote to you last. I am sorry. I haven't felt right for some weeks. I have slowed up a good deal, but apparently not enough,[1] for last Friday, about 7 oclock, I had a bad attack of angina. It was pretty bad for about 25 minutes. Dr. Haskell got down quickly and gave me two nitro-glycerine tablets, followed by a hyperdermic which eased it. I stayed in bed the next day, and Sunday. Now I am allowed to do a little light housework, if I am strict about lying down flat at least half the time. I am taking digitalis, and keep nitro-glycerine tablets close by me in case of another attack. It seems my heart is now enlarged and my blood pressure is high.

Dr. Haskell approves of going south on my account now, as well as Roberts. I came to New York last night, am now waiting for papa, who is coming down from Albany (he had two readings there, on the 27th and last night) and also Irma, John and Jacky, who are coming in from New Haven to have Thanksgiving dinner with us here at the Webster. Tomorrow afternoon we go on to Washington. Papa speaks on Saturday there, at a luncheon of the National Ass'n. of English Teachers. [Vice President] Henry Wallace speaks also at the luncheon, and a woman teacher from somewhere. I think that will be about the hardest thing papa has ever done as he is the last of the three.

Then on Monday he speaks at Clarksburg, [West Virginia] and on Tuesday we start for St. Augustine. If we like it, there, we'll get a small house; if not, we'll go on to Miami. I'll wire you as soon as we have a permanent address.

We'll see the Cowards either this evening or tomorrow at lunch, and perhaps plan to visit them on our way home. We'll also see the Torrences[2] sometime tomorrow.

The Drinkwater book is so dull that Carroll wasn't interested in it, and I thought it might serve you as a reference book, and that it was a good idea to get it out of our house at the Gulley, because it speaks so poorly of papa, and he might open it some day and be very much upset. Just throw it away if it is useless.[3]

Carroll, Lillian and Prescott are driving down to Florida after Christmas vacation begins, so Prescott won't lose any school. They will get a small house near us for three months. I am expecting we can get little homes for $25 each.

Willard [Fraser] has taken his brother's job temporarily as assistant manager of the State Liquor Store in Billings while Marvin goes back to selling automobiles. It is $200 a month, and the family needed money desperately. I hope and believe there will be something better for him in the spring. From their reports Robin is thriving wonderfully. We are thinking a little of getting out a small book of Marjories poems. I think papa is very reluctant to broach anything to any magazine, but I would just love to have something in either the Atlantic or the Yale Review.

I will write again in Washington, a short letter.

I *am so* sorry the children have chicken pox.

You, my dear, will have to slow up. You mustn't let the

girls expect some excitement at the book shop *all* the time. You simply cannot stand it.

Lots & lots of love   MAMA

[1] EF took over the care of Robin after her mother died, and the task became too much for her.

[2] RF dedicated "A Passing Glimpse" (*PRF*, p. 248) to poet-playwright-editor Ridgely Torrence in admiration for his book of poems *Hesperides* (1925). See EF to Lesley Frost, [11 November 1917], n. 1.

[3] John Drinkwater frequently praised Edwin Arlington Robinson at RF's expense. A review of books which Drinkwater either wrote or edited suggests three possibilities for EF's reference: *The Muse in Council* (1925), *Twentieth Century Poetry* (1929), or *The Outline of Literature* (a one-volume edition in 1931).

EF to Lesley Frost Francis

The McAllister Hotel, Miami, Florida,[1]

DEAR LESLEY, —   Saturday afternoon [December 1934]

Excuse this garish paper. I may as well use it as long as its supplied. This is a hotel recommended by Orton Lowe, an old acquaintance of papa's, who teaches [English] in the Univ. of Miami. He is away just at present, though. We are more or less bewildered travelers. We arrived last night, and we have made enough inquiries today to find out that rents anywhere in *this* region, are way beyond our means, even if we wanted to stay here, which we don't. We should find it too like a resort for miles up and down the coast. The Davisons[2] are here, somewhere. Ted is off lecturing and we have been trying to get Natalie on the telephone all day, but she doesnt seem to be in. Ted is teaching for one term.

Tomorrow morning, at 7.20 we are starting on a trip to Key West. Papa has always wanted to go there, and the train goes over narrow bridges, & c a lot of the way, so its like going over the water. We might have tried to find a house there, but they say Hemingway lives there, so it is out of the question. We shall return here Monday forenoon, and perhaps go across the tip of Florida to Sarasota, on the

Gulf Coast, by bus. They say there are several villages on
the coast, south of Sarasota, where rents are cheap, and you
can get fruit and vegetables for almost nothing. However,
after floundering around, I imagine we shall end up at St.
Augustine, as being the most interesting place, even if it
isn't as warm as down here. I am sure we don't want to lie
around on beaches, anyway. You can imagine how the
money papa has just earned by four lectures, is melting away.
His lecture in Washington, before the National Institute of
English teachers was about the most successful he has ever
done, I guess. The whole crowd rose in homage, as he stood
up — and clapped with great enthusiasm when he finished.
Then he went out to Clarksburg, W. Va. on a reading, and I
went down from New Haven, where I had spent three days
with Irma, to Washington, to meet him. We stayed two
nights and had lunch with Mark Sullivan and his family
the day we were both there. Mark Sullivan is the noted
newspaper correspondent, you know, who writes special
articles for the Tribune three times a week.

Then Papa called up Justice [Benjamin N.] Cardozo,
of the Supreme Court, (whom we met at Williams, when
papa and he were taking [honorary] degrees)[.] He is a
bachelor, but he invited papa in for a call in the evening
— and was very kind and complimentary.

I am lying down fully half the time during each day,
and eating very carefully — and think I can avoid getting
overtired before we get settled some where.

I am thinking of you and the children a lot. Please,
please try to take things as easy as possible, won't you?

I'll write again in a few days, to let you know what is
happening to us, and I'll let you know our permanent
address as soon as we get one[.]

Lots of love,   MAMA

1 This was the Frosts' first trip to Florida.

² Edward Davison. See RF to Lesley Frost, 3 August 1928, n. 6, and EF to Lesley Frost, 20 September [1928], n. 5.

EF to Lesley Frost Francis

DEAR LESLEY, — Miami, Wednesday evening [December 1934]

We haven't had especially good luck in finding a home this trip. We have decided on Key West, but there are drawbacks. The house we are going into is right on the water. It has an upstairs and downstairs. The owner, a 50 yr. old widow lives upstairs. She doesn't possess a radio and is said to be very quiet. The rent is only 35 per month. We have been looking more around here but rents are absolutely awful. We saw Natalie [Davison] last night. She is looking well. We didn't see Peter, as he was sick with a throat infection, but the youngest, Lesley, is a nice plump little girl. Ted is away lecturing.

[Irma's son] Jacky has so few books, and I don't really know what to get him. As soon as you get this, will you send Miss Manion the names of two or three of the nicest books Elinor & Lee have, so that she can mail them to Jacky. Have them addressed to John P. Cone, Jr. *153 Cold Spring St. New Haven, Conn.* Two would be enough, and have the reading part easy enough so he can read them himself.

We are going down to Key West tomorrow, and can go into the house and get settled the following day, I expect.

I am feeling desperately homesick. It doesn't seem as if I *could* stay down here three months. It's a bad disappointment not to see you when you come east after Christmas. Don't mention this homesickness of mine in your letters.

It has been cold here for two days, but we have been in a steam heated hotel. It has been almost down to the freezing point. From the papers, I judge *you* have had *terribly* cold weather.

It seems such a long time that we've been out of communication with you all. No mail from any one. Write a few words as soon as you get this — to *Key West* Florida. I don't know the street, but we'll tell them at the P.O. of course, and I'll let you know the address in my next letter.

Lots of love   MAMA

EF to Lesley Frost Francis

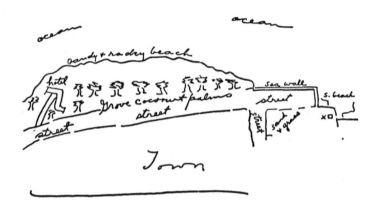

DEAR LESLEY,-   [Key West, Florida, 27 December 1934]

I am surprised you dont know where Key West is. It is the jumping-off place of North America, at the end of a long line of long narrow islets called keys, that curves south and then west, from Cape Sable. The railroad, to reach it, goes over many miles of shallow ocean, on piles driven down through a number of feet, or yards of water. It is a rather old place, being first a hang out for pirates, then a town where "salvagers" of wrecked ships lived. Salvaging was a process of taking off all articles from a ship wrecked out here on the reefs, and selling them later at a public "auction." A small fleet of privately owned sail boats was kept in readiness, for the purpose. It wasn't much better than piracy. Later, a lot of Cubans moved over here, to make hand rolled cigars, and avoid the tariff. Not very long ago the machine made cigars took the place of hand rolled ones, and the population here declined, gradually, from 27,000 to 12,000. It is 1/3 whites, 1/3 Cubans, 1/3 Negroes. I'll tell you more about it some other time. The little sketch shows you our location. A cross marks the house we are in. A sea wall separates the yard from the ocean waves, and in the corners of the wall outside are bits of sandy beach, which are supposed to belong to this house. In the forenoon & early afternoon, a few people come in, but we have it all to ourselves in the early forenoon and evening. I waken as early as ever and it's lovely to see the dark water and the cloud effects as the sun rises.

I'll tell you more about the house, and the woman who owns it some other time. She lives upstairs alone, and is out most of the time. It is certainly balmy here — just a trifle damp, but I don't think enough to harm Lillian. I suppose you are flying today. I am thinking of you. I suppose Carroll, Lillian and Prescott started from South Shaftsbury yesterday. We found an upstairs apartment down in the old residential part, near the school, where there is "atmosphere", and also a garage. The rent of the two places comes to very little, considering.

I hope you will enjoy your New York and Cambridge visits. Write when you are expecting to go back to Rockford. I am glad the children were well over their measles before it was time for you to start.

It's grand that everything is going as well at the college. It seems strange that Gordon & Roberta[1] have turned against the region. It must be pure nerves. Miss Snell, at Mt. Holyoke, told papa that *you* were sort of pining for New England. I guess it was just Roberta's own feelings that made her say it about you, to Miss Snell.

I will write again in a few days. Papa and I send much love.   MAMA

P.S. Papa is feeling very well. I am very weak and listless, but I am following all of Dr. Haskell's directions, and don't anticipate another attack if I am very careful.

I was sorry not to see Mr. & Mrs. Coward, but we had to leave New York sooner than I expected, and I wasn't able to do a thing while there. Please give them our warm regards. Do you think they would like to have us spend a night with them on our way back? But it would probably be better to stay at the hotel and go there for the evening.

[1] Gordon and Roberta Chalmers. Dr. Chalmers was the newly inaugurated president of Rockford College, Illinois, where Lesley was teaching. Again — as in earlier letters — both RF and EF were deeply involved in their daughter's successes and frustrations. This is the first of many letters touching upon their concerns with Lesley's treatment at Rockford.

EF to Lesley Frost Francis

DEAR LESLEY,— [Key West] Tuesday morning [late winter 1935]

This morning the wind has risen to quite a gale from the southwest, and the waves are dashing up and spraying over the sea wall. The wind has been blowing quite hard for three days. I hope this is the climax and that tomorrow will be calm again.

I didn't write you, I guess, that Ted and Natalie Davison are in Miami this winter. He is teaching at Miami University. We invited them down, and they came Saturday, and stayed until Sunday evening.

They both seemed more likeable than of yore, and we had quite a pleasant time. They were very agreeable to Carroll and Lillian, and we all had a picnic together on a lovely part of the shore Sunday noon.

Ted has part charge of the summer English school at

Boulder, and he said he was intending to ask you out there to do a little work in the school this summer. You might not want to do it, but I suppose it would help at Rockford in the matter of prestige. It would probably only last three weeks, and you could leave the children with Rosa again — or you could drive them out, and Margaret Bartlett could engage a housekeeper for you and find a small inexpensive house. Rents are very cheap there.

You didn't tell us how it came out between Gordon and Miss Drew about the literary magazine. Did he give in? It all sounds very worrying. Is the available money so limited that Gordon cannot get rid of her, but he can take her work away from her, just as Meiklejohn did with Davy Todd.[1]

Irma writes that Jacky has measles. He had hardly recovered from a *very* bad attack of grippe, followed by chicken pox before he even got out of bed. It certainly distresses me. Poor little boy — and poor Irma.

When you write, tell me something about Mildred and her husband, in Cambridge. Are they colored. But I remember now they are Italians. Would the husband know anything about farm work? I was just thinking of the *possibility* — of their being with Carroll & Lillian.

Well, I mustn't write any longer.

Lots & lots of love, dear   MAMA.

[1] David Todd, 19 years RF's senior, was director of the observatory which he helped plan and build and professor of astronomy at Amherst from 1881 to 1920. He was then named professor emeritus.

RF to Lesley Frost Francis

DEAR LESLEY: [Key West, late winter 1935]

We admired your enthusiastic flight piece.[1] You have a good time in it[,] the writing runs free and the result is a work of one kind of art.

Your account of the day-to-day changes in your situation at the college keeps us somewhat excited. The villainesses of the plot we grow to hate. I have been on the point once or twice of advising Gordon what to do with them. You seem to speak as if he thought of firing at least one. But I hadnt supposed it possible to fire a full professoress any more than a full professor except on proof of moral terpitude. His only way that I can see is to take away their importance bit by bit. For instance why doesn't he at one stroke end all faculty editorship of the college magazine on the ground that the girls should be made entirely responsible for it as grown up children. Luckily I have written Gordon nothing. Things are changing too rapidly in your mind for me to act on them accurately from this distance.

Your last two letters show a growing interest in Boulder this summer. Elinor hasnt believed you would be interested: so I have been sluggish in pressing the matter with Ted Davison. Before I really go after the job for you I want all things considered. I get a new slant on everything from what you say in one breath about credits for a master's degree, publicity employment, and your future with the Chalmers should they go elsewhere. Nothing is worth building very great hopes on. Still I'm inclined to wonder again if a degree wouldnt be a legitimate prop in your life. I couldn't see you seeking it in English exactly. You would be laying yourself open to too many snubs and humiliations. The[re] would be a look of originality if you could get it in some part of Latin, say Mediaeval Latin or in Latin in general or in Greek or in Greek and Latin. You would be welcomed to that forsaken department and having done well in it would give you distinction in any department. I mean it would add to you[r] dignity as a teacher of English. Or if you feel any decline of your ability to learn by heart and acquire vocabulary you could go into philosophy or history. Economics I should avoid as I should a best-selling novel.

But if you are serious about the degree I dont see what you would be doing at Boulder. You couldnt teach there and submit to being taught at the same time. You'll have to decide for teaching or being taught. Then I can go after Ted for the Boulder job or take up the question of where you will work for your credits this summer. If you are going in for Latin you will want to find a half an hour a day for memorizing some Latin verse or declension or conjugation right away. You'll have to get the rust off. I have been thinking a lot lately that a unique position would be with one leg in the English department and the other in the classic setting an example in both of getting the furthest possible away from linguistics and scientific nonsense in the art of literature. I've been reading some Latin again lately — Helen Waddell's book Mediaeval Latin Lyrics. You ought to see it. Henry Holt publishes it here. But this isnt what set me thinking. I have long had these thoughts about how Latin could be redeemed by the right live literary teaching — scholarly but not so that anybody would notice it. It was in my head all the summer I was in California reading Lucretius De Rerum Natura.

Of course I think Gordon might let up on you still more as teacher if he is going to burden you with his publicity. But be careful not to be too particular at the beginning of any job. The only questions to concern you should be Can you get the two poetry courses down to a pleasant routine that won't cost you too much time and energy and can you see in the ideas of Gordon and your additions to them a real chance to go large. All his inclination toward a really bookish college fills me with approval. Gee I could ring endless changes on that. Even in Latin I should set myself to lead a class into buying non-textbook looking books.

I wish I could have seen Gordon for a talk when he was as near as Atlanta. What has he to suggest as to where you should seek your credits and how? Do you want me to ask him if he would let you off with only one course? The danger I see there is that it might be the beginning of your tapering to nothing in the teaching.

Be nice to Harriet Monroe and her staff particularly Morton Zabel.[2] Have you had any of them out?

Affectionately   PAPA

[1] Lesley, always the adventurer, had taken a 3 1/2-hour flight from Chicago to New York over Christmas recess. Her write-up of the experience had appeared subsequently in a number of newspapers around the country.

[2] See RF to Lesley and Marjorie Frost, [1924]. Zabel was then associate editor of *Poetry*.

RF to Lesley Frost Francis

DEAR LESLEY: Key West, 23 March 1935

No news and no further advice. I merely wanted to say Elinor and I share your prejudice against the idea of adult education. Beyond a certain point lessons in school (day or night school) are degrading. You've had enough. You would be outraging yourself if for any reason on earth you subjected yourself to being teacher-taught. We've all of us come to that conclusion several times before. It costs something every time to come to it. Let's not get where we will have to come to it again. (Just the same I think it would be a novelty if you got up your Latin secretly and the first thing they knew you were reading some rarer Latin poets with a group at Maddox House a few times next year.)

You make the crowd around you, even some of the better ones, look as if they had wrinkles in their souls. They may be better than they seem to us. Their ways however are not our ways. You should not be broken to fit their mould. With the best intentions in the world both Gordon and Roberta may be quite capable of designs on you that might be fatal. You have to look out. And you'll have to get out if the position gets too false. As you say, the whole thing can be thought of as a flyer in the academic.

What do you think of Kantor's[1] verse? I see he has a book out. What do you say to McLeish's Panic?[2] Elinor and I are not going to be poisoned with poetry as a care any more. You'll have to tell us about what is passing. You are young and tough-spirited.

We are leaving this hot-bed for the open air next Wednesday (March 27)[.] To Santa Fe, Carmel, Greenwich Village, Montmartre, and Peterboro, add Key West. Arty Bohemias! I have stayed away from the others. The Lord delivered me into this one to punish my fastidiousness. Don't make my sentiments public or it might follow me to the grave. We got here and then panic-stricken said things to the FERA[3] who found us a house to live in. I exclaimed when I heard that John Dos Passos might live up stairs: "My God two authors in the same house! It would be a regular word-factory." It was an unguarded moment — and made enemies of Dos Passos and [Ernest] Hemmingway. Never mind. But the story that grew out of it must be left to die if it will.

Uneasiness about such things and about Carroll waiting round and about the hotel servants tanning on what we were lead to suppose was our private beach have kept Elinor from getting the start upward we hoped for. She thinks the moist warmth of the tropics has been bad for her. I don't think we can tell. Anyway it will be good to get back to Amherst.

My immediate schedule looks rather full: Miami University (at Coral Gables), Foxcroft, Virginia, Normal Schools at Trenton and Glassboro, N.J. then my two public lectures on "Before the Beginning and after the End of a Poem" at Amherst, then Milton Mass., University of New

Hampshire, Dartmouth Harvard and Yale. Then one more honory degree — this one at Elinor's St Lawrence University. This last is supposed to be kept secret.

Waves waves waves all the time, though not very large in this shallow sea with a reef-barrier like a south-sea island. The water is exactly seventy five feet from our door by measuremen[t] made just now while the letter waited. Enclosed for Lee and Elinor is a grass burr I got making it.

Let me know if and when you hear from Boulder. Also let me know if you dont hear in two weeks.

Affectionately   PAPA

[1] MacKinlay Kantor, best known for his prose fiction.
[2] Archibald MacLeish's *Panic*, a play, was published in 1935.
[3] An arm of the W. P. A., the Federal Emergency Relief Administration.

RF to William Prescott Frost

DEAR PRESCOTT: Franconia,[1] 22 August 1935

Last night we had a good rain and a little lightening that sucked the electric lights low every time it flashed. That reminded me of your lesson in electricity on Monday. I hope it went off well. Write me about it will you? Electricity has come into use in my life time. When I came to New England in 1885, there wasnt a telephone in the city I lived in, Lawrence, Mass., and there wasnt an electric light. At least I didnt know of any. The telegraph had been going for quite a while. The wires were everywhere even in San Francisco. We used to loose our kites on them. But most electrical developments have taken place with me looking on. I have even worked in the [Lawrence] mills on the electric lighting system and spent part of a year in the dynamo room. And still I haven't paid enough attention to the biggest thing in the present-day world to understand such a thing as a transformer or an electric metre. A radio sender is a complete mystery. You'll have to educate me in all this some day. What do you suppose happens when a lightning flash draws down the house lights?

Bears as usual up here. They have been killing lambs. Hodge has a man out hunting. I ought to bring a gun when I come.   Affectionately   GRAMPHA

[1] RF and EF had left Florida in early April. As soon as his lecture schedule and Amherst duties allowed, they retreated to the gully farm in South Shaftsbury. Following a pattern of many years, they made a late-summer visit to Mrs. Fobes's guest house in Franconia for hay-fever relief. See RF to Carol Frost, 18 September [1933], n. 1.

RF to Carol Frost

DEAR CAROL: Amherst, 7 October 1935

We both liked the apple-crating poem for the genuine satisfaction it takes in the life you are living. It has a great deal more of the feeling of real work and country business than anything of mine could ever pretend or hope to have. Your true way is straight ahead as you are going in farm work as it affects you in thought and emotion. You are bound to achieve a different [... style...] from other writers if you can stick to both the farm work and the poetic art. Anyway that is my opinion. The two things firmly kept should be good fun and should land you somewhere. All art is a dangerous life. It is apt to end in artiness in silliness and in folly. It *generally* does. All business is safer. I mean a life of business exclusively. But the best life of all I should think would be a life of business and the family expressing itself in one art or another. You are in a very strong position on your apple farm to make dashes out from into poems.

I notice your syntax and grammar go all right in your sentences.

Dont forget to speak to Mr Fineman about the Dane.

Dont forget to give some apples to Mr Howard.

I have just started in on the box you gave me.

Affectionately   PAPA.

RF to Lesley Frost Francis

DEAR LESLEY: [Amherst, 8 October 1935]

Elinor and I saw Louis [Untermeyer] (at his fifty year birthday party Oct third), We saw Ellen and Alfred Harcourt at their house where we stayed over night, we saw the Blumenthals who are going to make the book of Marjorie's poems and I saw at the New School some girl who roomed with you and took a great notion to you on your way back from Europe this last time, but I have gone and forgotten her name. All this was on our recent expedition, I might add that I saw Raymond Holden[1] at Franconia on his way back from New Brunswick where he had been fishing with Otto Mallory[.] Raymond spoke as if his book had gotten away to a good start and he was surprised to hear I thought it very autobiographical. Probably he has to assume that attitude to insure himself against suits for libel. He will have a hard time convincing Grace she isnt in the book.

All but the Blumenthals (who never met you) talked about you and wondered how you liked Rockford College. How do you like it this year? That is the great question. It didn't sound to me as if you were being treated right about that freshman class. I can't stand any dirtiness from Gordon. You'll have to tell me frankly that Gordon Roberta and the new teacher in your department are satisfying you or my family pride will drive me to action. Damn them. Let's hear the facts. Then we can consider whether I will visit the place this November. If I come it will probably be toward the last of the month.

I thought we would call Marjories book If I Should Live to Be a Doll, just for the strangeness of the thing. We dont want it to savor the least bit of memorial lugubriousness. The poems are good enough for publication regularly, though I doubt if we would have the heart to submit them to public criticism. We'll use her picture with them and I have a poem of my own for a foreword.[2] I'll write you out the poem.

Remember me to anyone with whom it will do any good[.]   Affectionately   PAPA

[1] See RF to Lesley Frost, 9 December 1917, n. 2, and 8 February [1920], nn. 1 and 5.

[2] "If I Should Live to be a Doll" was one of 26 poems by Marjorie which RF and EF arranged to have printed in a book finally entitled *Franconia*. The small memorial volume was produced later in 1936 by Joseph Blumenthal's Spiral Press. No photograph was included, nor was RF's poem for a foreword, "Voice Ways." (*PRF*, pp. 301-302).

RF to Carol Frost

DEAR CAROL: [Cambridge, Massachusetts, March 1936]

Well here we are in the middle of the great world again and it is greater than ever as we came back to it [from Florida]. The flu we dreaded for me I hardly got at all (I had it a little): but Elinor has had it hard. She has been in bed a week and will probably have to stay there most of the time for several days more. She had a temperature of more than a hundred for three days: and she looks pretty well exhausted. I wish to goodness we could see her really strong and happy. Everybody here is thinking of her. She has had flowers and flowers sent to her.

After the unfriendliness of Florida I might say the coldness of Florida the warmth of New England toward us has almost taken our breath away. I've never been welcomed anywhere with the noise and enthusiasm I met with at my opening lecture.[1] You'd think I was some musical hero. I suppose the audience wanted to show their approval of having an American give the lectures after so many years of foreigners in the chair. I've usually been treated well, but never like this anywhere. People usually keep such excitement for athletics and, as I say, for music. It was hard to understand. I wasnt at my best. I was too scared. They didn't care how I did. They were out to make me glad I had come back to the college I ran away from thirty seven years ago. Of course I have been in and out around the place quite a lot in the years between, but not so anyone would notice it. It was very dramatic for a quiet life like mine. I thought you'd like to know. My books seem to spread wider all the time. When Elinor gets up I expect we will be a good deal out being entertained. I hope she can stand it.

I finished the manuscript of my book, A Further Range, and left it with Henry Holt & Co the last day of February. It should be out April 20th. That means further excitement for the aged adventurers.

You'll be back on the farm by then, getting ready for the dormant spray. We'll be thinking of you coming up the coast pretty soon now. How many days does it take? Three to New York? I suppose you might have bought your ticket clear to Boston and landed in our front yard. Tell Prescott not to rock the boat. Maybe the March winds will rock it for you. I hope Lillian doesnt get too seasick.

We are having fine sunny weather, though fairly cold. It freezes hard at night and stays hard in the shade still. But in the sun the water runs everywhere from the big snow banks in the city streets. Winter got the better of them this year. The snow was never properly cleared away.

Remember me to Orton Lowe, poor man. I can't help contrasting the wretched University he is struggling in with the real Universities I know up north. I'll never forget the night you and I and he and President Ashe sat in the dark car and talked about what made a good college president. I pitied Ashe too.

Affectionately   PAPA

[1] RF gave the six Charles Eliot Norton Lectures at Harvard in March 1936 under the series title "The Renewal of Words." His over-capacity audiences were loudly enthusiastic, and he and EF were warmly entertained by President James Bryant Conant, Mr. and Mrs. Theodore Morrison, and others.

[2] Lowe was Professor of English at the University of Miami, Coral Gables, Florida, established in 1925. Bowman F. Ashe was the college's president.

RF to Lesley Lee Francis

[Post card]

DEAR LEE   South Shaftsbury, 28 June 1937

Here's a picture[1] of a good little mother affectionately bringing up a good little doll baby. The little mother is called Madonna. I suppose you see Madonnas everywhere in Mexico.   Affectionately your G.F.

[1] The face of the card is a reproduction of George B. Luks' "The Little Madonna" in the Phillips Andover Academy's Addison Gallery.

EF to Lesley Lee Francis

DEAR LEE,-   [South Shaftsbury, summer 1937]

I guess you don't remember this farm of grandfather's and grandmother's. You came here several times when you were a little bit of a girl, but you are quite a big little girl now, aren't you? Grandfather and I have been up here about a week, and I have been busy getting the house in order. Yesterday, Elizabeth came up from Amherst. You saw her last fall. You remember that she gave you and Elinor your breakfasts don't you? Now she will do the work for me, so I shall not be so busy. There are a lot of wild strawberries up on the hill, and Elizabeth and I will go up and pick some pretty soon before it rains. It looks a little like rain. I wonder if it rains much down in Mexico.[1]

Prescott finishes his lessons in about two days. He said yesterday that he was going to rest for about a week from all writing and then he was going to write a letter to you. Grandfather and Carroll and Lillian send a lot of love to you, dear.

I will write again soon.

Lots of love   GRANDMOTHER

1 Lesley, with her daughters Lesley Lee and Elinor, spent most of the year 1937 living in Mexico — first on a ranch in Tampico Province, then in Mexico City, and finally in a rented home in Cuernavaca.

RF to Lesley Frost Francis

Hotel Stonehaven, Springfield, Massachusetts
DEAR LESLEY!   [30 September 1937]

I dont know whether you had any letter from Elinor about the operation we were afraid she would have to undergo. She had the operation this morning Thursday September 30th at ten o'clock in the Springfield Hospital Springfield Mass. You can write to her there. Be careful to give her all the courage you can for the future and at the same time all the credit she deserves for having come throug[h] a worse ordeal than we expected. She had her right breast removed. You will know what that means. Wonderful care was taken of her. She was to have risked it yesterday, but we all got scared at the condition of her heart and her general weakness. Doctor Sweet, the operator and Doctor Haskell debated whether she hadnt better try it with a local anaesthetic. In the end, though, the decision was for ether, and she lived through it. Thats some of the battle. She came out of the ether well. She never has lost her mind from ether or I mean her mind has never run wild. She was talking sense though terribly little of it by noon. Of course there is a hard night ahead of her tonight and I suppose a critical week or so. Beyond that we mustnt any of us look. We must all try to be cheerful and untroublesome in any years there are left. She's a brave one. She's been too brave. I have no doubt she will figure out for herself the danger she is in. But we are going to shut our eyes to it by agreement with the doctors. No one outside is to be told. There's a hope that the worse fears may not be realized. We will live on the assumption that they wont be. Anyway if we get through the next three weeks we have some precious time on earth to make the most of. I don't see yet just what to do with it, but one thing is sure we must indulge her longing for quiet and economies. You'll be coming home pretty soon. You didn't tell us whether you had got your tires and your license. Elinor read your preface just before we came down to Springfield. I haven't had the heart to hear my praises at a time when I feel to blame for being alive.

Affectionately   PAPA.

I am at this hotel. But it will be better for you to write to Amherst. My mail will be brought down.

EF to Lesley Frost Francis

[Amherst] Wednesday morning

DARLING LESLEY,-   [13 October 1937]

I have been home since Sunday, and am gaining every day — but shall not go down stairs until next Sunday.

We have good help so do not worry about us in the least. Everything is going fine, and we quite like your idea of going over to Florida. There is no hurry about your leaving Mexico though — and we think you could come North and over to Florida on a Mexican license Why not? Florida licenses are *very* cheap, we remember, and I don't think they require a driver's license. So you could get one there as soon as you arrived.

I am awfully sorry you have been so upset about my operation. I didn't think you would be if it was successfully

over before you heard of it. *I* wasn't frightened about my
heart, as Dr. Haskell has said twice in the last year and a
a half that it was improving a lot. As soon as the doctors
had seen my electro-cardi[o]gram they were reassured.

I shall be very relaxed and quiet for a long time — and
there is no need of any worry.

Am so glad Lees eye is in good shape. I'll write again
soon[.]   Lots & lots of love   MAMA

EF to Lesley Frost Francis

DARLING LESLEY,-   [Amherst] Thursday, 21 October [1937]

We do not expect to go south until around December
1st. It occurred to us the other day that it might be exciting
for us all to go to Mexico, and Robert wrote to you about it.
I don't really believe, however, that it would be the best
thing; we will decide as soon as we hear from you in answer
to his letter. Other wise, we will go to Gainesville, Florida,
and will send you money to go across, and find a house or
two there for us.

I had a letter from Mrs. Payne the other day, asking
about you. She is just having her teeth out, and will then
"go into hiding" for awhile. She would like to have you &
the children stop there on your way, if it came at the right
time. It isn't worth while, for you to go out of your way for it,
of course. While in San Antonio we got acquainted with a
young married woman about your age (through a letter of
introduction from Louis) & she spoke of wanting to know
you. She is an Alpha Phi, and is a very nice person. She &
her husband who is considerably older, have no children
and have a large house. He is a successful dentist. If San
Antonio isn't much out of your way, you might like to write
to her, & speak of seeing her as you go through, and
perhaps she might invite you & the children to stay there

a night or two. I *wish* San Antonio had more sunshine. I'd *love* to stay there another winter.

For some reasons, I'd like to go to Arizona & try that. The chief reason being that it would be easy to get Robin down to stay with us. Of course you could go there as well as to Florida. If we don't have her this winter, we'll have her next spring to stay through the summer.

It will be fine to have you & Elinor & Lee with us through the winter.

I am dressed and downstairs half the day now. This is a *gorgeous* day after 2 days of rain, and I have walked a little way down the road this morning.

Much love   MAMA

RF to Lesley Frost Francis

[Portion of letter missing]   [Amherst, 25 October 1937]

[...] immediately about what life would be like in both places. Theres food, there's water there's beds there's insects there's sunshine there's humidity theres political danger, there's the friendliness of the natives to us Yankees to consider. Be sure to touch on all those and anything else you think of. Then also theres the renewal of your passport. We'll have to think quickly. Wouldnt it be fun to break such new and unusual ground as the West coast of Mexico? But you have to remember we are not young and rugged. We mustnt be ambitious to live too dangerously.

Elinor is doing well and even better than could be expected. She came down stairs yesterday a little while, though I doubt it was very wise. Ethel [Manthey-] Zorn scolded her. She's staying upstairs for lunch today.

Of course we would include Carol Lillian & Prescott in any plan. We had thought of Gainesville Florida as a tung nut possibility to give Carol something to keep him out of unhappiness. The nuts are prospering we hear and already there is a factory processing the oil. Idleness is terribly hard on Carol.   Affectionately   PAPA

EF to Lesley Frost Francis

DEAR LESLEY,-   [Amherst] Wednesday, 27 October [1937]
Of course there are misgivings about Gainsville, or any place we might decide to go to, but I guess Gainsville it will be this year. I know that Lillian would prefer any place to Florida, because of her fears that Carroll might break loose again over that girl, but Robert seems inclined to ignore that danger, because he believes Florida is so much better for him (for Robert, I mean[).] I believe that Carroll will be all right. He seems quite steady and contented lately.

I am enclosing check for $100 and will send $50 check tomorrow. I think probably rents will be quite cheap in Gainsville, as it isn't a resort. We should all be near each other this year — as its such a waste of gasoline as well as of time and energy to go back & forth between houses every day. You will have to stay in a tourist camp while you are searching the town. Furnished houses & apartments may not be plentiful in such a place, of course. Papa has an idea you might find a small double house for us, and for you & the children, so that we shouldn't have all our meals together, and then a small house or apartment close by for Carroll & Lillian. If you found a *very* cheap unfurnished house or apartment, it might be worth while to put in a little cheap furniture ourselves, but probably it would count up to too much. You will have to use your judgment.

Northern Florida is very full of lakes, and I imagine there would certainly be one or more near Gainsville, and we could drive to the ocean for a picnic at least once a week.

You *might* decide on taking a fairly large house for you folks & Carroll, Lillian & Prescott — if there was a small one near for papa and me. It will be a difficult business to decide on just the right quarters — and it might be that you'd better not make a final decision on more than one place before we arrive, which will be just about Dec. 1st.

I will write again tomorrow when I send the other check.

I am getting on fine, and I assure you I am being *very* careful not to overdo.

I hope you folks will get out of Mexico safe and well.

Lovingly   MAMA

EF to Lesley Frost Francis

DARLING LESLEY, —   [Amherst] Friday, 29 October [1937]

I shall breathe easier when you are out of Mexico. I hadn't realized you were running *quite* so many risks.

I believe I should send you another $100 check, to be on the safe side. You will turn the money into express checks and *hide* some of them. Or perhaps I'll send two $50 checks and then you can use your judgment about cashing both of them in Mexico. You will have your own Nov. check from Mr. F. of course[.]

The address of the lady in San Antonio is Mrs. Franz Joseph Stumpf 602 Augusta St. San Antonio. The house is down in the center of the city.

Papa has been *excessively* busy, this far, with lectures out of town and things here at the college.

Perhaps we'll write our next letter to the Mexico City address — Please give us the ranch address again, and write or telegraph when you leave Cuernavaca.[1]

Lots & lots of love   MAMA

[1] RF and EF joined Lesley and her daughters in Gainesville, in early December. A rental was also arranged for Carol and his family. Robin came on from Montana. It was to be both a festive and final family get-together.

Never Again Would Birds' Song

Be The Same 1938-1963

Much of life — both its beauty and its pain — moved beyond the threshold of easy words in the last quarter-century of Robert Frost's career. Marjorie, the promising poetess of the family, had died. Elinor succumbed to her weak heart. Carol, neither the poet nor the farmer he might have wished, committed suicide. Irma would require care in a mental hospital. Yet Frost continued to write poetry, much of it deceptively playful. He busied himself with his "barding about" and was frequently involved in cultural "affairs of state." Although his personal correspondence dwindled, he took a special delight in writing his grandchildren. A few people played an increasingly important role in his life. At the end, life-toughened, the recipient of more honors than he could possibly count, America's preeminent poet was still committing to paper much that was otherwise difficult to say.

RF to Carol Frost

DEAR CAROL: [Gainesville, Florida, late March 1938]

Well, youre hard at work up there and that must be some comfort. I hope you have an interesting summer. You'll be getting new trees and baby chicks and I suppose putting on the dormant spray. There was nothing Elinor wanted more than to have you take satisfaction out of that home and farm. I wish you would remember it every day of your life.

We plan to have the funeral[1] either on Friday April 15th or on Monday or Tuesday of the week following. Something will depend on when the minister can come. I am going to ask Sidney Snow of Chicago to read some poem or two she liked and some not-too-religious verses from the Bible. Stanley King says we can use either the College Church or the Chapel. But the chapel means more to me. It is a beautiful room and the pulpit has been one of my chief speaking places. I don't know whether she ever heard me there, but she was always waiting anxiously at home to hear how my talk came out. The Chapel has had so much to do with our position at Amherst that my sentiment is for it. Maybe Otto will know of a place for us to keep out of sight there. We'll see.

Lesley is getting Rosa down from New York to take care of the children while she comes north with me for the funeral. After the funeral we can all drive over to Derry and scatter the ashes out in the alders on the Derry farm if the present owner will let us. By all I mean just the family and perhaps one or two of our closest friends.

I shall be working hard myself at lecturing in May.

Affectionately PAPA

[1] After a succession of heart seizures, EF died in Gainesville on 21 March. Her body was cremated. A memorial service was held at Amherst College's Johnson Chapel on 20 April with 19 friends serving as honorary bearers: Fred

Allis, Reginald L. Cook, Sidney Cox, Bernard DeVoto, George Roy Elliott, Donald Fisher, Dr. Nelson Haskell, Robert Hillyer, Stanley King, Otto Manthey-Zorn, David McCord, Frederic G. Melcher, Paul Moody, Theodore Morrison, Wilbert Snow, Lawrance Thompson, Richard Thornton, Louis Untermeyer and George Whicher. RF was not able to carry out his intention to scatter his wife's ashes on the Derry farm; more than three years later, her urn was buried in a family plot which RF had purchased in the Old Bennington Cemetery, in Vermont.

RF to William Prescott Frost

DEAR PRESCOTT: Gainesville, 8 April 1938

Lillian tells us you are back in winter up there.[1] The Florida papers haven't failed to mention the fact. Anyone might think you would mind it more by contrast with the warmth you have been having for months down here. I found it different from that. I seemed to mind the spring cold in the north less for having filled myself up with sunlight all winter in the south. I believe I have had enough of heat to last me for a while. The nights are already too hot for me. I almost get a bad throat from trying to sleep uncovered. I have a week or so more to stand.

It is strange about your short wave radio set. You must get it to working somehow. Elinor was so anxious to have you have it. I'm going to tell you something just this once for you always to remember. I shall never speak of it again. Not more than a month ago she told me you were a great favorite of hers. She said you had a good mind and, more important still, a good nature. She never knew a boy or girl she liked better. She was going along way out of her usual way to say all this. She was seldom outspoken in praise. Dont forget.

We'll keep such things locked in our hearts and when we write each other a letter as we must once in a while, we'll speak of the ordinary things that happen to us and occur to us in our everyday life. Tell me especially about any ideas you have in mechanics. When you write a good essay

or story for your Calvert [School] teacher, you ought to
make me a copy of it with your pen or with Carols typewriter. I've got to be entertained.

Affectionately   YOUR GRANDFATHER

Lesley is in your house and I am in the Thomas Hotel.

[1] Grief-stricken by his mother's death, Carol returned quickly to the South
Shaftsbury farm with his family. Lillian wrote RF to assure him of their safe
arrival, and this is his response.

RF to Lesley Frost Francis

DEAR LESLEY: Concord Corners [Vermont] 7 September 1938

Pay not too much attention to my arguments with
myself. I have been having long long thoughts in the last six
months and the upshot is not yet. That was too much of a
letter I wrote you yesterday. I mustn't give way to the
troubles of my mind like that.[1]

When you come Saturday — and be sure you do —
please bring along a pair of my pants from the small closet
in my room at Carol's house. I need a heavier pair than
I have with me for the cold weather we are having. Take the
pair that has no coat to match it. That can be your guide.
I have the coat here.

Bring your tennis racket. You wont want to stay long
at the Untermeyers, but maybe there'll be time to get in
a game.   Affectionately   PAPA

[1] RF and Lesley had a sad-angry confrontation after EF's death. As
daughter and as mother, she feared and resented his overpowering needs; she
and her daughters had their own lives to live. The letter to which RF alludes
is not to be found.

RF to Lesley Frost Francis

DEAR LESLEY: [Boston][1] Wednesday, 30 November 1938

This afternoon at four thirty I shall be reading to a
Harvard audience and Tuesday evening I shall be reading

with you in Washington. My fear of these things beforehand
has largely left me. I have done my ten or fifteen this fall in
Ohio Pennsylvania New York and Massachusetts with
almost perfect calm. Something strange has come over my
life. I shall never be the scared fool again that I used to be.
Nothing can more than kill me. I happened to remark at
the De Voto table that I might turn to prose in ten years
from now and their eight year old piped up "You, you'll be
dead in ten years." I really enjoyed the rudeness. The devil
of it is that except for the flu threat I seem more alive than
I ever was. You should see me in trials of strength and
suppleness with men much younger. I even excel in some
events. I pass the time away with the lectures and with
a good deal of the society of a very few people here. Kathleen
Morrison[2] has made my apartment pleasant and taken an
interest in my mail and my lecture engagements. You must
be grateful to her for having helped me through my bad
time. Lillian I know would have been only too glad to take
care of me and make me one of the family at the farm. But
the burden of that household would have been too much
for my spirit. I am best as I am, though the hours alone are
sometimes pretty desolate. I read a little — write almost
none. There has been talk of my going to Greece for a long
visit with the MacVeaghs[3] and I have just been invited to
Tahiti by Norman Hall.[4] I doubt if I could stand the
journeys alone. The last invitation however has put it into
our heads that we might all make up a party, you and I the
Morrisons, the Weekses[5] (he's the editor of the Atlantic
and a great friend of Norman Halls,) Helen and Raymond
Everett and maybe Charlie Curtis and his wife. I would
want to take some children, your two, Prescott, Bobby
Morrison, and maybe the Everett girls. Prescott is old
enough to go as scout leader. This is more than a notion to
occupy my mind. I am at the plans for it, and mean to

bring it off. Spending the money will be part of the fun. The only thing I hate to do with money is pay bills.

Your report to Lillian on your work was the same as to me. Very hard isn't it? Maybe you will learn ways of shedding some of it as you go on. Maybe you will have to try to work up out of it into a degree and more regular teaching. I shall be anxious to hear what you are thinking. I'm glad Cobb has proved such a useful friend.

I guess I'll take a night train down and arrive Tuesday morning at 7.45[.] Lets try to have a good time of it.

Affectionately   PAPA

[1] After EF's death, RF resigned from Amherst College, sold his home there, and undertook many lecture engagements. In September 1938, he moved into an apartment at 88 Mt. Vernon St., in Boston.

[2] Mrs. Theodore Morrison, wife of one of Harvard's English faculty, who beginning in mid-1938, assumed a many-faceted role in the management of RF's life and affairs. See RF to Carol Frost, [March 1936], n. 1, and [late March 1938], n. 1.

[3] Lincoln MacVeagh, editor, publisher, U. S. Ambassador to Greece.

[4] James Norman Hall, co-author of the Bounty trilogy (1932-34).

[5] Edward A. Weeks, Jr.

RF to Lesley Frost Francis

DEAR LESLEY: [Boston, December 1938]

Two behaviors not too bad in New York at the New School and so home in a bed train all right. Kathleen had Raymond Everett in to tell us what he thought of the Holts' proffered contract. I could see it was disappointingly good from his point of view. None but a bad publisher, he said, could give an author such good terms. They are these alternatives: (A) I promise them only my poems and they start now at $250 a month and raise that to $300 a month for the rest of my life from the publication of my next book of poems; (B) I promise them both verse and prose and they begin at once with the $300 a month. For the last ten years my books have averaged just about $300 a month. The guarantee merely means their undertaking to strain their resources to keep me selling. One additional clause under B: if I promise everything now they will turn all my royalties from 10[,] 12 1/2 and 15 percent into 20 percent and so make all future royalties. The falling out of faithful friends is the renewal of contract much to my advantage. I didn't go for to get the better of them. I merely set out to get away from them, or make them eat crow for treating me so badly this year. I suppose Richard Thornton's quarrel with Herbert Bristol was to blame for their mishandling of me.[1]

I had a really good time in Washington with you. I shrink from the exile in Florida. The days go by better with the help of those who care for me in my restless old age. You kids count with me and having you to think of and see something of means a great deal. But there are things I have to look for outside where there are no family memories for complication. You must come to be grateful to Kathleen for her ministrations[.] The closest criticism will discover no flaw in her kindness to me I am sure. We must all be a lot together when we can. She will press nothing of course — as she has pressed nothing. If I find myself almost a member of the Morrison family (in my entire detachment) the pressure has been all mine from the moment when both Kathleen and Ted together merely suggested that I come and live near them in Cambridge. They had forgotten the idea when I picked it up to decide me against going to live in New York.

Here is the hundred dollars for your Christmas. Make it as gay as you can for the children. You furnish the young spirit.

Very important: I left a scarf with you I think. I must have it right away. Will you mail it?

Your position looks perfect to me.

Affectionately　　PAPA

Couldn't you ask David for fifty dollars?

1 It is likely that RF's contract, calling for a straight 20 % royalty, was without equal. This arrangement was Holt's response to RF's third threat to leave the firm. (For information relating to his first, see RF to Lesley Frost, 25 January 1919, n. 3.) Thornton and Bristol were Holt executives, the former its president and Frost's consistent champion.

RF to Lesley Frost Francis

DEAR LESLEY: [South Miami, 3 February 1939]

It is alot to me that you are having things so much your way these days. There is nothing much new about me except that I came through the two weeks with the Morrisons pretty well considering all there was on all sides to dissemble. I am alone now in a rather desolated house. The plan of my well-wishers is to ship me off for a few days' change to Cuba in the company of Mr and Mrs Paul Engel who are my neighbors in another of the Allen houses.[1] That should bring me back here toward the last of next week. week. I can't stay on in Florida, I'm afraid after the last of February. My first lecture is to be at Tufts College on March 3. After that a deluge. I think it would be better for you than for me to remind the Allens of their invitation. I'm sure they will want you.

Carol had found nothing in Homestead and given it up. When I got here he had all but decided to take a rather expensive house at West Palm Beach. I interposed to make them look Coconut Grove over. They are settled in a large house on the other side of town from me at $75 a month for February and March. Their trip down cost $200. The trip back will be another $200. The total extra cost will be upwards of $600 that might as well have gone toward a better house in South Shaftsbury. They have begun to see it that way. They talk as if this were their last winter south. I am not seeing them often. It isnt good for us to be together.

I remonstrate with Carol for running past stop signs and I only start an argument. He says everyone runs through them. The next day he has a small head on collision with a man uninsured. It cost us twenty five dollars. I didn't complain a word — merely said we were lucky it was no worse. He said Lillian had called his attention away to look at something. I feel all the time I ride with him his eyes are off the road ahead too often. I'm no judge and I dont want to be one. He is not well disciplined and it is too late to do anything about it. Let's not worry. Prescott is out of school. I may offer him money to do some real work for me this spring when he gets back to Vermont.

Wont it be great if you can get a book of childrens stories going.[2] You are late in overcoming your selfconsciousness in writing. Its about time you came out in writing with the naturalness you have in talk. You arent as happy in talk when I am present I guess. It is as if I was always present when you wrote. You have me to get over.

Me — I am miserable living round with people all the time. I have always had hours and days to myself alone. I feel on draught from dawn to dark. It can't last. I have no idea how it is going to be stopped though. Not as yet. My entanglement has had critical moments when it looked near openly declared trouble. The future of Europe is easier for me to see into than my own future.

I wrote a preface for Holt's new edition of my Collected. It has a name The Figure A Poem Makes.[3] Its fault is that it is a little or a lot too condensed from my talks.

I dont believe in carrying poems to editors as you carried Mrs Aldrich's. It does neither her nor you nor me any good. Only the bullying power of an Ezra Pound ever thrust poems down a publishers throat. Experience will teach you. You cant use the device of saying to a pupil for top mark: "That is better than an A poem. It is good enough to print."

You'll lose standing with the pupil if you do. It cramps an editors judgement when he is approached the wrong way. I merely tell you.

Affectionately   PAPA

[1] RF and the Theodore Morrisons were guests on the estate of the author (William) Hervey Allen, an early lecturer at Bread Loaf and author, among other works, of *Anthony Adverse* (1933). Other guests included the Iowa poet Paul Engle and his wife Mary. RF remained beyond the Morrisons' departure.

[2] See RF to Lesley Frost Francis, [9 November 1939], n. 1.

[3] A new *Collected Poems* was issued by Holt in mid-February 1939. For the text of "The Figure A Poem Makes," see also *Complete Poems of Robert Frost 1949*, pp. v-viii. Not in *PRF*.

RF to Lesley Frost Francis

DEAR LESLEY: [South Miami, February 1939]

I'm relieved too. I told Kathleen some time ago I hated to see you undertake such a monstrous big job when you might be on the verge of freedom from all money worries and the need to work hard. I wish you could get away from schools entirely. We seem to hang round them unwanted. I mean our family. My mother lacking normal school never earned more than $400 a year to keep her two children on — and herself. Lacking a degree, I had to be satisfied with $300 each [of] my first two years at Pinkerton for part time and then eight hundred and eleven hundred for the next two years respectively for full time. I was on the ragged edge of the profession. The Rev Chas Merriam got busy with George Palmer at Harvard to see if a degree couldnt be made easy for me at the age of thirty six. I saw George Palmer in the matter and he advised me to read Shakespeare. Even my kindest patrons in education were suspicious of me for my irregularity. They dont remember it now, but they were. It's time you broke the family habit. It brings on an old sickness to hear the words the safety-people use in rejecting you. It seems to me it might be a lesson to you not to look for advancement among them by favor of me and your friends. Your appointed way should be more and more clear to you. It will be by knowledge or achievement you will make your mark, you mark my words. Spanish is the plain and simple way perhaps. The more ambitious we wont talk about. There will have to be a buckling down to long hours of work and rework though.

I'll not neglect Mrs Dykstra and I am not aware of neglecting the Clem Smiths. Something was said by her I think at one party at the Joneses about my coming to have dinner with her even if Clem wasnt able to be there. It wasnt followed up. I now go to din[n]er with wives of absent husbands. I never did such a thing in my life before. I couldnt have thought of such a thing.

Arrange it with Auslander[1] as you see fit but hurry and consult Kathleen at 88 Mt Vernon St about the date. She is now arranging dates with Gordon at Kenyon. So hurry. Tell her why it cant be fitted into my Virginia schedule. Tell her your politics demand that I come this year if at all possible.

My work here comes on too slowly and runs into too much expense. Never mind. Nothing matters ever anymore again here or here after.

To hell with the Boyntons and all such. I could have told you so in the first place but refrained for fear of discouraging you. Affectionately PAPA

When I get home I'll simply call the Smiths and say blandly I thought you were going to have me to dinner.

[1] The poet Joseph Auslander.

RF to Lesley Frost Francis

[En route to Boston] Havana Special
DEAR LESLEY: 25 February 1939

Just a note in passing — I can't stop this time. I shall start another season of lectures March 2 and I must have a day or two with Kathleen first. I had a really beneficial visit at Hervey's. Hervey is a great friend, almost of the devotion of Louis [Untermeyer]. He has bottomless wisdom in metaphor and story. I never realized his importance to me before. He and I have reached a point of frankness where we can tell each other exactly what we want of each other. For instance he could say right out to me that for worldly reasons if for no other, he would like me to be good, but that doesn't mean too good. He recognizes that all my thinking must start from the obligations I am under to Kathleen and she under to me for what she has done to bring me back to life. He thinks as I think all can be managed right and seemly.

Also he could be perfectly outspoken about his situation with regard to your visit there. He and Ann both want you. All the little houses at the Glades are going to be full for [a] while however. So that the best way for you would be to come to the San Sebastian Hotel at Coral Gables, have Hervey hire you a small car for your stay (he knows a place of renting) and be in and out with the Allens and Chapins for tennis and things. Paula and Henry Chapin would be your tennis people. He is a poet of a book or two and a gentleman farmer and vinyardist at New Hope Penna[.] They are a few years older than you. Her father was the famous Henry Van Dyke, poet, preacher and professor at Princeton University. They are good company. They took care of me third in succession. The Morrison pair began it. The Paul Engles went on with me. The Chapins finished me up fairly brown — not as brown as some winters in the sun, but browner than some. My advice would be for you to go there on this arrangement. I will pay all your bills for the hotel and car. (Hire the car, Dont waste time driving down.) Get train reservations very early so as to get onto the best train. I am on only the second best. I know none of them will neglect you. They are really full at the Glades except for one part of one house, that must be kept for Herveys brother who may be out of the hospital soon if he lives. I must tell you sometime the story of all Hervey's troubles. But — if you aren't sure you are attracted to the Gables and San Sebastian and would prefer the Casa Marina (a hotel and a fine one) at Key West say so and I guess that can be managed. The proprietor Peter Schutt is a friend of mine and would be good to you and then there are the Hemming-ways who seem very friendly. Mrs Hemingway[1] played tennis with us this year when we were down there. I liked her.

Did I tell you I went to Cuba for a week with Paul and Mary Engle. We went down to Camaguey saw several cities besides Havana and plenty of sugar cane and royal palms. The land is rich; the people are miserably poor. Everywhere beggars and beggar-vendors. We saw one great beach to beat the world and on it a car with a Vermont license which on inquiry proved to belong to friends of yours the heads of the art department at Bennington College — Bee's friends — I forget their name. It was one of the only two American cars we saw outside of Havana. We had a pleasant more than pleasant meal with them by the most transparent ocean water I have ever looked into. Paul and Mary had two long swims in it. I am not much on foreign parts. I favor that beach for you to resort to someday though. To me the best of the excursion was the flight both ways in the big Pan American plane and especially the swoop and mighty splash into the bays on arrival.

We have just passed the rebel city of Charleston South Carolina — the Boston of the South. Both cities live on their past. One however licked the other.

Affectionately   PAPA

The unsteady hand is railroad[.]

I ought to add that Carol Lillian Prescott and Robin seem better than in the years when we were too much with them for our good. Carol came down perverse and surly, but he improved on being let alone. Or so I imagine. I have played cards with them six or eight nights and had a couple of long rides with them. They have been fishing on their own considerably. They are not lucky so far in life. They catch no fish. The mongrel dog has just brought forth eight more, much more, mongrel pups, for them to drown. Nobody else's experience profits them the least. I told them they couldnt take care of a bitch. I couldn't. You could see a little of them — not too much.

You had better write to Mrs Allen and considerately say your idea and mine was you should stay at the San Sebastian and have Hervey find you a car to hire — that is if you decide on visiting them. They'll give you a good time.

1 Pauline Pffeiffer, Hemingway's second wife.

RF to Lesley Frost Francis

DEAR LESLEY: [Boston, 1 March 1939]

I am home at 88 Mt Vernon Street. Somehow mixed with my own recent mail I found this letter of Elinor's. I suppose you must have given it to me when I was away from my desks and files and I must have put it into one of my traveling bags with the confusion of letters and manuscript I always carry around. It belongs to your early days at Wellesley [in 1917]. My, my, what sorrow runs through all she wrote to you children. No wonder something of it overcasts my poetry if read aright. No matter how humorous I am[,] I am sad. I am a jester about sorrow. She colored my thinking from the first just as at the last she troubled my politics. It was no loss but a gain of course. She was not as original as I in thought but she dominated my art with the power of her character and nature. I wish I hadnt this woeful suspicion that toward the end she came to resent some thing in the life I had given her. [Four lines deleted.] It seems to me now that she was cumulatively laying up against me the unsuccess of the children I had given her. She was a person of the soundest realistic judgement. But here I think she was radically wrong for once. She failed to see she wasn't giving you the time she patiently gave me. You are coming out all right in your way. Irma will come out all right too. (I have just had a letter from Larson to tell me how very well [Irma's husband] John is doing in his office. That gratuitously from a hard man!) A way will be found to put Carol on his feet. You'll see.

But today I had a shock that was sympathetic with the way Elinor would have taken what I heard on the telephone when I called up John at Hanover. While I was lost in my travels so I couldnt be reached anyway Irma was discovered to be suffering with a large tumor and operated on at the Hanover hospital. That was last Friday. Everything went off all right and she should be at home tomorrow (Thursday March 2) with a prospect of better health than she has had. I dont suppose you realized there had been anything very wrong with her. I knew she was rather worse than she used to be. Be sure to write her a good encouraging letter. She'd like to know I told you how Larson had been bragging about John. That is I guess she would. It cant be that what a woman lays up against a man is his success out where she can only imperfectly share it. Mind you I dont care if she does. I am prepared for any sadness in the structure of the universe. Go out and get all your own success. But do it cooly and deliberately without importunate haste. Keep well, look well. A woman has to look well. You have the basic good looks to build on. In one way and another I keep hearing of you as having made your place in Washington.

I begin a series of five lectures in your old birth town[1] tomorrow night. My subject will be "the success of a poem." My second subject will be Four Poets and a Half — meaning Emerson Longfellow Bryant Poe and Sill.[2]

For me a great deal of letter lately. What?

Affectionately   PAPA

It occurs to me to add: the more I think of it the surer I am your trouble with Gordon was like that of my new publisher Bill Sloane with John Farrar,[3] the clash of two minds designed to meet more distantly as equals. John Farrar now recognizes that he can brook no equal in his office. Hervey was talking about Bill Sloane's plain case.

[1] Lawrence, Massachusetts. See EF to Lesley Frost, [September 1920], p. 99, n. 2.

[2] Five of RF's favorite poets. See Arnold Grade, "A Chronicle of Robert Frost's Early Reading," *Bulletin of the New York Public Library*, vol. 72, no. 9 (November 1968): 611-628.

[3] William Sloane joined Henry Holt and Company early in 1939 after a brief tenure in the firm of Farrar and Rinehart. See also EF to Lesley Frost, 20 September [1928], n. 4.

RF to Lesley Lee Francis

DEAR LEE: [Ripton, Vermont, summer 1939]

I get the Mexican cards from you and Elinor in Bucksport Maine. I suppose I am to infer from that you are hearing from Lesley. She wrote me one long letter from New York just as she was leaving, but I haven't heard from her since. The picture post cards seem beautifully peaceful. I guess she hasnt run into any revolution down there. I was afraid when she set out that Mexico might not be a very safe country to venture into just now. You two children must feel home sick a little for Cuernavaca if thats the way you spell it. You were partly brought up there. And so were you partly brought up in Cambridge. No doubt Mexico City Cuernavaca (if thats the way you spell it) and the ranch in Limon will always have an attraction for you to draw you back. Sometime you'll go back.[1] Maybe more than once. You'll learn Spanish and translate some Mexican poetry into our language. No you wont bother to translate it. You will learn it by heart in Spanish to say to yourself along with poetry in American when you are alone and have no books with you to read. I knew someone who had poetry enough to last him reciting it all the way across the Atlantic Ocean. He liked to read when he had books, but he could get along without them. I wonder what you have to read in camp and if you have any time for reading. What *do* you do with the days? I have been hoeing in the vegetable garden, laying out a small baseball field and talking to various and sundried people.[2] Sunday I expect Carol Lillian and Prescott to come and get me for a quick visit at South Shaftsbury. I haven't climbed a single mountain yet this summer, We may get on top of [Mt.] Mansfield before fall. I wish I could see you. Aren't we scattered all over North America. I dont know whether you have any use for money where you are. If you haven't, you can save the dollar I enclose[.]

Affectionately — YOUR GRANDFATHER

[1] See EF to Lesley Lee Francis, [summer 1937], n. 1.

[2] This was RF's first summer on the newly purchased Homer Noble Farm, a short downhill walk or drive from Middlebury College's Bread Loaf campus. The understanding was that the Morrison family would occupy the farmhouse and RF would live and work in a cabin, later enlarged, overlooking the north pasture.

RF to Lesley Lee Francis

DEAR LEE   [Ripton, 17 July 1939]

It does my heart good to hear from your mother what

a fine camp she left you in. It looks as if you would have plenty to do till you see her again, painting in oils and water colors, working in clay metal and leather sailing ships and paddling canoes and playing with boys girls and councillors. You won't get lonely. Me I live alone in a little house by a roaring mountain torrent. Yesterday I went off three or four miles to eat my lunch alone in a mountain pasture. I like to be alone probably better than you do. I'm older. Dont think of me as alone all of the time. One or two or three nice people stay with me part of the time.

What a scattered family we are at the moment, you and Elinor in Alamoosooc Island Camp, Bucksport Maine your mother on a lump of coral called Bermuda in the middle or the Atlantic Ocean, Prescott and Jack building a boat I understand at Concord Corners in northern Vermont with John and Irma (your Aunt and Uncle as a matter of fact), Robin two or three thousand miles out west in Montana the third largest state in the Union, Carol and Lillian (your Uncle and Aunt respectively) diversifiedly farming in southern Vermont at South Shaftsbury to be exact and your Grandfather here in Ripton Vermont (in case you need his address to write him a letter in prose or verse.) Of course you must have guessed before this that the one writing you this letter is this same

GRANDFATHER.

RF to William Prescott Frost

DEAR PRESCOTT: Boston [1 November 1939]

I have some brand new paper so I think I will write on it to tell you I didnt catch the cold you had or didnt have. I got back to my home on Beacon Hill the next noon after I left you and the rest of the family, the dog and its kitten so abruptly. On the way I came on the enclosed picture of the almost total eclipse of the moon showing that the shape of the light portion is very different from that of a crescent.[1] I dont know what I was thinking of when I said they were the same. The crescent is the shape of the daylight coming over the edge of the moon: ☽ It grows till the inside line is straight across the middle: ◖ Next it gets what is called Gibbous. The inside line bulges: ◑ The order is crescent moon, half moon, gibbous moon and full moon. Thats the way light dawns and spreads over a ball. All sorts of things can happen in the eclipse of the moon depending on how big the shadow of the earth is at the moons distance from us (which varies because the moons path like all other sky paths isnt circular but eliptical) and depending on how the shadow cuts across the moon. ☾ ⊙ ⊙ Etc. Etc. There would never be any straight line across the middle of the moon. It would always be a curved line from the first bight of the shadow. Some people still believe the world is flat. The earth's shadow on the moon, since however the earth is turned it shows a curve, is the best proof we are a ball. Did you hear me say I saw a sect of people in Florida who believe the world is a hollow ball and we are inside of it with all our sea and land and the sky in another sphere contained in ours. In their church there was a nice mechanical model of the universe inside the world like a stone in a fruit. The shell world was split on hinges to open up and show the internal continents on the concave surface and the sun moon and stars on the inner ball. It was supposed to teach them in their lives to look inward for the great and universal things — into the mind and into the soul. Hervey Allen said he was going to try to buy the model as a curiosity. Thats not a very respectful way to treat other peoples religion. Queer religion — and I guess pretty well petered out. The minister looked sad and deserted. He seemed not to have many followers around. Science had about done for such a childish religion.

Write me some trapping letters if anything happens. Hunting too. I saw a deer in the market today.

Affectionately   GRANDPA

1 Once again in these letters RF shares a lifelong interest — this time in astronomy.

RF to Lesley Frost Francis

DEAR LESLEY: [Boston, 9 November 1939]

You would do a graceful favor where it would be appreciated if you would send a first of your Not Really[1] inscribed to John and Virginia Adams of Springfield Ohio. Another might well go to the lady who took Elinor and Lee off your hands while you were round making friends out there. I heard nothing but you and the children talked about in my short stay in Springfield. I liked the Adamses better than I had hoped. They liked you and the children too much for you to act as if you had forgotten them. You might find time to write them one of your famous letters. I thought I would tell you and not leave it to some small bird.

I did fourteen lectures and travelled two thousand miles in fifteen days last month. Last night I was with another of your friends Marion Dodd. She publicly professes the greatest affection and admiration for you. I believe she has come to mean it with the mellowing years. So you may as well accept it as one more support where support wasn't looked for. She is still a powerful bookseller. She had me a large audience in some hall and put me through a lot of autographing afterward at the store. I really shouldnt have been that near Amherst. But she would have me and I didn't like to seem a victim of Amherst distaste — I mean of my own distaste for Amherst. I saw Green there. He said you visited the Jones Library in the summer and carried off books. Make me a list of what you took will you? — so

I wont be wondering what became of this and that in the future. Green took it on himself to decide what books I ought to have sent me in Boston.[2]

I am going to say one thing more on a particularly serious subject and then keep still forever. You were entirely wrong in your understanding of that poem of last summer and I was completely right. The aversion expressed made me sure of the separation implied. My instinct had been right from the beginning. Lets leave it at that whatever the outcome.

Pray for me if you feel you must but let it be only on general principles as you would for any mortal in the toils of life.   R.

[1] *Not Really* — the first of Lesley's three children's books to date — was published in 1939.

[2] Charles R. Green, librarian of the town of Amherst's Jones Library, provided temporary storage for RF's books when the poet sold his Sunset Avenue home. After some of these books were shipped to 88 Mt. Vernon Street, Boston, the 400 remaining titles were card catalogued by Green for RF's protection. The packet of cards, long thought to be lost or destroyed, was discovered by the editor and one of the Library's curators, Winifred Sayer, on 6 February 1967. The top card bore the following notation: "Books in J.L. attic on Jan. 20, 1939. R.F.'s poetry books, — Benet, Snow, Untermeyer et al and his own and most of his modern books were sent to him in Boston in September 1938..."

RF to Carol and Lillian LaBatt Frost

DEAR CAROL AND LILLIAN: [Boston, November 1939]

I had a good look at Lesley and the kids in Washington and she tells me she wants to spend Christmas with you at South Shaftsbury. That will be fine — having the four kids together. Now if Willard would only turn up and John and Irma bring Jack over from Hanover you would have a real house party. I suppose you could all sardine in somewhere. You could bring beds over from my house if necessary and make the whole place a dormitory.

Dont be too disappointed if I decide not to join in. It is

so much colder up there in the mountains than here by the ocean. I am making an experiment I am anxious not to make to[o] hard on my health. I dont want to be too long in the south this year or any more forever. I know I have to have a little extra sunlight: but if I manage carefully I hope to get along with a very little extra. The managing is the point. I rest from lecturing from now on (I did my last till spring at the New School in New York Tuesday the 13th) and I keep out of crowded places.

My idea would be for you four to set out for Florida a few days ahead of me say about January 5th and wait for me at the Thomas Hotel till I arrive. Then after a few days with friends and a lecture at the University we could go on to visit Hervey Allen for a week or two or three at Coconut Grove. (He wants us) We could run down to Key West for a look over the new highway. Then I want to look over the Homestead region again for a possible cheap refuge from the cold in future.[1] You may decide not to make the annual break with your farming in Vermont if you have your house enlarged and a better heating plant put in. Then again you may think you will enjoy life more going away every winter. There's a lot to consider, and it should be considered, pretty soon now. We'll talk it all over in Florida. The question is how you will be best off when you haven't me any longer to depend on. I speak like a life-insurance man don't I?

Well go in and give the children as gay a Christmas as you know how. The enclosed check is for that pleasure and for nothing else.   Affectionately   PAPA

[1] RF's Florida plans were delayed by the need for an hemorrhoidectomy in January. After leaving the hospital, he recuperated in Florida and arranged to purchase a small acreage near Hervey Allen in Coconut Grove. Parenthetically, it should be noted that Coconut Grove and South Miami are two small, contiguous Dade County communities southeast of the city of Miami. The political boundary fell between Allen's estate and RF's property.

RF to William Prescott Frost

[Special Delivery]

DEAR PRESCOTT   Boston, 12 October 1940

Disaster brought out the heroic in you.[1] You now know you have the courage and nerve for anything you may want or need to be, engineer, inventor or soldier. You would have had plenty of excuse if you had gone to pieces and run out of that house crying for help. From what Lesley reported to me of her talk with Lillian in Pittsfield Friday I judge you were in actual danger there alone with your unhappy father — unhappy to the point of madness.[2] You kept your head and worked your faculties as coolly as a clock on a shelf. You've been tried more than most people are in a whole lifetime. Having said so much, I shan't bring up the subject again (for a long time anyway) either of your bravery or the terrible occasion for it. Let's think forward — I don't mean in big terms all at once, but just taking the days as they come along with a more natural and comfortable interest than I fear you have been permitted for some years past. You are fortunate in the friendship of such splendid people as the Hollidays. I took a great liking to them. They are a great new beginning for you. The spell you and Lillian have been under is broken. You and she can think with some sanity now. So can I with you.

Lillian says Carol thought nobody loved him. Pitiful! His mind was one cloud of suspiciousness. And we cared so much for him that his cloud was our cloud. We tried to enter into his affairs and sympathise with him. We spent hours, you and Lillian of course more hours than I. We could do him no good. Well he has taken his cloud away with him. His difficulty was too hard for us to understand. We never gave it up. He ended it for us. We shall have difficulties of our own ahead, but they will be simple and straightforward I believe. You and I and your mother have the healthy clearness of ordinary plain people. Lesley is that way too. So also is the Kathleen who has set me on my way onward again. We are the tough kind.

You write me and tell me how your mother is and what she's talking about. When she can spare you, come down and we'll see what we can do for amusement. Maybe Kathleen can arrange with Bunty Sage's father for our visiting some laboratories at Technology.

Affectionately   GRANDPA

[1] Letters written to Carol and those commenting on his restless ambitions reflect RF's concern for his son over many years. On or about 1 October 1940, Frost visited with Carol and devoted a few days to what he hoped would be a constructive and therapeutic conversation. A week later, on 9 October, Carol committed suicide. Only his son was on the farm; Lillian was in Pittsfield, Massachusetts, recovering from serious surgery.

[2] "My memory is clear... I was nearly sixteen... there was never any violence or threat of physical harm to be inflicted on anyone except by my father on himself." William Prescott Frost to editor, letter dated 5 February 1971.

RF to Lillian LaBatt Frost

DEAR LILLIAN   Boston, 12 October 1940

You're going to make it easy for me from now on by telling me always right straight out what you think best for yourself and Prescott and then if it is within my means and ability I will do it. I shan't have to guess so miserably any more. That is the great gain for me from our tragedy. I'll make suggestions if you want me to and I won't if you dont want me to. I suspect you will be making plans as you lie there in bed. But don't think you have to hurry. The immediate future is taken care of. You are to stay where you are till you are strong and then you are to live with Prescott at the [John] Hollidays[1] for awhile.

I mustnt blame you for not making me realize the actual danger you and Prescott have been living in. You couldnt tell me. You didn't know yourself any too clearly. You were of course kept in confusion of mind by Carol's confused suffering. We forgive the poor boy. I'm sure he was fond of both of you. His desperation was due to his not being able to accomplish anything for you. He couldnt be sensible about his ambition for you. He overworked and he thought too terribly hard. I see now that his overstrained reasoning tended toward his destroying you all together as included in his failure. Still he said things to me when I was up there a week ago that indicated a wish (I see now) to save you and Prescott from his own doom. You know better than I what he thought about. None of us will ever understand him entirely. There is no use in going over and over it. Two things are sure: he was driven distracted by life and he was perfectly brave. I wish he could have been a soldier and died fighting Germany.

I dont suppose you will be sitting up to write very soon. Have Prescott tell me how you are — and have him tell Lesley too. Be sure to keep us informed. I shall have to go to Iowa for a few lectures toward the end of the month. We ought to know a lot more about you by then. I feel absolutely satisfied with Prescott's home. You have real friends in the Hollidays. I'll write you a sheet of my news now and then and Kathleen says she will write too. Let us know when you are able to read books and magazines.

Affectionately   FATHER.

I'll put the money in the Bennington First National Bank for you to draw on.

¹ Friends in South Shaftsbury.

RF to Lillian LaBatt Frost

DEAR LILLIAN: [Boston, October 1940]

It's fine to hear that you are getting well and will soon be back in South Shaftsbury with Prescott. I enclose a check for you to endorse to the Hospital. Send me any other bills there are to pay in Pittsfield.

Let me caution you not to write anything to Irma. You know how she is — only a little less strange in the mind than Carol was. You will realize more and more that Carol's misunderstanding of life had been growing rapidly worse in the last year. I spent most of Saturday night when I was up there trying to clear his conscience of guilt and his mind of worry. I thought I had done him some good. We had a pleasant ride down to see you and we had a natural good dinner together at the Hotel. But he spoiled my confidence in the end by saying that I had got the better of him in argument. He wasnt satisfied. It had got so nothing satisfied him. What showed he wasnt right in the mind was his returning again and again to your not being able to have any more children. I tried to make him laugh at his own foolishness there. That wasnt all. He said many things that I didnt know what to make of. He had many fine qualities. He was devoted to work, he was fond of little children and animals he was idealistic truthful and brave. And he thought everything of you and his mother. But his mind had in it a strange twist from childhood that no wrench we could give it could seem to straighten out. You helped him of course more than any of us. I failed with him. Do my best with money or advice it was always the wrong thing. I dont mean I think he resented my kindness. I wanted more than anything to sooth his anxiety, and he wouldnt be persuaded. Apparently he talked all his last night with Prescott the same way he talked all his last night with me. Prescott will probably tell you about it. But probably you know what it was already. A mixture of unreasonable guilt and anxiety. He couldnt seem to hold in mind anything comforting said to him. I tried to make him look forward to Florida. Florida was all right but he said he didnt see where the money was coming from to get back from there. I was in a terrible state of wondering if it wasnt my duty to have him examined by a mental doctor. But where might that have landed him? Better this way than a life in an institution. I am not going to keep on with this kind of talk.

Outsiders needn't hear a word of it. He is entitled to have those who loved him think only the best of him forever now. — Affectionately FATHER

RF to Lillian LaBatt Frost

DEAR LILLIAN: Boston, 18 October 1940

I hope to hear soon from Mrs Holliday or Prescott or Lesley or the Doctor that you are coming on well. It occurs to me that since there is no will, all your property including your money in the banks (unless that was on joint account) will be tied up till the estate is settled. So you had better send some money to the Benningon bank in your name to write your checks on. I enclose two hundred for October and November. There's a lot of arranging to talk over but that will be easy now (too sadly easy) and it can wait till you are out of the woods and the hospital. Isn't it one of the best things ever that Prescott and you have such friends as the Hollidays.

It's getting cold: we'll have to be thinking of Florida soon. I shall be in Iowa for several days from October 26th on and be seeing Paul and Mary Engle. They are terribly terribly sorry. Many people cared for Carol much more than he seemed to want them to care. Such a misunderstanding a whole life can be !

Affectionately FATHER

RF to William Prescott Frost

DEAR PRESCOTT: Boston, 10 December [1940]

I havent forgotten how we won our membership in the Hobby Club. Me, I have not a hobby. That is to say I have no side interest for rest or relaxation. I doubt if you have any. Everything is straight ahead in front of us as much play as it is work and as much work as it is play. All I encounter turns into thinking. All you encounter turns into thinking of another kind — scientific. I must send you along the two copies of the Technological Review Mr Sage had sent to me.

Here's twenty five dollars to buy Christmas things for yourself and others.

Affectionately GRANDFATHER

RF to Marjorie Robin Fraser

DEAR ROBIN: Boston, 17 December 1940

It's a long time since I saw you last. You've probably grown so I wouldnt know you if I met you on the streets of Boston or even Billings. I remember how you used to look. You looked like a good little girl who deserved a letter now and then and who would probably soon be able to write letters herself. You must try to live up to the fact that you come of literary people on both sides of your family. I write and your mother wrote and you ought to have seen the good letter I just now had from Willard. Tell him from me if you see him how glad I was to hear of the pleasant talk he had with my friend the Vice President of the United States of America [John Nance Garner]. I had a pictorial history of the great state of Montana (third largest state in the Union) from him for Christmas. I want you to have something from me for Christmas. But I am not allowed to go out into the big Christmas shopping crowd for fear I will catch a flu bug and then not find any present very interesting or useful. I cant buy you a hat because I dont know what size your feet are. I cant buy you glasses or a handkerchief because I dont know how long your nose has grown. I can't buy you any funny toy because I don't know how much of a joke it takes to make you laugh. So I'm stuck unless you'll take the enclosed check and buy for yourself just what will do you the most good for the shortest time. I dont ask that it shall last more than till New Years. Some of the very best things in the world aren't very lasting. You may have to wait till you grow up before you agree with me. Please deal with Mr. Albin in person at his store and give him my regards. And remember me to Willard if you see him and to your grandparents and all the family. Merry Christmas[.]

Affectionately   YOUR ALTERNATE GRANDFATHER

RF to Lillian LaBatt Frost

DEAR LILLIAN: Boston, 13 January 1941

I have been delayed a little by shortage, but I knew you would be all right while you waited. Here is my check for one hundred and twenty five dollars.

I'm off for Florida day after tomorrow — that is on Wednesday January 15 at 8.20 AM and expect to arrive in Miami Thursday at 3.30 PM. My address will be Coconut Grove for the next few weeks. I shall stay in the village while directing the building of the Hodgson houses.[1] I shall have very little heart in this under the circumstances. Five acres is much too much for us now.

I shall have to come all the way north again for the one night of the Poetry Society Dinner in New York February 1st when I am to get some sort of medal and speak.[2]

I heard Prescott had a good time at Stony Water! and I heard that you were looking well.

Remember me to Prescott and the Holidays and try to make Prescott write.   Affectionately   FATHER

[1] Having purchased the land in South Miami, RF planned to proceed with the erection of two small prefabricated cottages produced by Hodgson Homes, Dover, Massachusetts. The retreat came to be known as "Pencil Pines."

[2] RF was awarded the Society's Gold Medal 31 January 1941.

RF to Lesley Frost Francis

DEAR LESLEY: [Miami, 12 February 1941]

Here it all is but the short stories. I cant seem to find that black book of them high or low — so far. I had a hard enough time of it finding your preface. I have so many boxes I dont know what to do. And they are all mixed up with your boxes. I put things away on some sort of principle but it isnt long before the principle goes out of my head. I hope I was always that way. I'd hate to think I was getting worse in the memory of ideas: for if I am I dont know how I am going to write the books ahead of me which will be nothing but a more or less orderly arrangement of things already said and thought.

The prospect at Washington[1] seems very good and would be perfect but for that one little cloud on your scholastic record the lack of a degree that has yet I suppose to be noticed. Maybe if you dont make *too* much of it by blush or stammer they wont. Of course they can't expect you to put the children away. You don't mean that. If they are off your hands during school hours and their board is paid for at the King Smith Studio School probably everything will be all right. It will be great.

In my search for my stories I found two or three by you in an old note book of our English days.[2] Do you remember doing one you called a House Cleaning about an old woman (very thoroughly described — she had a head that in

excitement bobbed like a Phoebe's tail) who tumbled
everything out of her house in fear of an oncoming forest fire.
Another about a beetle in the grass was called A Reflection.
Then there was the short piece I have always remembered
about the swallow's looking like a bow that flew away with
the arrow. There was a lot about Marjorie in it. The writing
was so extraordinarily straight forward and simply effective.
There wasnt an exclamation point or exclamatory adjective
in the book. I'll send it to you if you say. It has other reasons
for being preserved: a list of French words Elinor was
cramming into her mind at the time I suppose with a view
to going to France to live when we should get round to it
and an itemized account (apparently in your hand) of some
chickens we hatched and started to raise and what Old Joe
cost us in the garden and what we got out of the garden. I
wish there were more of it. Thats the way I am now —
mostly retrospective. Pretty much everything is behind me
— except a little promotion so to speak. Any prose I write
will be for the purpose of widening the circle of my poetry
and increasing our chances of being remembered. Beyond
that I dont care. Every thought has carried me nearer the
answer to the conundrum: what reason could Stanley have
given the trustees for letting me go that would satisfy them
and yet not seem inconsistent with my remaining friends
with Amherst College. I got the last clue from Otto [Man-
they-Zorn] the day Carol and I went for the last belongings.
He said I had never had technical standing as a full professor.
I could have been dropped at any time and I never had the
least claim to a pension. Then I was completely deceived —
by some inadvertancy, I suppose. George Olds in declining
health failed to fix me on the institution as he promised.
I can do the rest myself. I was kept on from year to year out
of some rich mans pocket. And the rich man was Stanley
King himself. He could obtain merit with the trustees by

protesting himself unable to tell me that. Hence all the mystery. I feel all the more wronged — though relieved.[3]

Affectionately   PAPA

[1] After three years as director and teacher at Washington's King-Smith Studio School, Lesley established her own studio school at 2003 Kalorama Road. It is apparent, however, that initially she maintained some ties with King-Smith.

[2] Three of the Frost children's notebooks survive in Lesley's care. The first, written in 1912-1913, contains prose, poetry, and French vocabulary in Lesley's hand. The second, dated 1913, is "An Important Year By Four Children Dedicated To Papa & Mamma." Chiefly prose, the notebook also contains maps, diagrams, and assorted lists giving specifics of the family's life in Derry and Plymouth, N. H., and in England. The third, "On the road to Fleuraclea," is an assortment of her writings which Lesley presented to her father on Christmas morning 1913. The stories to which RF refers are not in these notebooks.

[3] As noted earlier, RF resigned from Amherst College following EF's death in 1938. In reflecting upon his relationship with the college, he fancied that there had been a plot of considerable proportions to remove him from his long tenure there. Although he would return to Amherst in 1949 on a life appointment as lecturer, RF, the college, and members of the Frost family were to suffer disappointments and misunderstandings which have continued to this date.

RF to William Prescott Frost

DEAR PRESCOTT: [Cambridge,[1] 29 September 1941]

Enclosed find check of twenty five dollars toward the rest of what I still owe you. You know so many things probably it is unnecessary to tell you you will have to endorse it.

Knowledge is of two kinds, one is acquired from other people and one you think up yourself. The first you can go about getting wholesale, the second you have to venture into very cautiously. It is of course possible to go wrong in the first. Many are doing so at the present moment in their easy acceptance of what the gover[n]ments are ladling out to them for war purposes. But you can be made the biggest fool of by your own originality. It is the only knowledge that can lift you into the higher ranks; you have got to have some of it to be anybody at all in law science art or business. But it is the more dangerous and as I say must be stepped out into or onto as onto the thin ice of early winter. A safe way with ideas you consider your own is to write them down privately some where and leave them for a year and then try them to see how good they seem. Some of them will seem less original than they did when new, and some of them will seem plumb foolish and some will have lost all meaning: you wont see what you could have meant anymore than as if you couldn't read your own hand writing. Suppose I write down now I would be willing to regard Russia as just one more Democracy along with the United States and England if I can be shown that Stalin hasnt been elected to his office of head of the Russian government any oftener than Roosevelt has been to our Presidency. That seems like a good joke to me now[.] The question is will it seem like it a year from now. It is the same in every department, medicine mechanics or what you will. The President Milliken we met in Passadena had the idea that cosmic rays were thrown off by God kicking his heels in idleness outside of space. The idea doesnt hold up — thats all the trouble with it. Nils Boar had the idea that the particles within the atom were arranged and behaved like a minute solar system. The idea of an exploding universe is attractive. The redness of all the more distant suns isnt the proof of it it was judged to be three or four years ago. You have to begin with a tiny idea now and then when young and see how you come out with thinking. You have to get going and find yourself as a thinker by trial and error. That is if you dont want to be a mere servant of other minds and live obediently to their dictation.[2]

The word knowledge started me off on all this. Otherwise I might have remarked the Dodgers won it.

Ill send along the Technology Reviews when I have got my capacity out of them.

My best to all four of you up the beautiful staircase in Bennington[.]   Affectionately   GRANDFATHER.

Cash the check right away.

1 In the spring of 1941, RF moved from his Boston apartment to a home he had purchased at 35 Brewster Street in Cambridge.

2 This letter further reflects RF's active interest in scientific matters and in the relationship between science and religion. Robert A. Millikan studied the origin and intensity of cosmic rays in the 1920s and early 1930s by using high-altitude balloon probes. His earlier work with electrons prompted RF's "A Wish to Comply," *PRF*, pp. 391-392. The Danish physicist Niels Bohr was a pioneer in postulating the structure of the atom.

RF to Lesley Frost Francis

DEAR LESLEY   [Cambridge, 17 November 1941]

This has to be short. I am off for Ripton. Doesnt it seem unreal, my apparition among the monuments of Washington? We'll remember it. Plainly I was most justly taken sick at the thought of that mismanaged banquet. Was Archie[1] imitating as usual? Or did he have the same idea independently?

Here is fifty dollars for either the past trip or the one to come as you've a mind to regard it.

Affectionately   PAPA

1 The reference is apparently to Archibald MacLeish, Librarian of Congress, who had recently received two honors: he was named director of the newly established U.S. Office of Facts and Figures, and he was awarded *Poetry's* Levinson Prize.

RF to Lesley Frost Francis

DEAR LESLEY   Coconut Grove, Florida [February 1942]

We've brought the two small houses[1] on a little way further, we've had three and five weeks in them and now leave them to our neighborly neighbors the Hjorts to keep an eye on till we come back next year. I wish you could use them for a few months either to write a novel in or get the girls away from the scarlet fever Lillian has to worry about for a change. The three-room house is already almost too pretty to abandon. The two room house exactly twenty five feet across a grassy and flowery court from it is comfortable and convenient. The three-room is to have an open fireplace soon. The two room has a small woodstove against the blue northern. The stores are a mile and a quarter off at South Miami. We walk or bicycle to them. We got along without a car this year for practice in economy.

Wednesday the twenty-fifth we set off northward on the same train, but part company at Jacksonville. Kathleen to go on to Cambridge, but I to Auburn Alabama for a lecture at the University of Alabama on February 26. On Monday March 2 I lecture at Gainesville for Clifford Lyons[2] and on Tuesday March 3 at Stetson University in Deland. I ought to come back to see to the building of the fire place for a day or two. I figure to be free to set out for Washington by Friday or Saturday the sixth or seventh and would reach you the afternoon of Saturday or Sunday. Whatever you have in store for me in Washington and at St Johns College must come right in there. I must be back in Cambridge by the eleventh at latest to start wrestling with my income tax. I *could* get to Washington on Saturday if you had something for me Saturday night. I leave the end here somewhat elastic for you. Wire or write me in care of Clifford Lyons. The last mail I pick up here will be on Tuesday February 24. Is that all clear?

You would like the Hjorts. He is a Professor of physics at the University. His children are two daughters of twelve and fourteen, the older the leading student in her class at her high school. They farm their ten acre piece. They have all sorts of fruit and ducks hens and turtles. No dog. But the Allens have two dogs left (now completely recovered from the mange) and as you know they are settling down just round the corner from us to make Florida their voting place and bring their children up in the public school five minutes up the road.

I have seen more than usual of Hervey [Allen] and listened to about a fifth of his big new novel.[3] It sounds all right. All about Indians and Fort Pitt in the seventeen fifties. He is a case study in his reduced circumstances. He is all tightened up with anxieties, real or imaginary I cant guess which. If it is as bad as he thinks it is, he is a tragedy of the income tax. He seems to spend part of his time every year going over his profits and losses with the income tax collectors. Thats really all thats been the matter with both Anne and Hervey — finding themselves poor when they and everybody else thought they were rich. They have come a swift fall from butlers chauffers and the Surf Club clear down to the possibility of having their proudest possession Bonfield[4] taken to satisfy the commissioner of internal revenue. They may rent Bonfield if they dont have to have it sold. I take Herveys side against a system that puts such a heavy penalty on enterprise and creation.

Well, you say when and what.

Affectionately   PAPA

Davis Road
Route 2
Coconut Grove
Florida

Correct address for here but write or wire to me in care of Clifford Lyons University of Florida Gainesville Florida

---

1 See RF to Lillian LaBatt Frost, 13 January 1941, n. 1.

2 Clifford B. Lyons was an instructor in English at the University of Florida who had thoughtfully assisted the Frost family at the time of EF's death.

3 *The Forest and the Fort*, published in 1943.

4 Bonfield Manor, the Allens' winter home in Oxford, Maryland.

RF to Lesley Frost Francis

DEAR LESLEY: [South Miami] 6 March [1942]

My telegram of yesterday meant I was still to[o] hoarse and voiceless to risk undertaking anything for Saturday night. If I do the one in Richmond Tuesday it will be as an experiment to see how I stand the strain. Florida has been no special good to me this year. I have had two of its summer-like colds. My suggestion would be that you find out from Kathleen [Morrison] right off now when I am to be in New York for the Junior League and try to get St Johns to have me not further than two days away from their date either before or after.

Great luck the scarlet fever didn't come off.

I have nothing but sorrow for Irma — and John too — yes and Jack and Harold. But for some reason they seem not to want my sympathy. At least they give me no chance to show it. No one writes to me to tell me anything. I send Jack five dollars a month. You'd think or rather I'd think they might have him sit down and practice writing on me if only to the extent of a few words of thanks. I shall send them a present to help out in this emergency. I see John sports a good looking letterhead. I trust it means he is doing business.

You have good friends in Gainesville. I could tell by the way they spoke of you there this week.

You mustnt be too hard on the British in their day of adversity. I hate to hear them starting to free India under fire. If one were fanciful he might venture the figure that it sounds like the Empires death bed repentance. Neither do I quite like their fawning on us at such a time. Still it ill becomes a Frost not to sympathise with a nation that has done so much for our family. Possibly you calculate it has not been all good — good only for me and not for the rest of the family. I have no answer for that. Any way I am on their side. But what would Rudyard Kipling say — Had he lived to see this day — of having his poems edited by worlds-end-whimper T.S. Elliot — to rouse the spirit of the British to the Natzi level to meet the Natzi-greatness?

There are sarcastic things I could say to our own campaign. For instance: the New Deal has won one more victory than was to be expected of them in the field of internal politics (over the hearts of the proletariat); now lets see them win a victory or so in the field of external politics over real men. Churchill wont last much longer unless his affairs take a turn for the better: and if he goes it will be too bad for the Groton boys who love the mother country like a mother.   Affectionately   PAPA

RF to Lillian LaBatt Frost

DEAR LILLIAN   Ripton, 22 September 1942

Im glad the sonotone works and gladder still if Prescott is getting on well with his school work. I dont know how you feel, but I have been wondering whether Prescott should try to get into a military school for his last year or should be left to his pleasant associations in the Bennington High till the draft calls him to soldiering. It might not be too late to get him changed. You have probably thought it all over. The advantage of a year in a military school might not be very great. I dont know. You might talk it over with the Hollidays. Of course what they are able to do for Jack will probably save him from war altogether. Don't say I said so. I could wish Prescott could have got an appointment to West Point. But it is not for me to wish my own out of heroic danger.[1] You know best how his spirit is tuning up.

I have clean forgotten whether I have sent you this months check. Anyway here is a check. You can tell me which it is for September or October. I must try to have a regular date. I may have to ask you to keep down to one hundred — a hundred and ten till you get your earphone paid for. Affectionately FATHER

1 See RF to Lesley Frost, 20 May 1919, n. 7.

RF to Lesley Frost Francis

DEAR LESLEY: Cambridge, 8 October 1942

Home again at 35 Brewster. I will send you another book for the Wallaces.[1] At times I weaken toward the New Deal philosophy for liking them. After all they may be as right as they surely are nice. I tire of our political differences anyway. I have to laugh at the ingenuities of our rulers in making it out that our differences with the Russians never existed. I cant admit the differences dont exist. But tonight I am willing to waive them. Lets call it this as a Christian War because it is so Christian an act for the Russians to be fighting it for us and lets call it a Democratic War because I cant learn that Stalin has been elected as often as Roosevelt. But whats all that compared to the friendship of people? After we have shown our intelligence by judging lets abdicate judgement and have a good time together. (Dont forget to have Shafroth[2] put me on the mailing list of the Supreme Court if there is such a thing or tell me how I can be supplied with its decisions and dissenting opinions. — Speaking of the abdication of judgement.)

Two things more I want you to tend to right away before I have to set forth on my travels: the complete manuscript of A Witness Tree and the portrait of me by Enit.[3] I know you are too busy, but you must make time to ship me these. Dont you think they would come safelier by Railway Express?

I was glad to hear John [Cohn] was doing so well. They keep themselves pretty well off my mind. You should realize the difference in the feeling Lillian gives me. I have a long letter from her in answer to my question whether she and Prescott had any notion of preparing him for the thought of war by sending him to a military school. She says Jack Holliday finds his a strict dull place he may not stay in and then again he may. She says Prescott will have had so many hours of shop work in the B.H.S. that he can count on getting into some such service as ground work on the airplanes. Not that he would avoid duty at the front. Only of course he would want to be where his abilities and training would help most. He had been out hunting and had killed a grey squirrel. I shall say nothing more on the subject. Not everybody can be expected to like war. I wish though you could have heard Clifford Lyons when he was in here with his wife just an hour after I got back. He likes war and thinks eighty five per cent like it. He allows for the other fifteen per cent as "neurotics." He's good natured about it all but a little too hard perhaps. Life and Death! I've just been reading some Marcus Aurelius again.

And Ive just read David Cecil's The Young Melbourne and an able beastly poem (book long) by Max Eastman and some of Louis' Great Poems. Love to Lee[.]

Affectionately   PAPA

Have you heard from Rogers about Mexico?[4]
The Lyonses asked specially for you.

[1] Vice President Henry Agard Wallace, with whom Lesley recalls playing tennis at the Alexandria, Virginia, home of Justice Hugo Black.

[2] Will Shafroth was a divisional chief in the Administrative Office of the United States Courts.

[3] RF's A Witness Tree was published in April 1942. It included a frontispiece portrait by the photographer Enit Kaufman.

[4] Cameron Rogers was associated with the Office of Coordination of Inter-American Affairs. He frequently wrote and lectured on Mexico and South America.

RF to Marjorie Robin Fraser

DEAR ROBIN   Cambridge, 19 December 1942

It was good to see you again though only in a picture. You are getting bigger and older than I can believe. And there is your father beside you all dressed up for war. He makes a fine looking soldier and you make a fine looking soldiers daughter.[1] I'm proud of you both. Sometime before very long I hope we'll all get together within talking distance either in my house here in Cambridge Massachusetts right next to Boston or in your house in Billings Montana, or the house of your two aunts in Washington D.C. where your cousins Lee and Elinor are this Christmas or in Bennington Vermont with Lillian (another aunt) and Prescott (another cousin) or at my farm at Ripton Vermont where I have horses and cows, or at San Antonio Texas where the hotel had an eye in a post that opened the door for you when it saw you coming or at some other place as warm and comfortable. Remember me to your other grandfather and to your grandmother and to your other aunts and uncles. For Christmas Im going to let you buy your own present from me: So I enclose ten dollars. See that you do just what you please with the money. Have a happy time.   Affectionately   GRANDFATHER

[1] See Illustrations. Willard served with the infantry in the European Theatre of Operations 1942-45.

RF to Lesley Frost Francis

DEAR LESLEY: Cambridge, 21 December [1942]

The enclosed three checks and a Happy Christmas to you all! Remember me to [Willard's sister] Jeanne (with a Scotch last name like Fraser, she should spell her first name Jean or Jeanie shouldnt she?) I should have been

for having our Christmas all together here. I have four guest
beds and a canvas camp cot now in three sparate guest
rooms. I planned them for family reunions. The only thing
left out of my plan is a servant in the house. When invited
you must expect to do your own house keeping. But then
I do mine and I am not letting you in for any hardship
I dont cheerfully put up with myself. Please add the Putney
horse[1] to my giving this year; and the tax bill on the Gulley
which came in as a little surprise last week. I dont mind
such things after a moment's thought. I suppose Lillian's idea
was I ought to make up for what she calculated she lost on
you this summer. Once you start reasoning you never know
where you will end up.

That's why I refrain from reasoning too much about
the Germans. Louis [Untermeyer] is down living alone in the
Webster Hotel on the regular government job that Archie
[MacLeish] and Carl and Elinor Davis are on.[2] I couldn't
bring myself to it if I tried. Louis is writing a primer of
Americanism to be translated into all the languages of
Europe and distributed to the peoples of Europe. How can
he? — unless as an excuse to flee the failing farm and rest
from his wife. He says [his wife] Esther blames him for a
deserter. Deserter is a bad word in war time. But as long
as he isnt a deserter of his country and his country's
cause or causes. Becauses! Why are we at war? The best
construction I can put on it is that we and the British have
a property and a position the Germans would give anything
to get away from us: and that we arent fools enough to let
them. The position and the airs of easy assurance that go
with it are even more enviable than the property. They
would fain try how it feels to sit on top of the world —
recline on top of the world. It gives beautiful the manners
of the non-upstart and non-climber. Well if I dont look out
I'll be writing a primer myself. Whence the Natziism? That

grows naturally and swiftly out of the desperation of what the poor fools are attempting against a world roused from peace and comfort to meet them in arms. Louis now speaks with the official We. He says We expect the war to last about another year. I am only too willing to have them proved right. I wonder how much of a soldier Prescott will have been made into by then. I'm glad he got in in time to choose his service[.][3]

I have about decided to go down and have a look at the cottages in Florida late in January. I hope for a lecture or two to pay the expenses. I have one scheduled at Duke in Durham.

Find out will you how one subscribes for that Supreme Court Bulletin.   Affectionately   PAPA

[1] Both Lee and Elinor were enrolled at a private school in Putney, Vermont, and RF had rented a horse for their use there.

[2] The Office of War Information.

[3] Prescott, just 18, enlisted in the army on 7 December 1942. He opted for the Signal Corps and was sent to Camp Carson for basic training where he came down with pneumonia and further complications. These complications necessitated his medical discharge in the summer of 1943.

RF to Lillian LaBatt Frost

DEAR LILLIAN: [Cambridge] 28 December 1942

You must have wondered why I didnt mention the vice you sent me for my Christmas present. The Bennington postmark on it was December 17th. I got it today December 28th. It is what we have been told to expect. Now we know. The parcels sent by mail have been at a standstill nearly.

Sometime you must tell me how you made such a finished tool. Did you cast it and then grind it down on a lathe? I shall have to set it up on the mantelpiece as an ornament or else build a workshop for it. Lesley says the government isnt going to let you use your acquirements as a mechanic because of the sicknesses you have had. It seems a shame. Well, we should have learned by this time to take everything as the government wills it. The mails are slow, we get drafted or rejected. We dont complain. We got broken in by Fate before ever the government came along with this war to save our English cousins.

Affectionately   FATHER

RF to William Prescott Frost

DEAR PRESCOTT,   Coconut Grove, 1 February 1943

(Private William); I shall have to get used to these formidable army addresses before I venture to write to you directly. But you might write me directly some time when you are in the mood. You can help me get into closer communication with you by printing very plainly all I must put on an envelope for you. I haven't heard from your mother for a week or so. When I do I hope it will be with good news about your health. The last was that you were up around and all right. I suppose the sulphur medicine may take longer to recover from than the pneumonia.

I am down here again for the old climate. My exact address is Route 2 Coconut Grove Florida. I shall stay for about four weeks and Kathleen will keep me company most of the time. I have three or four oranges, two or three grapefruit, one mangoe, two loquat two calomondon and one banana to water. I may not be able to keep them alive if the govt decides to stop all fertilizers for citrus fruit. That will mean cutting off the orange juice and starving everybody of their vitimines A B C D E F G H I J K L M N O P Q R S T U V W X Y Z. The V for Victory vitimine is the one we shall miss most. The sun is warm here this year. I am getting more summer heat this winter in Florida than I got all summer in Vermont.

Speaking of Vermont, I wonder if you have noticed the Govt report that Texas and Vermont lead all the states of the Union in percentage of enlistments. Your state is a proud little state to belong to. I wonder if the explanation isnt that Texas and Vermont were once nations by themselves, won their own independence, and had each a flag of its own — a national flag not just a state flag. A history like that is bound to linger in the minds of its people and show itself in their character. That winter we all lived in Texas I heard plenty of proud talk about the state. When I told a Texan I thought Vermonters hated the idea of Govt relief, he said Texans were the same. Absolutely no one at first would volunteer to go on relief and a posse had to be organized to run someone down to be the first victim of Govt paternalism. Massachusetts is pretty well up on the roster and so is my birth state California. It surprises me to see states like Virginia and South Carolina once so warlike (in'61) now away down. New Hampshire was next below Vermont.

The sky overhead is almost never free from the noise of planes. They are of all kinds, from the big South America passenger planes we used to see off from the Coconut Grove airport to all sorts I dont know the name of. They say the boys who flew over Tokio trained here; also many of the Britishers now flying in Europe and Africa.

Did I tell you Clifford Lyons is up at the naval air base in Squantum near Boston teaching dead-reckoning air navigation? Like Larry Thompson[1] he is restless and dissatisfied at not being on active duty at sea or in the field.   Affectionately   GRANDFATHER

---

[1] Lawrance Thompson, named by RF as his official biographer in 1939, on leave from Princeton.

RF to Lillian LaBatt Frost and William Prescott Frost

DEAR LILLIAN AND PRESCOTT: [Cambridge, February 1943]

I am sorry sorry the furlough comes so soon and lasts such a short time. I wanted to see the soldier in uniform, the first in our family for a hundred years. I mean in the direct Frost line.[1] But I have a lecture to give at the University of North Carolina (Chapel Hill) on March 1st which determines the date of my journey north. I am lucky to be getting lectures still at here and there a college and feel I mustn't pass any of them up. I shall miss the chance to hear about soldiering at first hand. You must write to me Prescott. My chief interest in the war comes from your being in it. I dont listen to the radio commentators and I hardly look at the papers. The headlines seem to be written by people who dont know anything about war. I hope you get information in camp that means something. I think of you every day.

Affectionately   GRANDFATHER

Check enclosed for February.

[1] RF's great grandfather, Samuel Abbott Frost, served in the War of 1812. Samuel's forebears had served respectively as Indian fighter in Maine, commander of a Royal Navy frigate, and as lieutenant in the Continental Army. See John Eldridge Frost, *The Nicholas Frost Family* (Milford, New Hampshire: The Cabinet Press, 1943).

RF to Lesley Frost Francis

DEAR LESLEY: [Boston, 21 April 1943]

The two days I might spend in Washington for dinners would be Sunday May 2 and Monday May 3. Then I must have a reservation for the midnight Monday May 3 [train]. Will you get that for me — ticket for Boston too. I enclose check for twenty dollars to cover both. If nobody wants me for dinner either of those nights lets save the money for another time and save me too. I have few days to waste before I go to farming. There are a lot of chickens coming to be taken care of early.

I'm glad Prescott is all right. Being a soldier may do him lots of good and it might do him lots of harm to be rejected. Then again it might not do him harm to be rejected. You never know anything. I mean I never know.

Affectionately   PAPA

RF to Lesley Lee Francis

DEAR LEE   Ripton, 20 May 1943

The enclosed money is something special. You heard of the prize I recently had for a book of poetry.[1] I have had it three times before and it never before occurred to me that it would be more fun and make the occasion more memorable if I spread some of the prize over other people. You get twenty-five dollars for your share this time to spend as you please when you please. You might like to save the amount of a war bond. I insist on nothing. What you do with it is one of the Forty-eleven freedoms.

Farming has started. We have twelve tomato plants one foot high in pots, two hundred chickens in brooders and a new cow. There are many discouragements in the farmer's life. The old cow got at a bag of grain left open in the barn floor and got an overdose of feed that rather dried up her milk. But all we had to do was buy a new cow. That seems a simple thing to have thought of. But for [a] while we didnt think of it. We were too stunned to think perhaps — or too inexperienced — or too unoriginal. It looked as if we were stuck. The question is how important is originality. How original are you getting to be? I feel sure I must be getting more original every ten years. How else would I have thought up the idea of letting other people in on my prizes?

I can get more stuck up about having an idea than about winning any prize. The great thing is to have an idea. Most schools fail to point this out, and so fail to start the young on the right road.   Affectionately   GRANDFATHER

1 RF was, for a fourth time, awarded a Pulitzer Prize — for *A Witness Tree.*

RF to Lesley Frost Francis

DEAR LESLEY: Ripton, 9 July 1943

Lillian writes that she has had no word from you about what Lee and Elinor are going to do this summer. I thought it was settled one or both of them would come to South Shaftsbury. Before I make the suggestion I have in mind I should like to know your plans and possibilities. Are you having any vacation at all? If you are, why not spend it (you three together) in a house with a house keeper we have prepared for you right down here at the foot of the road by our mail box and the river. This is business I am talking and calls for an immediate answer, so we can hold on to the housekeeper with a definite promise. Your old Spanish School has been moved up to Bread Loaf to make room for soldiers in Middlebury: and I hear the Dean or his wife has been inquiring about you. You could hear some Spanish spoken without enrolling. You could get some tennis. We could all see a lot of each other. The housekeeper (at her expense) would take everything off your hands and set you entirely free to rest. The Spanish School lasts about three more weeks from the time you get this. Better than the Spanish School however would be the English [Bread Loaf Writers'] Conference if you want to wait till then. Consult your own convenience. Only let me know soon. The only bad week from our point of view will be from July 18 to 25. Better not come then. Ann [Morrison] is having her tonsils out. You havent told me about your new job, how you like it and how restricting it may be. You may be utterly essential and indispensible where you are. In which case I thought I would invite Lillian to bring the girls up to the same place. I shant say anything to her though till I have had your refusal.

Like long treed royal Odysseus I have made a new plan or had one made for me by Athene. I shall have a slighter connection with Harvard next year and a very considerable connection with Dartmouth, but of course without moving up there. I am to go up for seminars salons and such fourteen weekends and to march in commencement processions. My title will be Ticknor Fellow in the Humanities, which are still a concern of the stay-at-home President of Dartmouth. I call him that because he stays with his college and plans for it after the war — yes and even during the war. It is a strange denouement. I ran away from Dartmouth exactly fifty years ago. And here it is capping its forgiveness by bringing me back with the rank of professor.[1] But I have had a lifeful of such story-stuff. I shall see more of John Irma Jack and Harold.[2] John is teaching graphics in the army classes.

Read Max Eastman in the Literary Digest for July.[3] Just for confirmation in what we knew already.

Affectionately   PAPA

[1] An Associate of Harvard's Adams House since 1939, RF transferred his allegiance to Dartmouth in September 1943. He had studied there for three months in late 1892. Ernest Martin Hopkins was the college's president.

[2] Harold, born in 1940, was not quite 3; Jack was nearly 16.

3 *Literary Digest* ceased publication in 1939. RF had reference to Eastman's July 1943 *Readers Digest* article "To Collaborate Successfully — We Must Face the Facts About Russia" in which he scored American gullibility.

RF to Lillian LaBatt Frost

DEAR LILLIAN   [Cambridge] Friday, 24 September [1943]

I am afraid the letter I wrote you from Ripton Tuesday never reached you. My reason is that another I put into the

roadside letter box at the same time never reached its
destination. I mailed them both at the same hour of night
and foolishly raised the metal flag on the box to advertise
their presence. I mustnt make that mistake again up there
or any where. The letter to you contained no check, but was
partly an enquiry as to your immediate money requirements.
So the loss if it was a loss was only important if it lead to a
misunderstanding between us that left you waiting to hear
from me and me waiting to hear from you. The rest of it was
some advice about Prescott's taking strict health measures
to see if he can't beat the doctors' expectations. The doctors
base their expectations on averages, conscious themselves
that they will be proved wrong in a certain number of
pessimal and optimal cases. They cant afford to allow for
the exceptional persons who have the extra will to live and
get well. They can only be glad of such. I have known
young people who made over as hopeless a thing as a weak
heart. Some time I can tell you this part of my letter again
if you didn't get it in the first place. Let me know right away.

I have written and so has Kathleen to the people who
are to be your closest neighbors,[1] Elmer Hjort and his
family. Hjort is a professor of chemistry at the University
of Miami. He was at the University of Pittsburg before they
had to move down there to save their daughter Edith's life
after she had pneumonia several times. Edith has flourished
and is now in her third year of high school. She has a
younger sister Nettie Bell. The father mother and all of
them are the kind you'll like. You and Prescott will find
them helpful about the little farming you will want to do.
A little mild puttering outdoors on a carefully graduated
scale (five minutes the first day six the second seven the third
and so on up for a way) ought to do him good. Books will
kill him if he merely reads and lazes round in chairs and in
bed. Judiciousness in physical exercise is his salvation.

Every step of it must be watched for a while. I wish a spec[i]a-list could be found down there who could help him keep from catching cold. As I said in my other letter he must give up smoking, he must keep perfect hours (early to bed) and must eat well. Then comes the exercise almost scientifically self-administered. I preach a lot more than I have ever been moved to before. This is a terribly serious moment for us all. He has a cool head and a good one. He can save himself from the life the doctors have to predict from the law of averages.

I enclose the *regular hundred*. Tell me right back how much more you need for travel and tuition. I hope to see you both before you go. It wouldnt add much to your journey if you took in Cambridge on your way. My dates are like this: I go to Hanover every Friday and get back to Cambridge Sunday evening. My first lecture trip away will be after October 20 I think now.

A word about the Hervey Allens without prejudice and without malice. They have lost a lot of money and are unhappy about that and the loss of social position it may mean for them and their children. They have grown accustomed to expensive company and big doings. They are fighting to avoid too much of a comedown. I dont know how well Hervey's new novel The Fort and the Forest has succeeded. I hope well but I fear only fairly well. If the latter, Hervey will be in a more self absorbed and troubled state than last year and you must not expect any more attention from him than you accidentally get. We'll see how he is feeling when I get down.

Now about the houses while I think of it. I wish you and Prescott would take the two rooms in the two-room house for your bedrooms and reserve the bedroom in the three-room house for mine always. The sitting room and the kitchen in the three room house can be for all of us. There is a stove in the two room house the purpose of which is mainly to give the whole house a thorough drying out in the daytime once or twice a week. You have to be careful not to run it too hard and burn the house down. You couldnt sleep in the house if it were going at night. I got it to get rid of the dampness that bothers my throat in most houses in Florida. There may be days and evenings cool enough for you to want to sit by it. I mean sooner or later to build a chimney with an open fireplace at the three room house.

I think thats all for the present[.]

Affectionately   FATHER.

Elmer Hjort (pronounced jort) writes that he doubts if you need the electric refrigerator. You might leave it so that it could be sent if things got worse.

We traded mostly at Shumans store. We walked to it — it's not over a mile off on the perfectly dead level. You'll want to make friends with the interesting Russians named Thoro — especially if you like really good papaya[.]

1 Following his medical discharge, Prescott undertook studies at the University of Miami. He and his mother lived at RF's "Pencil Pines" retreat.

RF to Lesley Frost Francis

DEAR LESLEY: [Cambridge] 14 October 1943

I have mailed the play[1] in another envelope. I hope it gets there safely. The envelope isnt as strong as I should like. I must have the play back pretty soon. Please don't lend it round down there. I have a touch or two to give it yet.

You sure are giving them the great thoughts[.] I must read some of those chapters you lay out. Where can you get the books for a whole class?

I suppose Prescott and Lillian will be going past you this week. You will hear Lillian on the subject of a pension for Prescott. I have grave doubts of pressing for one. His is a border case that must be difficult to decide on. Prescott told me others with like ailment to his had been kept on and run through their training. I have some pride in the matter. I wouldn't want it said that all we Frosts had done for the war is get a pension out of it for never getting to the front. I dont want Prescott to develope a sense of having been wronged. He could if he got to arguing with the government. I know it is hard to take it from the authorities that he has no claim because he didnt get his injury in service. Of course he did. But as I say I don't see how we can afford to insist in a cause like this. Patriotism comes first and Lord, I'm sure Prescott is man enough to earn a living once he gets his start from his family.   Affectionately   PAPA

<hr>

1 *A Masque of Reason*, first published in 1945. *PRF*, pp. 473-490.

RF to Lillian LaBatt Frost

DEAR LILLIAN: [Cambridge, November 1943]

Here I am back again at 35 Brewster St. From your reports I judge our mild November has extended clear to Florida. There has been no frost yet in Massachusetts. You say you are still in the middle of insects and feeling the heat too much. Maybe the heat is to blame for your eye trouble.

Well the nation has come back to think the same way as Vermont.[1] Vermont only had to wait patiently for people to come to their senses. The kindness of hand outs has gone down in defeat to the kindness of discipline. I put it that way for fun. That is the way the Republicans ought to put it for effect. But Florida has kept [Sen. Claude] Pepper and the New Republic has Henry Wallace.[2] These are interesting times for Prescott to learn his voting in — and for Phyllis[3] to learn hers too. I hope they'll both belong to the same party. Parties aren't worth families disagreeing about.

The check is in this.

                         Affectionately   R.F.

[1] The 78th Congress reflected an increase of 46 Republican members and a drop of 50 for the Democrats.

[2] One of RF's frequent plays on meaning. Wallace was Vice-President of the U.S. and also a frequent contributor to *The New Republic* magazine.

[3] A friend, Phyllis M. Gordon, whom Prescott would marry in 1947.

RF to Lesley Frost Francis

DEAR LESLEY   [Ripton, 2 September 1944]

Here's seventy-five for the watch to carry to Paris — or even Berlin. I should think you would be having to learn a few more languages in a hurry.[1] French should come easy after your experience with one branch-off from Latin. So would Italian. I can get as far with Spanish as not trans-lating it into English but as seeing from the English on the opposite page in a bilingual book of verse how it would naturally mean what it means. None of those tongues are far removed from ours. The reason I suppose is because their separation doesnt go back to Babel.

About Irma. You'll have to think again there. It would never never never do to impose her on Lillian and Prescott after all they have suffered from the Frost derangement. It frightens Lillian to contemplate it. She's thinking of Prescott — not herself. We talked with Dr Hall (Richards brother) night before last at a dinner with the Brooks family. You would be grateful to him if you heard his interest in Lillian and Prescott. We have to be considerate of Prescott. There is probably a serious operation ahead for him. Dr Hall said he had never heard of anyone's getting over bronchiectasis without having part of his lung cut out.

It seems to me if you acted at once instantly you might find out for us if Vera[2] wouldnt be willing to board Irma and the baby for the winter in Cambridge ostensibly so that Irma could study her art (or work at it) a little and perhaps have the benefit of treatment by a good analyst. I know one of the most sensible in the world Vernon Williams and he would be glad to do anything he could for us. Of course it would have to be kept from Irma that he was anybody to me or that I had brought him into the case. We could have Rosalind Potter (33 Brewster St) propose him. You must take time from affairs of state to help me get this business right.

About Louis. He was up here with the Bill Sloanes for a day or two and you never saw anyone look more whipped. I could have told him he would never get out of it with a lawyer as he did with those other girls. He has hated Esther more than eight years of the nine he has been married to her. Her mouthy vulgarity wasnt made up for by her good farming and housekeeping. I didn't think she would go as far in the break up as asking for all his property and trying to ruin him and the Irish girl from Saratoga. I am telling him of the old song that says

> You'd better be off with the old love
> Before you are on with the new.

The war draws to a conclusion. You may not see much of it.   Affectionately   PAPA

---

[1] In 1944, Lesley undertook a series of varied assignments with the Office of War Information as assistant to the training director. Later she worked as cultural officer and lecturer with the State Department.

[2] Vera Harvey, a cousin.

RF to Lesley Frost Francis

DEAR LESLEY: [Cambridge, December 1944]

I dont feel as if I knew where you are with no address but that internationalism of an O.W.I. But it wont do for me to continue in that mood if I am intending you any Christmas money. You fortunately prefer money to things. I have no courage to go forth looking for appropriate things in late years. How much will it take to make you happy? Suppose I send you a hundred and the girls each twenty five and then pay you back for anything you spend getting up here for your vacation. It will be your Christmas present to me for you to come to Cambridge. I might wish to visit you in New York especially if you argued it would help you sociopolitically. But you wouldnt want me running the risks of travel in the Christmas crowd. I ought to stay pretty well put for the month ahead of me before I go south — if indeed I go, for all my mind is clouded with a doubt about reservations in the train. I plan to break throug[h] by breaking the journey into three sections — no, four — chair in Pulman by day to Washington — same by day to Farmville Va — sleeper from there to Athens Georgia — and sleeper from Atlanta to Miami. I hear your gang are already taking it as a matter of course that England and Russia are at war. It seems to me a plausible understanding of the trouble in Greece. I should be careful about where I said it out loud.

Sunday evening the 24th Christmas Eve Kathleen expects us all four, you me and the two infantae to have dinner at her house. It wont be a present giving affair. We're all too lazy tired this year for the hardships of shopping. We can have a perfectly good time playing and talking. [Portion of page cut and missing.]

RF to Lillian LaBatt Frost

Dear Lillian   [Cambridge, September 1945]

Late as usual. I enclose one hundred plus twenty five for the hurricane. Twenty five seems getting out of a hurricane pretty cheaply. Lets hear more of the damage or not damage. Theres a certain satisfaction in listening to the ruin we might have suffered but escaped by luck. I wonder how much the houses really stood up under. Such storms are spotty even at the center. Maybe we werent right in one of this one's spots. How did Hervey fare? The Hjorts' place sounds bad. Well we've passed that examination by the Lord and ought not to be subjected to another for five or six years by any law of chance I have heard of. But I leave that to Prescott's calculations. Once in five or ten years in Florida, once in fifty or a hundred in Vermont. Really never in Vermont over behind the mountains.

I go to Ohio (Kenyon and Wesleyan[)] for four or five days beginning Oct 11[.] Then comes Dartmouth for most of November.

We wound up a lot of our farming before we came away. The two horses Kay and Ann rode on down to Brandon and left with Pinkey Johnson. Candy the pinto has got pretty well over her fern poisoning. The chickens went to Brandon. All thats left at our risk is the old sow. A double-headed letter gave the first bulletin she had had fourteen and only rolled on one: then in the second bulletins one week later said she had rolled on seven more. Casualties at the rate of one a day. The sooner tis over the sooner to enjoy our money on ourselves. I dont know about the old cow; she has such persistent garget in one quarter. I guess we are drifting out of the cow business. We may not stay out of all this. Im an incorrigible. A little encouragement by the right kind of people to live at the Dow place (some good refugees perhaps) and we'd be back in again.

I wrote Prescott for his birthday. I'm not much good at birthdays but I thought his twenty first ought to be observed. If we were all down there together we could celebrate by going down the keys.

Affectionately   R.F.

RF to William Prescott Frost

DEAR PRESCOTT: Cambridge, 16 January 1946

I saw that last play just as plain as if I had been present in the Orange Bowl — even plainer than that perhaps. It was almost too much for the radio announcer to describe[.] He couldnt believe his eyes. He didnt want to believe his eyes. I could tell he had been on the side of the Irish all through the game. Probably he knew he was talking to an Irish audience away off up here. He even began the game with a warning that everything had been set by your chamber of commerce to have Miami win by fair means or foul. He showed a last minute hope that the smart Irish would pull something in fact the very thing Hudson pulled and snatch the victory out of the fire. He didnt know what to say when Hudson (was that his name?) snatched the bobbled ball and got away with it for the whole length of the field. He kept repeating "I guess its legal I guess its legal" as if there might be a chance it would be called back. Apparently there never was just such a play. Most of it was after the game was over. The goal was kicked long after the game was over. I was glad Hudson was a plain Florida High School boy and not a hired man from the coal mines or iron founderies of Pennsylvania or somewhere far from Miami. These bowl games don't get taken very seriously by the sports writers of the nation. There's too much chamber of commerce mixed up in them. But that was a fine one to listen to and with my minds eye watch. I enjoyed being there with you. It seems Elinor and Lillian didnt go to it.

I wish they'd build a special railroad into Florida for me when the war's well over. I hate this competing with the race track people for tickets. But I have my ticket now for this year — just got it yesterday and will be headed your way next Tuesday. That doesnt mean you will see me right off at once. I have to stop for three lectures, one in New York next Tuesday night, then one at the University of Georgia and one at Agnes Scott College in Decatur Georgia[.] I may and may not have one at Gainesville. I plan to have you meet me either on Sat Feb 2 or Sun Feb 3. I will let you know more definitely later.

Maybe they will build some more railroads when the flow of all our wealth abroad gets staunched and people get driven to work again. There's a great roaring and splashing in the vat as it begins to fill up again. I dont let it worry me[.] Every sign points to great times ahead. We are all power and plenty. Pretty soon Henry Wallace will be having to scare us again with our plenty.

A man finds cows worth thirty dollars apiece pigs three dollars and sheep fifty cents. He spends a hundred dollars and carries off a hundred animals. How many does he take of each kind? At least that's the way I understood the problem.

It will be fun to see you both again. I wish I could have found Elinor there too.

Is the boat in the water I wonder.

No fruit this year. Maybe some blossoms.

Anyway the houses didnt blow away.

Just as soon as we can we must get the basement windows closed with wire so as to keep the coral snakes out or starve them to death in there.

If I should want to write a Negro dialect story, how much an hour do you suppose I would have to pay a Negro for talking to me so I could learn Nigger idiom the way you learned German at the Berlitz School?

Affectionately   GRANDFATHER

Perhaps Kay told you in her letter Lee will have flown to Portugal by the time you get this. Lesley got the whole State Department stirred up over her passport and then the Spanish Embassy stirred up over getting it visaed. Pull pull! I'm no help in things like this!

RF to William Prescott Frost

DEAR PRESCOTT   [Ripton, 13 September 1947]

I'm glad you and Phyllis[1] are warming the Acton [Massachusetts] house. There must be things you and she will enjoy doing with and for it.

Here's a hundred dollars for your tuition and here's looking forward to seeing you soon a student at [Massachusetts Institute of] Tech[nology].

Love to you both   R.F.*

* What Lesley has taken to calling me.

[1] Prescott and Phyllis Gordon were married 12 June 1947, thus establishing another branch of the family. An earlier branch had been severed; Irma and John Cone were divorced and Irma was committed to a mental hospital.

RF to Willard Fraser

DEAR WILLARD   Hanover, New Hampshire [February 1949]

There's a copy of Come In[1] here that to the best of my recollection came from you for a signature or an inscription. Is it for you yourself or whom is it for? Tell me and I will rouse myself to deal with it.

Ben Miller has reported on you only this year. You did well in your first campaign he says, though you didnt quite win. You have to learn to take the set backs if you will run for office and ask for popular favor. The reason I dont show my sympathy with you is very simple: from this distance where I look on with cool detachment it seems absolutely certain to me that you will go far in politics, though if you go as far as Washington I should think it might not be good for your asthma.[2] Perhaps you have outgrown your handicap or have decided to go ahead regardless of it. I should enjoy thinking you had. You are the only son in law I ever cared for.

What a daughter you have in Robin. And how she comes on like a prairie fire. You know how bad I am about writing letters. I had rather get ten letters than write one. This is one of inquiry it may take you ten to answer. Tell me any news of yourself or her that you think will help me along.

I shall be as near you as Grinnell Iowa on the 21st of this month but that's not near enough for you to hear me talking literature from the college platform. I shall be thinking of you and Robin off there to the northwest.

Always your advocate   R.F.

By the time you get this digested the news will probably have been announced that I am changed from the George Ticknor Fellow at Dartmouth into the Simpson Lecturer in Literature at Amherst. I am none to[o] loyal at that level. As long as my friends stay my friends at Dartmouth I dont suffer too much from any desertion. I see too many colleges in a year to dote on any one in particular as the capital of education. But Amherst is being very good to me and especially in the length of the contract it makes with me. I have spent nineteen of my last thirty five years there. They are now taking me back for my next nineteen. I dont like to speak openly of finalities, but between you and me I dont suppose I have any right to expect but that that will about tell the story. Life's a span at most.

My best address from middle May to late September is Ripton Vt; the rest of the year 35 Brewster St. Cambridge Mass. I shall be six or eight weeks irregularly at Amherst.

1 *Come In and Other Poems*, first published in 1943.

2 Willard was an assistant to Sen. Burton K. Wheeler (D., Mont.), served for seven seasons as an archaeologist with the Carnegie Institution, and was Mayor of Billings, Montana, for three terms. A member of the U.S. Territorial Expansion Commission and active in other state and local groups, he stood for reelection as Mayor of Billings in 1971.

RF to Lesley Frost Francis

DEAR LESLEY   Ripton [Fall 1949]

You don't say you have received my Special Edition [of *Complete Poems 1949*] at 32 Bank St,[1] which I hear is other wise fully furnished. I must admit my imagination was much taken with what I may call the Bank St way of life. I'm glad to have someone in the family living it as my proxy. The same as I am glad to have Robert Hillyer scourging folly out of the Temple of Letters in Washington[2] for me and so saving me the publicality of having to do it for myself. Epaminondas[3] was like me there. I think I may have modelled myself on him unconsciously. Isnt it an oddity, by the way, that the one who set the rascals up in their authority should just at this moment be taking his seat in the chair at Harvard[4] that was not long since vacated by the one who turned the rascals out? And both these public figures are friends of mine and so are some of the rascals. I have had very uneven luck in my friendships. I have reached a poise, however, of taking them as they turn out. Louis [Untermeyer] for instance wrote me the warmest kind of an old time letter in recognition of my having brought round so many of the doubters and held my own with so many of the faithful. It is noticeable that he is saying nothing in print. I suppose he cant say much after what he did to me in the Yale Review. Virginia Moore's[5] son was probably at the bottom of that. "Oh well," as Justice [Harlan Fiske] Stone sighed over the Supreme Court and as I sighed in answer. At least I have a vague sense of having had this year the height of my success. It is entirely beyond anything I ever dreamed of or set my heart on. Its our elders that despise our unpromising youth. So they get dead and safely out of the way before they are proved wrong in their misjudgement of us. There are a few people I regret not triumphing over.

But it is with a mild regret that seldom comes over me in its unworthiness. Now would be the time for them to have to reappear and face my facts. Any earlier it wouldnt have been so hard on them. Any later we dont know what the situation might have become. "For we are poised on a huge wave of fate. And whether it will roll us out to sea" etc. etc. as it is written in Sorab and Rustum if I remember rightly. I haven't my Arnold here to verify it.[6]

Elinor and Malcolm[7] were enjoyable and so was Montana Robin. Both Robin and Elinor got upon the relatively high horse (known as Steeply for short of Steeple Bush) with Kay or Ann. Not a man on the place rides at all unless it is little Roger Dragon.[8] He's a real horseman. I groom and feed horses but stay on the ground like the ground crew in aviation. It all gets to mean more and more to me: so that if I never wrote another single line of iambics I could be as composed as a trappist trapping for the Hudson Bay Company which I once threatened to become. See Page in my Completed (if you have the copy mentioned[)].[9] I had a big garden do well this summer. I started some new fruit trees against my old age. And I caused another pond to be excavated against the next drouth. The spell must soon be broken though. Next month for another kind of pastures. I shall be singing To the Frenchman and the Indian he didnt do a thing[10] in the Lord Geoffrey Inn by October 10. My best Fall address however will be 35 Brewster and my declared residence henceforth with all my heart and vote will be Ripton Vt USA.

Enclosed find one poem written out to your order. You didnt name a particular one; so I let Kay choose. I never know what feet to put forward in such an emergency[.] Metrical feet.

I also enclose some printed matter from your Uncle John Moodie who seems bent on dying without benefit of clergy like a hard-headed Scot. He wants to hear from you he says. I notice his list of the greats in England who have espoused rationalism [includes] no names of poets or artists. Does that mean artists are worse or better than scientists.

Affectionately   R.F.

Cousin Johns address
    538 Worcester St
    Christchurch New Zealand

[1] New York City.

[2] Robert Hillyer questioned the representative membership of The Fellows of the Library of Congress in American Letters, decried their decision to grant Ezra Pound the Bollingen Award for "The Pisan Cantos," and urged that T.S. Eliot be dropped as Fellow and juror. See his "Treason's Strange Fruit,"*Saturday Review of Literature*, vol. 32, n. 24 (11 June 1949): 9-11, 28; "Poetry's New Priesthood," *SRL*, vol. 32, no. 25 (19 June 1949): 7-9, 38; Letter, *SRL*, vol. 32, no. 33 (13 August 1949): 21; and "Crisis in American Poetry," *American Mercury*, 70 (January 1950): 65-71.

[3] Fourth-century B.C. Greek patriot-statesman who withheld his eloquence until it could be used to best effect.

[4] Archibald MacLeish, formerly Librarian of Congress, was named Boylston Professor of Rhetoric in 1949, a chair vacated in 1945 by Hillyer.

[5] Louis Untermeyer's second wife.

[6] Ll. 390-396 of Matthew Arnold's narrative poem read:
"For we are all, like swimmers in the sea,
Poised on the top of a huge wave of fate,
Which hangs uncertain to which side to fall,
And whether it will heave us up to land,
Or whether it will roll us out to sea,
Back out to sea, to the deep waves of death,
We know not..."

[7] Lesley's daughter and Malcolm Wilber were married in July 1947.

[8] Son of caretaker-farmer Stafford Dragon of Ripton.

[9] "An Empty Threat," pp. 256-257 in *Complete Poems of Robert Frost 1949*. *PRF*, pp. 210-212. RF also imagined himself as a neglectful fur trapper at Hudson's Bay in a November 1915 letter. See *The Letters of Robert Frost to Louis Untermeyer*, pp. 17-18.

[10] From the college song, "Lord Jeffery Amherst."

RF for Lesley Frost Francis

[n.p., n.d.][1]

The course of true poetry is from more ethereal than substantial to more substantial than ethereal. What begins lyric may be counted on if not broken off by death or business to end epic. By pure poetry some would seem to mean poetry purely not substantial at all that's an extravagance of theory. But where has there ever been any such thing with success? It may have men tried for the purpose of sinning with originality. The result if any would be of scientific rather than esthetic interest. Such notion relegates to the realm where in the cyclotrons [?] nothing is perceptibly becoming something. That would be funny if it wasnt wicked. The surest thing we know is that the scale of words [?] is not quadruple none some more most but eternally triple merely some more most. Nothing can be done with nothing. Nothing but weight can put on weightiness. The moist diaphenous wings carry a burden pollen from flower to flower. No song without a burden.

What begins as lyric may be counted on if not broken off by death or business to end as epic. The principle was never better exemplified than in way the fine poems of Hervey Allens and through the years to a book heard round the world it was translated from admiration to so many languages. The book was a novel in prose but only a poet could have written it and its very name rang with poetry. Unquestionably it is best regarded as just one more poem on top of all his others longer than all the rest put together an epic that had come in the disguise of prose to get past our modern prejudice against the epic. Hervey Allen would have wanted it taken as part and parcel of his life in poetry. He would live to regret it in the Elysian fields if it wasnt.

1 RF's warm regard for his Florida neighbor Hervey Allen led him to commence a preface, or appreciation, of his friend's work. This appreciation was neither completed nor used. One version and a partial revision — without editing, just as they appear on three small pages of a folded sheet — appear here for the first time. The only addition has been to signal a separation between

the two drafts. Here RF declares his debt to Plato for images and ideas from the *Apology* and the *Ion*. The "book heard round the world" is probably *Anthony Adverse* (1933). The last line of the revision suggests that RF wrote this piece some time following Allen's death in 1949. These drafts were probably sent to Lesley as an enclosure in a letter.

RF to Lesley Frost Francis

DEAR LESLEY: South Miami, 19 January 1951

All this interest in my origins can't help making me aware of such scraps as the enclosed. You should own the Bluebird piece.[1] I dont know how it survived. The other sheet is older and shows that I did keep a note book at times in spite of my distrust of writing anything down except in final form for keeps. Theres what came to be later the title of one of the freshest things I ever dashed off.

If you are willing I think you ought perhaps to visit Irma and take her out for a walk and a ride once in every two months or so. Its terrible for you to have such a duty. It may be too much for you. I'd give you seventy five dollars to do it with. You think it over.

What you broached about more education is much more important. The year at the school of diplomacy might be the very thing. You are alive and in the running. You mustnt be sacrificed for anyone who has hopelessly lost her chance. The money could I suppose be found for your year. You would be earning some of it and I could supply some.

Affectionately   R.F.

[1] Originally entitled "The Message the Crow Gave Me for Lesley, One Morning Lately When I Went to the Well," the poem, in modified form, became "The Blue Bird to Lesley." Its shorter descendent, "The Last Word of a Bluebird," is found in *PRF*, pp. 135-136.

RF to Lesley Frost Francis

DEAR LESLEY: Ripton, 20 June 1951

You neither shocked nor displeased me by the sudden

new turn you seem to have taken. New York wasn't good for you. Getting out of it I hope means putting the Reds and all anxiety about them behind you. Texas is an old favorite state of mine.[1] I came within a night's sleep of buying a farm with a miniature Colorado Cañon on it out between the towns of Boerne and Comfort the winter we spent there. It is so big it probably has many kinds of climate all of them none too good probably, but it has all sorts of history and all sorts of possibilities for its denizens. You will probably end up a captain in the Texas Rangers to the credit of the Frost family. I have travelled through parts down there all lighted up at night with oil wells on fire. A financier friend of mine says the state has wherewithal to gas us all, the whole country for four hundred years. It came into the Union as such an overwhelming threat that it was put under contract never to cut itself up into more than four states, so it wouldn't pack the U.S. Senate with southern Democrats. Make the most of it. (I didnt say make the best of it.) I can't live in all the states of the Union at once. I do pretty well to live in four and to have lived in two or three more. For the rest I have to get my sense of being an All American out of having family representatives in New York Montana Washington D.C. and the state we are talking about namely Texas. You speak as if you were doing something about oil for your new friends. What a harsh lean land New England seems in comparison with what Texas flows with. Plenty ought to make the people generous natured and happy to live with.

Affectionately   R.F.

[1] Both as onlooker and unlucky investor, Lesley had become interested in oil prospecting. She took a position as driver-companion to Mrs. Andrew Belcher of Dallas, Texas.

RF to Lesley Lee Francis

DEAR LEE

Ripton, 22 August 1951 the day your letter came. I hope this answer reaches you in time.

You saw my poem about Columbus before you went away I assume, or I would write it out for you now. A funny think happened to it with Douglas Freeman the Lee-historian when I was at his house in Richmond last spring. Two funny things in fact. To take up the first one first: "I venture to say" he said after hearing it read, "I venture to say you were possibly months writing a historical piece like that". You can imagine my embarrassment. I should lose his respect if I confessed to a research man like him that I wrote the whole eighty four lines of it without consulting a single book in one night. He would think I was talking literary mysticism if I told him what was true in a sense that I had been all my life writing it. So I stumbled around with "Yes in a way" and "Poetry is of course not managed just like history is it?" Then after a long pause the second thing happened. With true scholarly gravity he asked if I knew that Ferdinand and Isabella werent making Madrid their capital in 1492. He got up and led me to the encyclopeadia for correction. My lines go like this.

> And to intensify the drama
> Another mariner da Gama
> Came just then sailing into port
> From the same general resort,
> But with the gold in hand to show for
> His claim it was another Ophir.
>
> Had but Columbus known enough
> He might have boldly made the bluff
> That better than da Gama's gold
> He had been given to behold

The race's future trial place,
A fresh start for the human race.

He might have fooled them in Madrid.
I was deceived by what he did.
If I had had my way when young
I should have had Columbus sung
As a god who had given us
A more than Moses Exodus.

But all he did was spread the room
Of our enacting out the doom
Of being in each others way,
And so put off the weary day
When we would have to put our mind
On how to crowd yet still be kind. etc., etc.[1]

That's right out of the middle of the idea. But not a word from the old man for the idea of socialism in the "How to crowd yet still be kind." All he noticed was Madrid. I didnt defend it as I might by saying Madrid would serve well enough as a part for the whole of Spain. (Figure known as Synechdoche.) But I'll tell you what I did do to show my slight knowledge of the country you seem to have adopted for your second best. I offered to make the line read "He might have fooled Valladolid."[2] I couldn't give up "I was deceived by what he did" — the most emotional line of all. But I'm not sure that Valladolid might not be too hard for the audience.

I tell you all this to match you if I can in the entertainment your letter gave me. I like to hear of other countries and my folks real experiences in them. I'm no traveller and dont like travelogues. The only country I can have any interest in is the one I have lived in. You've struck out a genuine beginning of a career — whatever it may prove

to be. I enjoyed every word of your story. We'll be seeing
you soon.   Affectionately   GRANDFATHER

¹ The poem "America Is Hard to See" is in *PRF*, pp. 416-419. Included
here are the fourth through the seventh stanzas of a total fourteen. Except as
noted below, revisions are minor.
² This line change is reflected in the poem as it appears in *PRF*.

RF to Lesley Frost Francis

DEAR LESLEY   Cambridge, 19 December 1951
     Lets think of all the pleasant things there are for
Christmas.¹ I was just telling someone since you had gotten
wings (thanks to the Wright Bros) you were able to be in all
places at once — Dallas Tex Cambridge Mass New York
N.Y. and Pensacola Fla. all so cheerful and merry.
                                   Affectionately   R.F.

¹ For RF, the year had had its unpleasant aspect-surgery for skin cancer.

RF to Lillian LaBatt Frost

DEAR LILLIAN   Ripton [September 1952]
     It's a long time I've been getting deeper in debt to you.
Carelessness was partly to blame. Dont be afraid I was
assuming too much from your new business venture.¹
You've done wonders so far if I am any judge. But it will
take another year of course to get you and your partners
on your feet. Patience is essential. Anyway enclosed find
five hundred.
     I'm sorry you've got to go on down to get good water.
Who would have expected to find a glacial deposit of
kaolin so deep in the earth? Are you sure the stuff isnt
leaking into the pipes from the side somewhere instead of
from the bottom? You're lucky that the spring on the
Potter place holds out. Water here on our place is as scarce as

oil seems to be in New England. I'm poking round ever[y] where for new sources.

Lesleys marriage was good family news.[2] We liked Joe for himself and also for his politics. He takes his opposition to the New Deal more calmly than Lesley but they are very congenial.

And Elinor's improvement is good family news. I was stunned when I heard of her blow.[3] Here we go for another tragedy I thought. It's hard to believe its all right yet. But Lesley is sure it is. Lesley says there is a possibility you may go down to help about the infants for a while later. I wish you had had oil heat in your stone house so there would have been no ashes to bother you. Would it cost too much to change to oil?

I stay here till October fifth sixth seventh eighth or so. I believe I have to begin at U of Virginia on the tenth. I shall be visiting Prescott and Lesley in Washington then. I did hope to look in on you again at South Shaftsbury before winter, but I seem tied up here.

Affectionately   R.F.

Remember me to the Simmons[.]

1 Lillian and her partner, Marjorie Simmons, operated a restaurant at the stone house in South Shaftsbury during the summers of 1952 and 1953.

2 Lesley married Joseph W. Ballantine, retired diplomat and teacher, on 23 August 1952.

3 Lesley's daughter was stricken with polio.

RF to Lesley Lee Francis

DEAR LEE: Ripton, 30 December 1953

Your present was the best mail I got for Christmas. You'd think I might be weary of poetry and the ambitions of poetry after all I have seen and known of both in the last sixty five years since eighteen eighty nine when I wrote my very first poem and named it La Noche Triste in the language of your adoption. But I still prick up my attention to a fresh note of thought and feeling. These are true little poems, firm and shapely. You make your point every time as so few rhymsters seem to feel obliged to do nowadays. An Evening's Mood is one, with that splash of rain on the dirty window. At Home is another. You do it with delicate touches and gentle insights.

> A different pattern in each heart
> And mould to every thought
> Have given life its secret part
> Which man must not defy

You wouldnt have written that at any time but now and in any place but Washington among the One-worlders. They will learn the lesson. I shall keep the book, not among my books, but among the papers I pack with me wherever I go. I mean the things of my own I haven't yet published or havent yet put the last touch to. Send me some more when you have them. Write me some poetry or politics from Spain and I'll see if I cant be roused to write you a letter back. I always like to hear about Spain for some reason. I wish I had the enterprise to go there. My interest is probably more due to Prescott[1] than to [Washington] Irving — the story of Cortez in Tenochtitlan rather than the Abenarrage in the Alhambra. (Spell some of those names for me.) I should be up and going to Peru and Yucatan among other places on earth I fail of. I take it out in reading. [Thor Heyerdahl's] Kon Tiki didnt attract me. But its successor American Indians in the Pacific [:The Theory Behind the Kon-Tiki Expedition (1952)] is just my kind of travels.

Affectionately your   GRANDFATHER
Back at 35 Brewster St in a few days.

[1] William Hickling Prescott, author of the monumental *History of the Conquest of Mexico* (1843), a portion of which inspired RF to write the poem which he cites in the first paragraph of this letter.

RF to Lesley Frost Ballantine

DEAR LESLEY   The Lord Jeffery [Inn], Amherst [1 May 1954]

You gave me the idea last time there was some reason you couldnt buy the piece of land you wanted for Irma's house. I'm only too glad to hear different. Go ahead right off. Get the deed. When I see that we'll talk about building. I'd like pretty well to set eyes on the spot too if possible without Irma's knowing. The important thing though is of course the deed.

Ive been bothered a few days thinking out how to have the property held. I don't know what was the matter with me. The solution is of course the same as when we bought the Acton place. Only of course this time you and Irma must own the place together instead of Irma and me. That will serve all purposes at once. It will keep her from selling or giving away the place on any impulse or crazy notion, and if anything fatal happens to her no one but you will come into possession. We wont talk of any other possibilities.

The house can begin not much more than a box of a summer camp. But I think it ought to be something we could go on with for summer and winter if thought best. One good room now will do. We can talk about more later. I think there ought to be a good foundation of some kind — not just posts or piers. But we can talk about it.

I shut into this letter two separate checks — one for the land and one for four month's of my part of her keep — June July August September. Is that right? I want to be punctual in my contributions.

I take some satisfaction in seeing her establishing residence outside in the world though it's in a state that hasnt nearly as good a asylum to go to as she had in New

Hampshire. Lets hope we can fix her up there on the farm to stay.[1]   Affectionately   R.F.

Be sure to have the deed made out in your name and hers together.

---

[1] Beyond what is apparent in these letters, RF devoted considerable time and thought to Irma's wellbeing. He arranged a succession of living accommodations for her which culminated in a comfortable custodianship in Vermont.

RF to William Prescott Frost

[Typescript]

DEAR PRESCOTT: Ripton, 17 August 1962

You and I don't keep track of each other. You may be packing up right now to go West. You may have gone. In that case I've nothing to count on but for the post office to forward this.

I have to report for myself that I also am on the move to go places. You probably won't have heard because it is a sort of state secret not meant to get out in general that on August 28th I am off to Russia to live there ten days and then come back here not to go on anywhere else. I thought if you were still in Washington and free I might have a meal with you folks on Monday the 27th, the day before I fly. I shan't be able to see you when I come back because I am landing in Boston. As you may guess, this is a sort of errand I am on, not a sight-seeing junket. I shall have an interpreter with me and Freddy Adams to keep me from falling out of the plane. And Stewart Udall will be on board on his way to Siberia. I shall be doing the usual thing — the preliminary talk and the reading from my book to audiences, many of whom will not understand my English. I can be a little political but I mustn't be too political. I let myself in for getting into such a big thing by accidentally getting friendly with the Russian Ambassador.[1] Put your mind on supporting me.

I shall want to hear more about Eugene when I see you and now and then in the days to come. I don't believe I ever had a letter from you, did I?

Ever yours   R.F.

[1] As a result of a May 1962 meeting between RF and Soviet Ambassador to the United States Anatoly Dobrynin which had been arranged by Secretary of the Interior Stewart L. Udall, RF undertook a ten-day cultural exchange visit to Russia in late August. Both of his companions later wrote books on the venture which was also widely covered by the press: Frederick B. Adams, Jr., *To Russia With Frost* (Boston: The Club of Odd Volumes, 1963); F.D. Reeve, *Robert Frost in Russia* (Boston: Little, Brown, 1964).

RF to Lesley Frost Ballantine

[Typescript]   [Peter Bent Brigham Hospital, Boston]
DEAR LESLEY: 12 January 1963

You're something of a Lesley de Lion yourself. I am not hard to touch but I'd rather be taken for brave than anything else. A little hard and stern in judgement, perhaps, but always touched by the heroic. You have passed muster. So has Prescott. You have both found a way to make shift. You can't know how much I have counted on you in family matters. It is no time yet to defer a little to others in my future affairs but I have deferred not a little in my thoughts to the strength I find in you and Prescott and Lee, and very very affectionately to K. Morrison and Anne Morrison Gentry, who are with me taking this dictation in the hospital, and to Al Edwards in all his powerful friendship. I trust my word can bind you all together as long as my name as a poet lasts. I am too emotional for my state. Life has been a long trial yet I mean to see more of it. We all liked your poems. It must add to your confidence that you have found a way with the young.

R.F.

RF was hospitalized on 3 December 1962 for a series of tests and subsequent surgery for a urinary tract obstruction. On 23 December he suffered a heart attack, and Lesley flew from New York to be with him. He apparently rallied. Once home again, Lesley wrote him "I think of you as Robert Cœur de Lion." This last letter is his encouraging response. Alfred C. Edwards, former chief executive officer of Holt, Rinehart and Winston, was a friend of many years' standing. RF stipulated Edwards as sole executor and trustee of his estate. Seventeen days after this letter was dictated, as a result of cumulative complications, Robert Frost died. His ashes were interred at the Old Bennington Cemetery in Vermont alongside Elinor and four of their children — Elliott, Elinor Bettina, Marjorie, and Carol. Below his name is inscribed "I had a lover's quarrel with the world." The inscription below Elinor's reads "Together wing to wing and oar to oar."

Afterword

We make ourselves a place apart
Behind light words that tease and flout,
But oh, the agitated heart
Till someone really find us out.

ROBERT FROST's poem "Revelation"[1] appeared in *A Boy's Will* a year before he wrote his son Carol the post card which launches readers into *Family Letters*. The first stanza serves as appropriate warning to anyone seeking The Truth in a bundle of letters. Be on your guard, the speaker of the poem insinuates. We are under no obligation to clothe ourselves in consistency. We live and write slant. However, the speaker adds feelingly, we do want to be found out. We want to be known.

Frost was a prolific letter writer, and those letters which survive help us to know him better. Incoming and outgoing mail were important to him, and for many years of his long life the pattern of his days was influenced by post office hours and pickup schedules. In his letters he vented a broad spectrum of emotions, he played games — some fairly innocent and others more dangerous —, he counselled and wrote detailed advisories, he rehearsed his thinking, he sought clarity, and he probed for response. Spelling and punctuation were never his prime concerns, but an ambiance of ideas was. The family letter, then, is a special part of his literature, an uncalculated sharing, an act of love.

The letters in this book offer a generous blend of people, places, and ideas. Like Frost's memorable conversation, they move nimbly from subject to subject with a slender thread

[1] *PRF*, p. 19.

of unassailable logic. They combine a mastery of words and their tonalities with a complete awareness of audience. An early note to the "Kids"[2] includes a depressing picture of Ellis Island and a minor touch of the heroic: "There was one man down there who shot himself while we were there rather than be sent back. And there were mad people and sad people and bad people in the detention rooms. I don't know how I ever got Merfyn out of it." Years later, aware that the recipient was a six-year-old grandson, Frost thoughtfully printed his sentiments in block letters spread across three large pages.[3] A Christmas letter to a granddaughter[4] defeats a distance compounded of age and geography: "I remember how you used to look. You looked like a good little girl who deserved a letter now and then... I want you to have something from me... [but]... I can't buy you any funny toy because I don't know how much of a joke it takes to make you laugh... [B]uy for yourself just what will do you the most good for the shortest time."

But by no means is all of it child's play. On a day in autumn, Frost sat in his Boston apartment and proceeded to write what surely must have been two of his most difficult letters. One was to Prescott[5] who had been alone in the house three days earlier when his father — Frost's son Carol — committed suicide. The other letter was to Lillian[6] who, in addition to recent surgery, now had to contemplate the tragedy of her husband's frightful act from a hospital bed miles away from home. So many thoughts must have crowded in on the poet as he wrote, yet what he managed to communicate in both his letters was comfort, support, and admiration for their strength.

[2] RF to Frost children [February 1915].
[3] RF to William Prescott Frost [late winter 1931].
[4] RF to Marjorie Robin Fraser 17 December 1940.
[5] RF to William Prescott Frost 12 October 1940.
[6] RF to Lillian LaBatt Frost 12 October 1940.

Occasionally Frost's letters are well wrought essays. Notable among these is one in which he dwells graphically on the "unheroic heroics" of military flying while grappling knowledgeably with a flight instructor's jargon.[7] In another letter, after devoting two brief paragraphs to home matters, he moves into a lengthy and psychologically acute discussion of expository writing.[8] A third letter devotes nine pages to the intentions and lineage of the imagist movement in poetry.[9]

Elinor Frost — seldom as relaxed or revealing as Robert — is beside and a bit behind her husband in these letters, just as she was in life. No liberationist, however, should be too quick to misunderstand. She was no less opinionated than her husband, and their views frequently collided. Hers was an enormous influence — both in family matters and in the shaping of Frost's poetry. She was a firm, intuitive, highly intelligent woman who brought order and discipline to the farmhouse of art. Her letters comment on the realities of frequent illness, the vicissitudes of moving, and the pressures of an irregular family income. She is burdened with family logistics, both of the world and of the heart.

Elinor lived for the present, for her family and for home. Because of this, perhaps, her letters seldom included the usual heading of place and date. Inevitably, however, as one conscious of and caught up in the daily round, she specified the day of the week and the time of day: "This is at half past nine, Tuesday evening... I feel sorry to go lately because the house seems so cosey and homelike..."[10] "Friday evening... I like this house better and better."[11] "Sunday

---

[7] RF to Lesley Frost 24 October 1918.
[8] RF to Lesley Frost 17 February 1919.
[9] RF to Lesley Frost [1934], p. 160 ff.
[10] EF to Lesley Frost [Fall 1917], pp. 5-6.
[11] EF to Lesley Frost [Fall 1917], p. 11 ff.

evening... we had all grown so tired of an empty house... You will like the house, I know..."[12] "... I almost think it would be better for her [Irma] to come home. And what about your coming home?"[13] "Wednesday afternoon... The house seems awfully cosy and homelike..."[14] "Sunday afternoon... I wish you could be here for a little while and enjoy this warm house."[15] Even trips to England and Florida were doubtful diversions: "I think we shall be satisfied with 2 months over there. I am already homesick."[16] "I am feeling desperately homesick. It doesn't seem as if I *could* stay down here 3 mos."[17]

In the 'forties Frost wrote a poem about a young family, weighed down with baggage and babies, who were passed-up by a clanging trolley because they stood on the wrong corner of the street.[18] Clustered together in dismay and bewilderment, Frost saw the family as one of the sculptor John Rogers' plaster groupings so popular in the last century. The Frost family were such "A Rogers Group," passed-up by the ostensible sureties of the nineteenth century and caught unprepared within the populated confusion of the twentieth. Few of them welcomed the change with anything approaching confidence and enthusiasm. They stood on the wrong corner, and "progress" passed them by. This fact is a key to their separate natures.

But Frost endured. Always the competitive athlete, the poet of prowess, he gauged the risks and studied the rules. Tennis, baseball, boxing, poetry, life — in a sense, they were all alike. To contend is always to risk failure, but the measure of a man is the nature of his response to winning

[12] EF to Lesley Frost [11 November 1917].
[13] EF to Lesley Frost [5 October 1918].
[14] EF to Lesley Frost [24 February 1919].
[15] EF to Lesley Frost [March 1919], p. 59.
[16] EF to Lesley Frost [August 1928], pp. 116-117.
[17] EF to Lesley Frost Francis [December 1934], p. 173.
[18] *PRF*, p. 391.   [19] *PRF*, p. 19.

or losing. It was therefore no mere coincidence that Frost displayed such extravagant admiration for professional athletes. Whether on the court, on the field, or within the arena, they were acting-out *his* drama and displaying those dearly developed traits of skill and courage for which he had the highest possible regard.

> *So all who hide too well away*
> *Must speak and tell us where they are.*[19]

Although there remains within them a quality of hide-and-seek which no reader should overlook, these letters illuminate the world of Robert Frost, both public and private. They do not bear The Truth, but many truths: Frost cared a great deal about his family; he was drawn in conflicting directions by the literary marketplace, and this posed crucial problems for him and for those he loved; he was proud and easily hurt, and there were times when he himself could not isolate the pain; he was intensely human and fallible and suffered from his readers' insistence that, somehow, the poet and his art must be one and inseparable; he was a natural teacher who tamed intricacy with metaphor.

Much of Robert Frost's life was a series of trials, but he would be the first to discourage any inclination to dwell on these. Better to say that he was tough-minded and indomitable, that he left behind him uncounted increments of beauty, perception, and revelation.

These letters are among them.

ARNOLD GRADE

Brockport, N.Y.
July 1971

Acknowledgments

An editor's debts are manifold and their acknowledgment a pleasure:

To Lesley Frost (Mrs. Joseph W. Ballantine) of New York City whose letters form the substantial nucleus of this book. Without her unflagging assistance and her gracious hospitality, this book would not exist. Most of the letters addressed to her have been acquired by the Clifton Waller Barrett Library of American Literature at the University of Virginia which concurs in their publication.

To Lillian LaBatt Frost of Panama City, Florida, for her kind assistance and for permission to publish letters written to her and to her husband Carol.

To William Prescott Frost of Panama City, Florida, Clifton Waller Barrett, and the University of Virginia for permission to publish letters written to Prescott Frost.

To Willard E. Fraser of Billings, Montana, for his kind assistance and for permission to publish letters written to him and to his wife Marjorie.

To Marjorie Robin Fraser (Mrs. David Beecher Hudnut) of Tiburon, California, for permission to publish letters written to her.

To Lesley Lee Frost (Mrs. Stanislav Zimic) of Austin, Texas, for permission to publish letters written to her.

To the Estate of Robert Lee Frost and Alfred C. Edwards, executor and trustee, for permission to publish the letters.

To the Estate of Robert Lee Frost and the firm of Holt, Rinehart and Winston, Inc., for permission to publish the poems in these letters. These are early versions of poems subsequently published in *The Letters of Robert Frost to Louis Untermeyer* and *The Poetry of Robert Frost*. All rights reserved.

To the late Laslo Boroshy and Kathleen Barnard for technical advice and the photographic reproduction of letters.

To my chairman, John Atherton, whose interest in Robert Frost and sympathetic adjustment of my teaching schedule were welcome expressions of support.

To Janet Kinnicutt and Wendy Bard who first transformed the letters into a working typescript; and to Debra Kolakowski who typed the final manuscript of letters and notes.

To my wife Mary Anne who helped read proof, quieted children, and patiently kept a home in which every flat surface was covered.

To Norman Mangouni, director of the Press, whose graciousness and tact have endured through the publication of two Frost books.

To Lawrance Thompson and James Cox whose interests in Robert Frost and readiness to check detail have made this a more complete book.

List of Letters

RF to Lesley Frost	[Amherst]	25 January 1919
RF to Lesley Frost	Amherst	17 February 1919
EF to Lesley Frost	[Franconia]	[24 February1919]
RF to Lesley Frost	[Amherst]	[late winter 1919]
EF to Lesley Frost	[Franconia]	[March 1919]
RF to Lesley Frost	Franconia	24 March 1919
EF to Lesley Frost	[Franconia]	[March 1919]
EF to Lesley Frost	[Franconia]	[March 1919]
RF to Lesley Frost	Franconia	3 April 1919
RF to Lesley Frost	Franconia	20 May 1919
RF to Lesley Frost	Franconia	22 May 1919
EF to Lesley Frost	[Amherst]	[October 1919]
RF to Lesley Frost	Amherst	4 November 1919
EF to Lesley Frost	[Amherst]	[November 1919]
EF to Lesley Frost	[En route to Amherst]	[December 1919]
RF to Lesley Frost	Amherst	28 January 1920
RF to Lesley Frost	Franconia	8 February [1920]
EF to Lesley Frost	[Franconia]	[February 1920]
EF to Lesley Frost	[Franconia]	[February 1920]
RF to Lesley Frost	Franconia	11 March 1920
RF to Lesley Frost	[Franconia]	[March 1920]
EF to Lesley Frost	[Franconia]	[March 1920]
RF to Lesley Frost	Franconia	18 March 1920
EF to Lesley Frost	[Franconia]	[March 1920]
EF to Lesley Frost	[Franconia]	[April 1920]
EF to Lesley Frost	[Franconia]	[April 1920]
RF to Lesley Frost	Franconia	23 April 1920
RF to Lesley Frost	Franconia	19 Sept. [1920]
EF to RF	[Arlington, Vermont]	[September 1920]
RF to Lesley Frost	Franconia	23 Sept. [1920]
EF to Lesley Frost	[Arlington]	[September 1920]
EF to Lesley Frost	[Arlington]	[September 1920]
RF to Lesley Frost	[Franconia]	[September 1920]
EF to Lesley Frost	[Arlington]	[September 1920]
RF to Lesley Frost	Arlington	[September 1920]

EF to Irma and Lesley Frost	[Arlington]	[September 1920]
RF to Lesley Frost	Arlington	14 October 1920
RF to Lesley and Marjorie Frost	[Amherst]	[1924]
RF to Lesley Frost	[Ann Arbor, Michigan]	[late fall 1925]
RF to Lesley Frost	Ann Arbor	17 April 1926
RF to Lesley Frost	[Ann Arbor]	[May 1926]
RF to Lesley Frost	S. Shaftsbury, Vermont	3 August 1928
EF to Lesley Frost	[En route to France]	[August 1928]
RF to Lesley Frost	Paris	21 August 1928
RF to Lesley Frost	[Paris]	23 August 1928
RF to Lesley Frost	Gloucestershire, England	11 September 1928
EF to Lesley Frost	London	20 Sept. [1928]
EF to Lesley Frost	[London]	[September 1928]
EF to Lesley Frost	London	1 October [1928]
EF to Lesley Frost	[London]	[October 1928]
EF to Lesley Frost Francis	[London]	[November 1928]
EF to Lesley Frost Francis	London	6 November [1928]

1929-1937 — A RECORD STRIDE

RF to William Prescott Frost	[Amherst]	[late winter 1931]
RF to Carol Frost	Boulder, Colorado	21 August 1931
RF to Carol Frost	[South Shaftsbury]	1 November [1931]
RF to Carol Frost	South Shaftsbury	19 November 1931
RF to Lesley Frost Francis	[n.p.]	[c. 1931]
EF to Lesley Frost Francis	[South Shaftsbury]	[January 1932]
RF to Lesley Frost Francis	[n.p.]	[1932]
RF to Carol Frost	Amherst	30 October 1932
RF to Carol Frost	[Amherst]	[November 1932]

RF to Carol Frost	[Amherst]	[December 1932]
RF to Carol Frost	Amherst	11 May 1933
RF to William Prescott Frost	Amherst	11 May 1933
RF to Marjorie Frost and Willard Fraser	[Amherst]	[May 1933]
RF to Carol Frost	Franconia	18 Sept. [1933]
RF to William Prescott Frost	Amherst	21 December 1933
RF to William Prescott Frost	Amherst	22 February 1934
RF to William Prescott Frost	[Amherst]	[23 February1934]
RF to Lesley Frost Francis	[n.p.]	[1934]
RF to Carol Frost	Billings, Montana	18 April 1934
RF to Lesley Frost Francis	Billings	20 April 1934
EF to Lesley Frost Francis	Rochester, Minnesota	27 April 1934
EF to Lesley Frost Francis	[Amherst]	[13 Nov. 1934]
EF to Lesley Frost Francis	New York	[November 1934]
EF to Lesley Frost Francis	Miami, Florida	[December 1934]
EF to Lesley Frost Francis	Miami	[December 1934]
EF to Lesley Frost Francis	[Key West, Florida]	27 December 1934
EF to Lesley Frost Francis	[Key West]	[late winter 1935]
RF to Lesley Frost Francis	[Key West]	[late winter 1935]
RF to Lesley Frost Francis	Key West	23 March 1935
RF to William Prescott Frost	Franconia	22 August 1935
RF to Carol Frost	Amherst	7 October 1935
RF to Lesley Frost Francis	[Amherst]	[8 October 1935]
RF to Carol Frost	[Cambridge, Massachusetts]	[March 1936]
RF to Lesley Lee Francis	South Shafts- bury	28 June 1937
EF to Lesley Lee Francis	[South Shafts- bury]	[summer 1937]
RF to Lesley Frost Francis	Springfield, Massachusetts	[30 Sept. 1937]
EF to Lesley Frost Francis	[Amherst]	[13 October 1937]
EF to Lesley Frost Francis	[Amherst]	21 October [1937]

RF to Lesley Frost Francis   [Amherst]   [25 October 1937]
EF to Lesley Frost Francis   [Amherst]   27 October [1937]
EF to Lesley Frost Francis   [Amherst]   29 October [1937]

1938-1963 — NEVER AGAIN WOULD BIRDS' SONG BE THE SAME

RF to Carol Frost   [Gainesville, Florida]   [late March 1938]
RF to William Prescott Frost   Gainesville   8 April 1938
RF to Lesley Frost Francis   Concord Corners [Vermont]   7 September 1938
RF to Lesley Frost Francis   [Boston], Massachusetts   30 November 1938
RF to Lesley Frost Francis   [Boston]   [December 1938]
RF to Lesley Frost Francis   [South Miami, Florida]   [3 February 1939]
RF to Lesley Frost Francis   [South Miami]   [February 1939]
RF to Lesley Frost Francis   [En route to Boston]   25 February 1939
RF to Lesley Frost Francis   [Boston]   [1 March 1939]
RF to Lesley Lee Francis   [Ripton, Vermont]   [summer 1939]
RF to Lesley Lee Francis   [Ripton]   [17 July 1939]
RF to William Prescott Frost   Boston   [1 Nov. 1939]
RF to Lesley Frost Francis   [Boston]   [9 Nov. 1939]
RF to Carol and Lillian
    LaBatt Frost   [Boston]   [November 1939]
RF to William Prescott Frost   Boston   12 October 1940
RF to Lillian LaBatt Frost   Boston   12 October 1940
RF to Lillian LaBatt Frost   [Boston]   [October 1940]
RF to Lillian LaBatt Frost   Boston   18 October 1940
RF to William Prescott Frost   Boston   10 Dec. [1940]
RF to Marjorie Robin Fraser   Boston   17 December 1940
RF to Lillian LaBatt Frost   Boston   13 January 1941
RF to Lesley Frost Francis   [South Miami]   [12 February 1941]
RF to William Prescott Frost   [Cambridge]   [29 Sept. 1941]
RF to Lesley Frost Francis   Cambridge   [17 Nov. 1941]

RF to Lesley Frost Francis   Coconut Grove, [February 1942]
                                  Florida
RF to Lesley Frost Francis   [South Miami]   6 March [1942]
RF to Lillian LaBatt Frost   Ripton   22 September 1942
RF to Lesley Frost Francis   Cambridge   8 October 1942
RF to Marjorie Robin Fraser   Cambridge   19 December 1942
RF to Lesley Frost Francis   Cambridge   21 Dec. [1942]
RF to Lillian LaBatt Frost   [Cambridge]   28 December 1942
RF to William Prescott Frost   Coconut Grove   1 February 1943
RF to Lillian LaBatt Frost
    and William Prescott Frost [Cambridge]   [February 1943]
RF to Lesley Frost Francis   [Boston]   [21 April 1943]
RF to Lesley Lee Francis   Ripton   20 May 1943
RF to Lesley Frost Francis   Ripton   9 July 1943
RF to Lillian LaBatt Frost   [Cambridge]   24 Sept. [1943]
RF to Lesley Frost Francis   [Cambridge]   14 October 1943
RF to Lillian LaBatt Frost   [Cambridge]   [November 1943]
RF to Lesley Frost Francis   [Ripton]   [2 Sept. 1944]
RF to Lesley Frost Francis   [Cambridge]   [December 1944]
RF to Lillian LaBatt Frost   [Cambridge]   [September 1945]
RF to William Prescott Frost   Cambridge   16 January 1946
RF to William Prescott Frost   [Ripton]   [13 Sept. 1947]
RF to Willard Fraser   Hanover,   [February 1949]
                                  New Hampshire
RF to Lesley Frost Francis   Ripton   [fall 1949]
RF for Lesley Frost Francis   [n.p.]   [n.d.]
RF to Lesley Frost Francis   South Miami   19 January 1951
RF to Lesley Frost Francis   Ripton   20 June 1951
RF to Lesley Lee Francis   Ripton   22 August 1951
RF to Lesley Frost Francis   Cambridge   19 December 1951
RF to Lillian LaBatt Frost   Ripton   [September 1952]
RF to Lesley Lee Francis   Ripton   30 December 1953
RF to Lesley Frost Ballantine   Amherst   [1 May 1954]
RF to William Prescott Frost   Ripton   17 August 1962
RF to Lesley Frost Ballantine   [Boston]   12 January 1963

Index

In the design of this Index, the editor has attempted to anticipate the needs of both general and scholarly readers. Most will seek a clearer understanding of Robert Frost's life and thought with all its obliquities. Others will want to appreciate Elinor Frost's role as wife and mother in ways and to a degree that were heretofore impossible. Still others will wish to understand both the fullness and the complexity of Frost family relationships. Most will be curious about people and places considered a part of the family record. Toward these ends, the reader will discover a series of subheadings under FROST, ROBERT LEE and FROST, ELINOR WHITE. Other entries are more selective; only representative references are provided for the children and other members of the family.

G

H

I

J